The Essential Guide to

Coding

in Obstetrics and Gynecology

Second Edition

The American College of
Obstetricians and Gynecologists

Women's Health Care Physicians

Suggestions and comments are welcome. Address your comments to:

ACOG Committee on Coding and Nomenclature
409 12th Street, SW
PO Box 96920
Washington, DC 20090-6920
Fax: (202) 484-7480
E-mail: coding@acog.org

ISBN 1-932328-19-X

12345/09876

ACOG gratefully acknowledges the contributions of the following individuals:

ACOG Committee on Coding and Nomenclature

Members, 2005:
Jordan G. Pritzker, MD, MBA, Chair
Allan T. Sawyer, MD, Vice Chair
Francisco Arredondo, MD
Gregory W. DeMeo, DO
W. Benson Harer Jr, MD
Gary S. Leiserowtiz, MD
Maria P. Lenaz, MD
Janet L. McCauley, MD

Liaisons, 2005:
Michael L. Berman, MD, Society for Gynecologic Oncologists
James T. Christmas, MD, Society for Maternal–Fetal Medicine
Robert L. Harris, MD, American Urogynecological Society
John T. Queenan Jr, MD, American Society for Reproductive Medicine
Craig J. Sobolewski, MD, American Association of Gynecologic Laparoscopists

Ex-Officio Members:
George A. Hill, MD
Barbara S. Levy, MD, ACOG Representative, RBRVS Update Committee
Sandra B. Reed, MD, ACOG Alternate Advisor, AMA/Specialty Society RBRVS Update Committee
J. Craig Strafford, MD, CPT Advisor
J. Martin Tucker, MD, Member, CPT Editorial Panel

Past Members/Liaisons:
Harry L. Stuber, MD
Scott D. Hayworth, MD

Editors: Terry Tropin, RHIA, CPC, CCS-P
Emily Hill, PA-C
Savonne Alford, RHIT

Staff: Albert Strunk, JD, MD
James Scroggs
Anne Diamond

Contents

Preface

The Essential Guide to Coding in Obstetrics and Gynecology is a compilation of coding resources developed by Committee on Coding and Nomenclature of the American College of Obstetricians and Gynecologists (ACOG). The committee felt that it would be helpful to combine the many resources available, including excerpts from ACOG's coding workshops, into one book. This provides a resource for Fellows and their staff members who are unable to attend a workshop.

This book was developed for the Fellow or staff member who is new to coding, is new to ob-gyn coding, or wants a review of general coding principles with examples applicable to an ob-gyn practice. Information is included about use of the *International Classification of Diseases, Ninth Revision, Clinical Modification* (ICD-9-CM), *Current Procedural Terminology* (CPT) codes, and Medicare rules, focusing on issues faced by the obstetrician–gynecologist. Each chapter ends with a quiz as a review of the chapter's major points.

A list of ACOG's coding publications can be found in Appendix A. In addition, ACOG's Committee on Coding and Nomenclature holds approximately 13 coding workshops each year at locations throughout the country. These workshops use an interactive approach to teaching coding to physicians and staff. Workshops cover gynecologic surgery, evaluation and management coding, Medicare documentation, and obstetric coding. For more information, please visit ACOG's web site (www.acog.org) or call 202-863-2498.

Physicians and staff also can submit specific questions about coding to ACOG staff. Questions can be submitted by fax (202-484-7480) or e-mail (coding@acog.org).

The Department of Coding and Nomenclature has a members-only online discussion on the ACOG web site. Members can post questions and review answers to questions asked by others. Fellows and ACOG staff comment on questions posted on this site (see Appendix A).

Each of these valuable resources addresses critically important aspects of coding for professional services. Taken together, physicians and staff should find the information needed to correctly code and obtain reimbursement for services provided.

Committee on Coding and Nomenclature

The Essential Guide to
Coding
in Obstetrics and Gynecology

Chapter 1

Coding: An Overview

Physicians often say, "I don't want to learn to code. I just want to treat patients!" In today's environment, it is essential that physicians have an understanding of coding rules to receive the money they have earned for their services and to avoid accusations of fraud. This chapter provides an overview of the coding systems used by physicians' offices and how coding affects reimbursement. More specifically, this chapter addresses:

- Why coding is important and how it affects physician practices
- The purpose of the main coding systems
- How these coding systems were developed
- How coding is related to reimbursement
- Why physicians should be involved in the coding process

Importance of Proper Coding

Today, physicians face increased economic pressure and increased scrutiny of their coding practices. Physicians who understand the intricacies of the coding system are more likely to receive fair reimbursement for their services and avoid accusations of fraud.

Codes condense a large amount of information into a short code description. Most medical procedures, diagnoses, and supplies are identified by codes. Health care providers, managed care groups, insurance companies, government agencies, and research organizations all use the same codes. This streamlines the reimbursement cycle from treatment to payment and makes it easier to monitor health care treatments and outcomes.

Physician reimbursement is determined by codes submitted to the insurer. Even in managed care environments, it is to the physician's advantage to identify services by proper use of codes. Physicians perform better financially if they:

- Select their own codes
- Understand the coding process
- Are involved in the reimbursement cycle

Payers want to be confident that they are receiving good value for their health care dollars. Also they want to ensure that services are consistent with the patient's insurance coverage. Services will be reimbursed only if they are appropriate for the evaluation or treatment of the patient's condition or both. This information is conveyed primarily

Correct coding implies the code selected is the most accurate description of "what" was performed and "why" it was performed.

through codes. The codes reported on the health insurance claim form or billing statement should be supported by documentation in the medical record.

Physicians are legally responsible for the codes they submit to payers. Payers scrutinize these codes for patterns of coding. The pattern can be used to create a profile of how a physician practices. This profile is then compared to similar physicians or groups. Questionable coding patterns or profiles may trigger a review by the insurer. The insurer may review either a single patient encounter or multiple encounters. If the pattern of coding suggests abusive or fraudulent billing, the insurer may impose sanctions on the physician or even exclude him or her from its plan.

Proper coding also can help streamline practice management. First, codes help physicians to get paid promptly for their work. The cost of submitting and appealing claims is estimated to vary from $8 to $20 per claim. Submitting claims right the first time saves time and money.

A practice also can use codes to monitor its income and expenses based on the resources used (physician skill, time, office staff, and equipment) rather than on the traditional net income method. Codes also can be used to profile the number and intensity of services provided by the practice. With this information, practices can develop better ways to meet patients' needs and use resources more efficiently.

Coding information provided by physicians to government and research agencies is used for outcome studies and clinical protocols. This information affects how physicians will practice and, more importantly, how they will care for their patients in the future.

Correct coding implies the code selected is:

- The most accurate description of "what" was performed and "why" it was performed

- Consistent with coding conventions and guidelines

- Supported by documentation in the medical record

Providers and their staff members must work as a team to ensure proper coding, thereby ensuring fair payment for services provided and avoiding allegations of false claims. When physicians understand the principles of coding and are involved in the coding process, coding becomes a management process instead of a management problem.

Main Coding Systems

There are three main coding systems:

1. *Healthcare Common Procedure Coding System* (HCPCS)

2. *Current Procedural Terminology*, Fourth Edition (CPT-4)

3. *International Classification of Diseases, Ninth Revision, Clinical Modification* (ICD-9-CM)

The Healthcare Common Procedure Coding System and CPT-4 codes describe what services were provided, and ICD-9-CM codes describe why the services were provided. For example, an office evaluation and management (E/M) service (CPT codes 99201–99215) is what was done. Pelvic pain (ICD-9-CM code 625.9) and endometriosis (ICD-9-CM code 617.9) are why the services were provided. Both the "what" and the "why" are necessary to justify the claim.

Each of these coding systems serves a different purpose and each is developed differently. The American Medical Association (AMA) and specialty societies, such as the American College of Obstetricians and Gynecologists (ACOG), help maintain the coding systems and provide standards and guidelines for their use. Not all insurers, however, follow these standards. Many insurers develop their own rules and may or may not inform physicians about them. This lack of consistency is a major source of frustration for physicians.

A number of resources have been developed by ACOG to assist physicians in resolving problems with third-party payers. In addition to this publication, there are coding workshops, a web site for questions and information, and several other publications that are available. A complete list of resources can be found in Appendix A.

The Health Insurance Portability and Accountability Act (HIPAA) of 1996 requires electronic transmissions of health care claims and encounter information to meet certain standards, including the adoption of a uniform coding standard. Under HIPAA guidelines, the only coding systems that can be used when information is exchanged electronically are ICD-9-CM, CPT-4, HCPCS, National Drug Codes, and Codes on Dental Procedures and Nomenclature.

Beginning October 16, 2003, HIPAA requires that physicians submit all initial claims for reimbursement under Medicare electronically. There are some exceptions to this requirement. They include:

- Small providers, defined as a provider billing a Medicare fiscal intermediary that has fewer than 25 full-time equivalent employees, and a physician, practitioner, or supplier with fewer than 10 full-time equivalent employees that bills a Medicare carrier;

- A provider that submits claims when more than one other payer is responsible for payment prior to Medicare payment;

- A provider experiencing a disruption in electricity and communication connections that are beyond its control;

- A provider than can establish that an "unusual circumstance" exists that precludes submission of claims electronically.

Understanding the Coding Systems

HCPCS

The HCPCS (pronounced "hick picks") was developed in 1983 by the Centers for Medicare and Medicaid Services (CMS) to report services and supplies provided to the government's Medicare and Medicaid programs. The HCPCS consists of two levels:

- Level I: CPT-4 codes are five-digit codes used to describe the cognitive, procedural, and material services provided by a physician's practice. They are developed and copyrighted by the AMA; CPT-4 is used by most payers to process claims.

- Level II: National codes are five-digit alphanumeric codes that include characters A–V and are grouped by the type of service or supply they designate.

Permanent National Codes

Some Level II codes are considered permanent national codes and are maintained by a National Panel consisting of representatives from CMS, America's Health Insurance Plans, and Blue Cross/Blue Shield Association. An example is the "J" codes; HCPCS codes that begin with a "J" describe drugs administered by a method other than oral administration. These codes identify drugs and dosages and are required under HIPAA regulations.

The Level II permanent codes most familiar to obstetrician–gynecologists are the "J" codes used to report drugs and "G" and "Q" codes used to report services provided by physicians and practice staff. Other Level II codes are used for services provided by other health professionals such as dentists and therapists.

Centers for Medicare and Medicaid Services updates these codes annually. Level II codes must be used for services reported to Medicare and Medicaid. For instance, CMS will reimburse for a screening pelvic examination reported using code G0101 (pelvic examination and clinical breast check) but will not reimburse for the same service if it is reported using an E/M services code. Other payers may recognize certain categories of Level II codes, such as "J" codes, for reimbursement.

Temporary National Codes

Other Level II codes are temporary national codes. These codes were developed so that an insurer can report a service that currently does not have a national code but will have one in the future. For example, new drug administration codes were developed by CPT, but will not be added to the CPT book until 2006. Therefore, temporary codes were developed for reporting these services in 2005.

Modifiers identify circumstances that alter or further explain a service or supply. There are different modifiers for each level of HCPCS. Level I modifiers are two-digit numeric codes found in the CPT book. Level II modifiers are alphabetic and are updated annually with the Level II codes.

Level I CPT-4

CPT-4 is the standard national coding system used to report physician services and procedures in the United States. Codes and their descriptions are developed and copyrighted by the AMA's CPT Editorial Panel. The AMA first developed and published CPT in 1966. Its original purpose was to:

- Encourage the use of standard terms in medical records
- Communicate accurate information about services to payers
- Provide the basis for computer systems and software
- Contribute information for administrative purposes

The first edition of CPT mainly described surgical procedures using a four-digit coding system. The second edition, published in 1970, contained diagnostic and therapeutic procedures and expanded to a five-digit system. It was not until 1983 that CPT was adopted as part of the government's HCPCS coding system used to report services provided under Medicare Part B.

CPT-4 codes must be used by state Medicaid programs and to report outpatient hospital procedures. The Health Insurance Portability and Accountability Act designates CPT-4 codes and their modifiers as a standard code set for the electronic transmission of physician and other health care services data.

The original goals of CPT have been broadened. CPT now is used for reimbursement from third-party payers, as a resource for research studies, and as a method for measuring resources used in the delivery of health care.

Changes in CPT Codes

CPT-4 is not a static coding system. Each year, revisions are made to keep pace with changes in medicine and medical practice. Therefore, it is critical that physicians use the current version of the CPT-4 book to ensure that they are reporting the current codes.

Any individual or group, including ACOG, may request a new code or modification of an existing one. Changing CPT is a complicated process that takes several years to complete. For services primarily performed by obstetrician–gynecologists, the process begins with ACOG's Committee on Coding and Nomenclature. This committee meets twice a year to consider requests for the creation of new codes or revisions of current ones. These requests may come from ACOG Fellows, ACOG committees, other physicians, or industry.

If the request concerns a new product or service, the coding committee requests advice from either the Committee on Gynecologic Practice or the Committee on Obstetric Practice.

Before submitting a recommendation to the AMA, the committee reviews the code proposal. The committee will most likely decide not to submit the proposal if the service:

- Can already be reported using one or more codes currently in CPT-4 (sometimes with the use of a modifier)

- Is a component of an existing code

- Is only rarely performed

- Does not require physician work or direct supervision from a physician or nonphysician professional

If the coding committee agrees that a new code should be added or a current code should be revised, an ACOG member develops a proposal. The proposal includes a detailed description of resources typically included in the service and the diagnoses of the patients who will receive the service. This description is known as a "vignette."

The code proposal submitted to the AMA includes this vignette, peer-reviewed articles, and journal information supporting the need for and effectiveness of the service. Approval of any drug or device used in the service by the U.S. Food and Drug Administration must be documented.

The vignette is then reviewed by the AMA's CPT Editorial Panel, which considers proposals to revise, update, or modify CPT-4. The panel consists of 17 physicians and health care professionals representing the AMA, the Health Care Professionals Advisory Committee, the Blue Cross and Blue Shield Association, the Health Insurance Association of America, CMS, and the American Hospital Association. The AMA's Board of Trustees appoints the panel members.

The CPT Editorial Panel is supported by the CPT Advisory Committee, which includes representatives from major specialty societies and member organizations of the Health Care Professionals Advisory Committee. This group reviews recommendations for new and revised codes and submits comments to the CPT Editorial Panel. The process requires at least 3 months of preparation and review before a recommendation is considered by the CPT Editorial Panel. The panel can decide to:

- Accept the proposal

- Table the proposal and reconsider it after additional information is obtained

- Reject the proposal outright

If accepted, the new or revised code is added to the next edition of CPT. The listing for the new code is a one- or two-line descriptor that condenses all the vignette's information regarding the components integral to the service.

CPT-4 Codes and Reimbursement

The process of assigning values begins once the Editorial Panel has approved a new code. Specialty societies, such as ACOG, survey their members to determine the relative physician work and practice expenses for the new or revised code. The surveys are designed to identify the resources typically included in the preservice, intraservice, and postservice periods and incorporates the vignette used in the CPT approval process. The surveys then compare the resources needed to provide these services to the resources needed to provide a similar service that already has a CPT code (called the reference service). This comparison is expressed in Relative Value Units (RVUs). For example, a hysteroscopic myomectomy

RVUs combine the relative costs of physician work, practice expenses, and malpractice expenses for any given service.

code (58561) uses more resources that a hysteroscopic biopsy code (58558). Therefore, code 58561 is valued as 15.46 RVUs whereas code 58558 is valued at only 7.48 RVUs in 2005.

A member of the specialty society then presents the survey data and recommended values (number of RVUs) to the AMA/Specialty Society Relative Value System Update Committee (RUC).

The RUC is composed of 29 members representing specialty societies, the AMA, the Health Care Professionals Advisory Committee, the CPT Editorial Panel, and the American Osteopathic Association. An Advisory Committee representing medical specialty societies and organizations supports the RUC. Members of ACOG represent ob-gyn physicians on the RUC. Members of subspecialty organizations represent ob-gyn physicians on the Advisory Committee.

The RUC compares the values submitted by the specialty society to those values assigned to similar services that already have a CPT code. The RUC recommends RVUs for the new or revised code to the CMS. Center for Medicare and Medicaid Services remains the final authority on relative values and other issues relating to the Medicare Fee Schedule.

Note that the surveys of the societies and the RUC consider only two of the three components that make up the RVUs for a code, the practice expense and physician work components. There also is an RVU component for the professional liability insurance required for the service. This component is calculated by CMS. See Appendix B for a discussion of the development of RVUs and determining Medicare reimbursement.

Routine preservice, intraservice, and postservice work included in the procedure is "bundled" in the new code and is not reported separately. The physician work and practice expenses for the routine service are reflected in the RVUs assigned. See the discussion of bundling in Chapter 8.

Many other payers have adopted variations of the Medicare Fee Schedule for their reimbursements. See Chapter 12 for a discussion of third-party reimbursement mechanisms.

ICD-9-CM

The ICD-9-CM is based on the *International Classification of Diseases, Ninth Revision* (ICD-9), of the World Health Organization (WHO), which is used worldwide to gather statistics on morbidity and mortality and for hospital indexing purposes. The ICD-9-CM, however, is used to describe the clinical picture of the patient. For this reason, the codes in ICD-9-CM are more precise than the codes in ICD-9.

The systematic classification of disease in the United States began in the early 20th century with the adoption of the Bertillon Classification of Causes of Death, later renamed the International List of Causes of Death. Revisions were minor until 1948, when the book was expanded into two volumes to include morbidity conditions. In 1979, the book was renamed the *International Classification of Diseases*. At that time, WHO assumed responsibility for subsequent revisions. The U.S. Public Health Service modified the ninth revision of the ICD by adding fifth-digit subclassifications to meet the clinical needs of hospitals and physicians.

Today, the ICD-9-CM coding system uses three- to five-digit codes to identify the patient's condition, illness, disease, signs, symptoms, or other reasons for seeking medical care. The current system is divided into three volumes: Volume 1 and Volume 2 contain diagnostic codes used by medical practices and Volume 3 contains procedural codes used by health care facilities to report their services.

Changes in ICD-9-CM

The ICD-9-CM is updated annually. Each year, the ICD-9-CM Coordination and Maintenance Committee reviews requests for changes. This committee includes representatives from the National Center for Health Statistics (NCHS) and CMS. The NCHS has primary responsibility for changes to Volume 1 and Volume 2. The CMS is chiefly responsible for changes to Volume 3. The director of NCHS and the administrator of CMS make the final decisions about proposed changes. These decisions are finalized in the spring and become effective October 1 of the same year.

The ACOG Committee on Coding and Nomenclature meets regularly with members of the ICD-9-CM committee to discuss possible changes in current codes or the creation of new codes. The ACOG committee also answers questions from the ICD-9-CM committee concerning appropriate terminology and definitions for conditions related to obstetrics and gynecology.

Because ICD-9-CM must be compatible with WHO's ICD-9, all requests for changes are scrutinized carefully. The classification headings and categories in the ICD-9 can be altered for the following reasons only:

- Entry contains typographical errors.
- Codes have become outdated because of advances in medical knowledge.
- A new disease has been identified.
- A code is too general.

Changes to subclassifications and subcategories can be made as needed.

In 1993, WHO published ICD-10. This version contains 5,500 more codes than ICD-9, enabling increased specificity in the reporting of diseases and recently recognized conditions. The ICD-10 contains 21 chapters containing alphanumeric codes. It currently is being used in some European countries. The ICD-10-CM is still under development by NCHS and will replace ICD-9-CM in the United States within the next 3–5 years.

ICD-9-CM and Reimbursement

The ICD-9-CM codes do not affect the level of reimbursement for physician services; payment is linked only to CPT-4 codes. However, claims that do not demonstrate clearly that the service was medically necessary may be denied or returned for additional information. The ICD-9-CM codes tell the insurer why the procedure was medically necessary. This is accomplished by matching procedural codes (CPT-4) to specific diagnostic codes (ICD-9-CM) on the claim form.

For example, a patient comes in for a colposcopy because of an abnormal Pap test result. At the time of the procedure, she also complains of vulvar pain. The physician notes that the patient has a Bartholin's gland abscess and performs an incision and drainage at the same encounter. The original claim filed is shown in Figure 1–1.

CPT Code	CPT Description
57460	Colposcopy of the cervix including upper/adjacent vagina; with loop electrode biopsy(s) of the cervix
56420	Incision and drainage of Bartholin's gland abscess

The modifier –51 is added to code 56420 to indicate that multiple procedures were performed.

The insurance company denied the claim because its editing software indicated that neither menorrhagia nor a uterine polyp is treated by incision and drainage of an abscess. The claim would have been paid if the claim had linked the ICD-9-CM code supporting the need for the incision and drainage to the appropriate CPT code as shown in Figure 1–2.

CPT Code	CPT Description
57460	Colposcopy of the cervix including upper/adjacent vagina; with loop electrode biopsy(s) of the cervix
56420	Incision and drainage of Bartholin's gland abscess

Claim forms have space for up to four diagnoses. Some payers read only the first diagnosis linked to an individual CPT-4 code (sections D & E in Figure 1–1) when processing the claim. Therefore, it is important to prioritize and link diagnostic and procedural codes accurately. The guidelines for proper ICD-9-CM coding will be thoroughly addressed in Chapter 3.

21. DIAGNOSIS OR NATURE OF ILLNESS OR INJURY (RELATE ITEMS 1, 2, 3, OR 4 TO ITEM 24E BY LINE)	22. MEDICAID RESUBMISSION CODE
1. 795.02 Pap smear of cervix with atypical squamous cells cannot exclude high grade squamous intraepithelial lesion (ASC-H) 2. 3. 4.	23. PRIOR AUTHORIZATION CODE

24.	A					B	C	D		E	F	G
	DATE (S) OF SERVICES					PLACE OF SERVICE	TYPE OF SERVICE	PROCEDURES, SERVICES OR SUPPLIES		DIAGNOSIS CODE	$ CHARGES	DAYS OR UNIT
	From			To				(Explain Unusual Circumstances)				
MM	DD	YY	MM	DD	YY			CPT-4/ CHCPCS	MODIFIER			
						11		57460		1		1
						11		56420	–51	1		1

Figure 1–1. Original Claim

21. DIAGNOSIS OR NATURE OF ILLNESS OR INJURY (RELATE ITEMS 1, 2, 3, OR 4 TO ITEM 24E BY LINE)	22. MEDICAID RESUBMISSION CODE
1. 795.02 Pap smear of cervix with atypical squamous cells cannot exclude high grade squamous intraepithelial lesion (ASC-H) 2. 616.3 Bartholin's gland abscess 3. 4.	23. PRIOR AUTHORIZATION CODE

24.	A					B	C	D		E	F	G
	DATE (S) OF SERVICES					PLACE OF SERVICE	TYPE OF SERVICE	PROCEDURES, SERVICES OR SUPPLIES		DIAGNOSIS CODE	$ CHARGES	DAYS OR UNIT
	From			To				(Explain Unusual Circumstances)				
MM	DD	YY	MM	DD	YY			CPT-4/ CHCPCS	MODIFIER			
						11		57460		1		1
						11		56420	–51	2		1

Figure 1–2. Corrected Claim

Chapter 1 Quiz: Coding: An Overview

True or False

1. CPT-4, ICD-9, and HCPCS Level II are the three main coding systems approved under HIPAA guidelines.

2. CPT-4, ICD-9, and HCPCS are updated annually

Choose the best answer

3. Physicians should be involved in the coding process because:

   a. They are legally responsible for the codes submitted for reimbursement

   b. They generally perform better financially than physicians who delegate all coding responsibility to staff

   c. They are the most knowledgeable about the service and why it was performed

   d. All of the above

4. Coding may be used to:

   a. Reimburse physicians for services to patients

   b. Compare the practice patterns between physician groups

   c. Manage administrative aspects of a practice

   d. A and C

   e. All of the above

5. CPT-4 is:

   a. Coding system for reporting physician services and procedures

   b. Maintained by CMS

   c. Directly linked to third-party reimbursement

   d. A and C only

6. Requirements for new CPT codes include:

   a. Service cannot be reported using an existing code

   b. Service must represent accepted standard of care

   c. Service must describe physician work or direct supervision by the physician

   d. All of the above

7. ICD-9 is:

   a. A coding system describing work performed by nonphysician professionals

   b. Used only by hospitals

   c. An essential component in the reimbursement process

   d. A system of alphanumeric codes

8. The vignettes used to apply for new CPT codes:

   a. Identify preservice, intraservice, and postservice activities

   b. Describe only intraservice and postservice activities

   c. Are used to help establish relative value units

   d. Describe the most difficult patient likely to require the service

   e. A and C only

Answers are listed on page 179.

Chapter 2

Basics of CPT Coding

Opening the *Current Procedural Terminology* (CPT) book for the first time can be daunting and mystifying—pages upon pages of numbers, symbols (circles, triangles, and arrows), and unfamiliar terms (separate procedures, surgical package, and add-on codes). Each symbol and term has a specific meaning that may not be apparent. Understanding the structure, logic, and basic rules that underlie CPT will help unlock the mystery. This chapter addresses:

- The basic organization of CPT
- The symbols and formatting system used in CPT
- The principles for selecting CPT codes

Following completion of the chapter, the reader should be able to:

- Recognize the symbols used in CPT
- Understand the use of the semicolon in CPT descriptors
- Find and select the appropriate CPT code for the services provided

Organization of CPT

CPT has been used as an administrative and billing code set for physicians. Now that CPT is a standard code set under the Health Insurance Portability and Accountability Act (HIPAA), it has acquired new roles. These roles include collecting data on new technologies, coding for services provided by other health care professionals, and tracking health outcomes and the quality of patient care. To meet these new demands, CPT has been expanded to three categories.

CPT consists of Category I, Category II, and Category III codes. Category I codes are the main codes reported and the primary focus of this publication.

Category I Codes

CPT-4 Category I codes consist of six sections plus an index. Each section has its own rules and conventions. The sections are:

1. Evaluation and Management (E/M) Services (99201–99499)
2. Anesthesiology (00100–01999, 99100–99140)
3. Surgery (10021–69990)

4. Radiology (including Nuclear Medicine and Diagnostic Ultrasound) (70010–79999)

5. Pathology and Laboratory (80048–89356)

6. Medicine (except Anesthesiology) (90281–99199, 99500–99602)

The sections are further divided into subsections. The subsections may include a specific component:

- Anatomic area (eg, Female Genital System is a subsection of the Surgery section)

- Procedure (eg, Urinalysis is a subsection of the Pathology and Laboratory section)

- Intensity of care required (eg, Critical Care Services is a subsection of the E/M section)

These sections and the code numbers within them are listed in numeric order, except the E/M codes (99201–99499), which are listed first. Obstetrician–gynecologists most often use the surgery section, which includes the Female Genital System and the Maternity Care and Delivery subsections, and the E/M services section.

Sometimes a procedure is placed where someone might look for it rather than where it logically would be located. For example, sperm washing for artificial insemination is found in the Female Genital System subsection within the Surgery section, even though it is not considered a surgical procedure.

The surgery section of CPT is divided into 18 subsections that group surgical procedures by organ system or anatomic site. Most of the surgical procedures performed by obstetrician–gynecologists are found in the Female Genital System and Maternity Care and Delivery subsections. However, any physician may report codes in any subsection, so obstetrician–gynecologists may report codes from the Urinary System or Digestive System subsection if appropriate.

Services included in the Female Genital System subsection are arranged anatomically. The following headings are included:

- Vulva, Perineum, and Introitus (56405–56821)

- Vagina (57000–57425)

- Cervix Uteri (57452–57820)

- Corpus Uteri (58100–58579)

- Oviduct/Ovary (58600–58770)

- Ovary (58800–58960)

- In Vitro Fertilization (58970–58976)

- Other Procedures (58999)

Services within these headings are grouped according to the type of procedure or service (eg, incision, excision, repair, laparoscopy, or endoscopy). Special notes found before some groups of codes provide additional instructions for reporting these services.

Category II Codes

These codes are intended to facilitate the collection of information about the quality of care by representing nationally established performance measures. These optional codes are updated biannually in January and July. They should not be used as a substitute for existing Category I codes.

Examples of these codes are:

0500F   Initial prenatal care visit (report at first prenatal encounter with health care professional providing obstetric care)

0501F   Prenatal flow sheet documented in medical record by first prenatal visit

0502F   Subsequent prenatal care visit

0503F   Postpartum care visit

These codes describe components that are typically included in an E/M service or test results that are part of the laboratory test or procedure. Therefore, they do not have their own relative value units.

Category III Codes

Category III codes allow specific data collection to assess the clinical efficacy, utilization, and outcomes of the described services. These services are typically new technologies or procedures not currently incorporated into routine practice. Medicare determines reimbursement on a case-by-case basis. This category is updated quarterly with changes posted on the AMA/CPT website. Recent additions include:

0071T   Focused ultrasound ablation of uterine leiomyomata, including magnetic resonance guidance; total leiomyomata volume less than 200 cc of tissue

0072T   total leiomyomata volume greater or equal to 200 cc of tissue

Index

Some services may not fall clearly in one section or another or may have multiple coding possibilities. The alphabetic index found at the back of the CPT book is helpful in locating the correct procedures and services reported using either Category I or Category III codes. Main terms are indexed according to:

- Procedure or service (eg, hysterectomy)

- Name of organ or organ system (eg, uterus)

- Conditions (eg, leiomyomata)

- Symptoms (eg, hemorrhage)

- Synonyms (eg, miscarriage and missed abortion)

- Eponyms (eg, Marshall–Marchetti–Krantz procedure)

- Abbreviations (eg, LH for luteinizing hormone)

The index lists a main term that may be followed by indented, more specific terms. For example, the main term "Hysterectomy" reads in part:

Abdominal
    Radical 58210
    Resection of Ovarian
    Malignancy 58951, 58953–58956
    Supracervical 58180
Cesarean
    After Cesarean Delivery 59525
Vaginal .58260–58270, 58290–58294, 58550–58554
    Laparoscopic 58550
    Radical 58285

The index may list a single code number, several codes, or a range of codes after a term. Even if only one code is listed, it is important to refer to the referenced code number in the body of the CPT book to ensure that it is the correct code. A code should not be selected using only the index. For example, the index lists:

Biopsy
    Vagina .57100–57105, 57421

Category I codes are a systematic listing of procedures and services.... Category II codes are optional performance measurement codes.... Category III codes are temporary tracking codes....

Codes preceded by the symbols ✚ or ⊘ do not require a modifier –51, even when reported with other procedures.

Codes 57100–57105 describe biopsies of the vaginal mucosa. Code 57421, however, involves a colposcopy of the entire vagina in addition to a vaginal biopsy. Therefore, it is necessary to review the full descriptors in the body of the book to find the most accurate code.

The index also includes notes under some entries that provide additional instructions or coding options. For example, under Amniocentesis, the index lists several codes, but also an instruction stating, "See Chromosome Analysis." This refers the coder to laboratory codes related to an amniocentesis if appropriate. Another example is the index listing for Abdominal Deliveries, which does not list any code numbers; an instruction states "See Cesarean Delivery."

Appendices

The CPT includes nine appendices in the back of the book. These appendices summarize key information and provide examples of E/M services. The appendices are:

- Appendix A: Modifiers. This lists all the CPT modifiers and their descriptors. Also included are modifiers to indicate Anesthesia Physical Status, those used for Ambulatory Surgery Center Outpatient services, and key Healthcare Common Procedure Coding System Level II modifiers. Modifiers will be discussed in detail in Chapter 9.

- Appendix B: Summary of Additions, Deletions, and Revisions. This lists all the changes made in CPT for the current year, including new, deleted, and revised codes.

- Appendix C: Clinical Examples. This provides clinical examples for E/M code descriptors. The examples do not cover all categories of E/M codes or provide examples for all specialties. The introduction to this appendix emphasizes that these are just examples and should not be used by themselves to assign a level of service for a particular patient. Evaluation and management levels of service are discussed in Chapter 4.

- Appendix D: Summary of CPT Add-On Codes. This lists all CPT codes that are considered add-on codes. These codes also are identified in the main text of CPT with the symbol ✚. Add-on codes do not require the use of a modifier –51 (multiple procedures). These codes are never reported alone but always are reported with other procedures. This symbol is found preceding a code number. An example of an add-on code is ✚ 59525 (subtotal or total hysterectomy after cesarean delivery).

- Appendix E: Summary of CPT Codes Exempt from Modifier –51. These codes also are identified in the main text of CPT with the symbol ⊘ preceding the code number. The codes do not require the use of a modifier –51 (multiple procedures). This code may be reported alone or with other procedures. An example is code ⊘ 90281 immune globulin (Ig), human, for intramuscular use.

- Appendix F: Summary of CPT Codes Exempt from Modifier –63. Modifier –63 is used to indicate that a procedure was performed on infants weighing less than 4 kg.

- Appendix G: Summary of CPT Codes Which Include Conscious Sedation. The codes for conscious sedation (99141 or 99142) would not be reported in addition to these codes. These codes are identified in the main text of CPT with the symbol ⊙ preceding the code number. Only one code in the female genital system or maternity care sections uses this symbol: code 58823, drainage of pelvic abscess, transvaginal or transrectal approach, percutaneous (eg, ovarian, pericolic).

- Appendix H: Alphabetic Index of Performance Measures by Clinical Condition or Topic. This section expands on the descriptions of Category II supplemental tracking codes. The appendix provides a description of the performance measure and information about the group that developed each specific measure.

- Appendix I: Genetic Testing Code Modifiers. This section lists two-digit alphanumeric modifiers used to report molecular laboratory procedures related to genetic testing.

General Coding Guidelines

Codes submitted to payers should reflect the most accurate code for the service and follow CPT's coding guidelines. Select the most specific code. The code must be the most accurate description of the service provided and be consistent with coding conventions and guidelines. Read any notes, instructions or other explanatory statements printed under subsections, headings, subheadings, and before and after codes. Know the bundling and unbundling rules used by CPT, your commercial payers, and Centers for Medicare and Medicaid Services.

CPT Coding Conventions and Symbols

Use of the Semicolon

The CPT uses the semicolon as a kind of shorthand to save space and to avoid repetitious wording. For example, CPT lists these codes:

- 57550   Excision of cervical stump, vaginal approach;
- 57555   with anterior and/or posterior repair
- 57556   with repair of enterocele

Code 57550 is called the parent code. Codes 57555 and 57556 both include the information in code 57550 that precedes the semicolon ("excision of cervical stump, vaginal approach") as well as the indented wording after the semicolon. Therefore:

- The full description for code 57555 is: Excision of cervical stump, vaginal approach; with anterior and/or posterior repair.
- The full description for code 57556 is: Excision of cervical stump, vaginal approach; with repair of enterocele.

Note that code 57556 does not include the anterior or posterior repair from code 57555.

In some instances it may be appropriate to report more than one indented code within the same series. For example, Hysteroscopy code 58558 is the parent code for the following procedures:

58558   Hysteroscopy, surgical; with sampling (biopsy) of endometrium and/or polypectomy, with or without D&C
58560   with division or resection of intrauterine septum (any method)
58562   with removal of impacted foreign body

If performed for medically necessary reasons, both codes 58560 and 58562 could be reported. A modifier –51 (multiple procedures) is necessary.

CPT Symbols

Many of the code numbers or phrases have symbols either before the code or enclosing words or phrases. Some of these symbols (✚, ⊘, and ⊙) were discussed previously in the section on CPT appendices. Other symbols are:

- ● A bullet means the code is new for the current year. This symbol is found preceding a code number.
- ▲ A triangle means the code description has been revised in the current year. This symbol is found preceding a code number.

▶◀ Arrows mean that the words or phrases between the arrows are new or have been revised in the current year. Arrows are found before and after phrases or sentences in a section's guidelines or in parenthetical statements after codes. Colored text also is used to identify changes easily.

CPT Modifiers

Modifiers are an important part of the CPT coding system. They indicate that special circumstances occurred during the patient encounter. These two-digit numeric codes are added to the end of a Category I code and designate circumstances such as:

- More or less work was performed than usual for the procedure (modifiers –22, –26, –50, –52, –53)

- An E/M service and a procedure both were performed during the session (modifier –25)

- More than one procedure was performed during the session (modifiers –50, –51 or –59)

- A procedure or E/M service was performed during the postoperative period of another procedure (modifiers –24, –58, –78, –79)

- More than one physician was involved in performing the procedure (modifiers –62, –66, –80, –81, –82)

Chapter 9 addresses the definitions and purposes of the CPT modifiers.

CPT Coding Guidelines

Physicians should report their services using the code that most accurately describes the service according to CPT coding guidelines. CPT includes general coding guidelines at the beginning of each section. The surgery section discusses which services are included or not included in the global surgical package. The E/M services section addresses how to select the appropriate type and level of visit code. There also are instructional notes at the beginning of most subsections or categories of codes.

Parenthetical statements, found throughout CPT-4, either: 1) provide additional guidance in selecting the correct code or 2) indicate that some codes from previous editions of CPT have been deleted. For example, wording following codes 57540–57556 includes two statements:

(For insertion of intrauterine device, use 58300.)

(For insertion of any hemostatic agent or pack for control of spontaneous non-obstetrical hemorrhage, see 57180.)

These notes provide important information about the appropriate selection and application of the codes. Physicians should become familiar with the guidelines and instructions for the categories of codes they use most frequently.

Unlisted Procedures

Sometimes a physician performs a service or procedure for which there is no CPT code. The physician may need to report an unlisted procedural code from the appropriate section or subsection of CPT. For example, CPT includes an unlisted procedural code for the female genital system (58999), for a laparoscopy procedure involving the uterus (58578), for a hysteroscopy procedure involving the uterus (58579), and for maternity care and delivery (59899). These unlisted codes are reported until a Category I or Category III code is established for the service. Sometimes an existing code can be reported with a modifier indicating more (–22) or less (–52) work instead of an unlisted procedural code. Because unlisted procedural codes do not include a specific description of the service provided, physicians must submit a special report describing the service and, if appropriate, the operative or encounter note with the claim.

Chapter 2 Quiz: Basics of CPT Coding

True or False:

1. Physicians can report codes from any section of CPT-4.

2. CPT-4 has a single category of codes that can be used to report services to payers.

Choose the best answer:

3. New codes are identified in CPT-4 by:

   a. A triangle (▲) preceding the code number

   b. A bullet (●) preceding the code number

   c. An asterisk (*) after the code number

4. The symbols ✚ and ⊘ mean:

   a. The codes are provisional CPT codes

   b. The codes describe new services

   c. The codes must be reported in addition to another service

5. New words or phrases are identified by:

   a. The symbol ●

   b. Enclosing the words with arrows (▶◀)

   c. The symbol ▲

6. CPT modifiers are:

   a. Part of the official CPT coding system

   b. Two-digit numerical codes

   c. Identify particular circumstances associated with the service

   d. All of the above

Answers are listed on page 179.

Chapter 3

Basics of ICD-9-CM Coding

The diagnostic code listed on the claim form does not determine how much a physician will be reimbursed; however, it can determine if the physician will be reimbursed at all. The diagnostic code provides the medical justification for performing the procedure. Therefore, it is important for physicians and coders to understand how to use the ICD-9-CM coding and its relationship to CPT procedural services coding. This chapter addresses:

- The basic organization of ICD-9-CM
- The conventions and punctuation used in ICD-9-CM
- The principles for selecting ICD-9-CM codes

Following completion of the chapter, the reader should be able to:

- Recognize the symbols and conventions used in the alphabetic and tabular volumes of ICD-9-CM
- Understand the basic guidelines for selecting ICD-9-CM codes
- Find and select the appropriate ICD-9-CM code for clinical situations

The ICD-9-CM

The ICD-9-CM consists of three volumes, each with its own rules and conventions. Volume 1 is the Tabular List of Diseases, Volume 2 is the Alphabetic Index, and Volume 3 lists procedures. However, physicians' offices use only the first two volumes to select the appropriate diagnosis to submit to a third-party payer. Some versions of ICD-9-CM, including the one sold by the American College of Obstetricians and Gynecologists, include only the two volumes used by physicians' offices.

Volume 1: Tabular List of Diseases

Volume 1 contains more than 12,000 codes to describe diseases, conditions, illnesses, injuries, signs, and symptoms. There are 17 chapters that classify conditions according to etiology or anatomic system. For example, Chapter 11, "Complications of Pregnancy, Childbirth, and the Puerperium," includes subsections based on etiology (eg, Ectopic and Molar Pregnancy, Complications Occurring Mainly in the Course of Labor and Delivery), whereas Chapter 10, "Diseases of the Genitourinary System," includes conditions according to anatomic site (eg, Disorders of Breast, Inflammatory Disease of Female Pelvic Organs).

The Tabular List of Diseases contains more than 12,000 codes to describe diseases, conditions, illnesses, injuries, signs, and symptoms.

The Tabular List of Diseases includes the following chapters:

1. Infectious and Parasitic Diseases (001–139)
2. Neoplasms (140–239)
3. Endocrine, Nutritional, and Metabolic Diseases and Immunity Disorders (240–279)
4. Diseases of the Blood and Blood-forming Organs (280–289)
5. Mental Disorders (290–319)
6. Nervous System and Sense Organs (320–389)
7. Diseases of the Circulatory System (390–459)
8. Diseases of the Respiratory System (460–519)
9. Diseases of the Digestive System (520–579)
10. Diseases of the Genitourinary System (580–629)
11. Complications of Pregnancy, Childbirth, and the Puerperium (630–677)
12. Diseases of the Skin and Subcutaneous Tissue (680–709)
13. Diseases of the Musculoskeletal System and Connective Tissue (710–739)
14. Congenital Anomalies (740–759)
15. Certain Conditions Originating in the Perinatal Period (760–779)
16. Symptoms, Signs, and Ill-Defined Conditions (780–799)
17. Injury and Poisoning (800–999)

Each chapter begins with an etiology or anatomic site and breaks it down into more specific sections, categories, and subcategories. For example, the chapter "Diseases of the Genitourinary System" (codes 580–629) includes the more specific section "Disorders of the Breast" (codes 610–611), which is divided into two types of breast disorders: "Benign mammary dysplasias" (610) and "Other disorders of breast" (611). Category 611 is further divided into 10 subcategories, including "Signs and symptoms in breast" (611.7). This subcategory is again divided into even more specific codes, including: mastodynia (611.71); lump or mass in breast (611.72); and other signs and symptoms (611.79).

Supplementary Classifications

There are two supplementary classifications in Volume 1. Unlike most ICD-9-CM diagnostic codes, these codes are alphanumeric. The two supplementary classifications are:

1. Factors Influencing Health Status and Contact with Health Services (V01–V84), referred to as "V codes"

2. External Causes of Injury and Poisoning (E800–E999), referred to as "E codes"

V codes are used to report factors influencing the patient's health and reasons she may encounter health care providers other than because she has signs, symptoms, or an actual illness. V codes are used to report an encounter with a patient who:

- Is not currently sick, but is being seen for some specific purpose (eg, group B streptococcus screening [V28.6]; well-woman examination [V72.31]; screening because of family history of ovarian malignancy [V16.41])

- Has received a diagnosis (disease or injury) and is being seen for a specific treatment of the problem (eg, chemotherapy [V58.1])

- Has a situation or problem that influences her health status, but which is not in itself a current illness or injury (eg, family history of breast cancer [V16.3] might be noted as a secondary diagnosis during a preventive visit [V72.31])

Many payers recognize and process claims with V codes, depending on the patient's coverage. If the reason the patient was seen is best described by a V code, then the V code is reported even if it means the third-party payer will not reimburse for the visit.

E codes are reported to indicate an environmental event, circumstance, or condition that resulted in an injury, poisoning, or other adverse effects. These codes are never reported as a principal diagnosis. E codes are reported to indicate accidents involving vehicles, poisoning, falls, fires or natural and environmental factors, submersion, or suffocation; adverse effects of therapeutic use of drugs; injuries inflicted by law enforcement agents; and injuries obtained in wars. E codes are not used frequently by obstetrician–gynecologists, but there may be state or insurer rules about reporting these codes.

Obstetrician–gynecologists might report E codes for a patient who has been raped (a code for the specific injury or injuries plus [E960.1] to indicate the rape) or for a pregnant patient who is seen because she has fallen down the stairs (code for the pregnancy plus [E880.9] to indicate a fall).

Appendices

Volume 1 also includes four appendices: 1) Morphology of Neoplasms, 2) Classification of Drugs by American Hospital Formulary Service, 3) Industrial Accidents According to Agency, and 4) List of Three-Digit Categories. These are not necessary for code selection and are rarely used by obstetric–gynecologic practices.

ICD-9-CM Coding Conventions in Volume 1

Specific coding conventions in Volume 1 provide additional information to assist users in selecting a code among the extensive list of diseases, conditions, illnesses, injuries, signs, and symptoms. These conventions include the use of inclusion and exclusion notes, instructions to use more than one code to indicate a diagnosis, and abbreviations to indicate unclassified or unspecified diagnoses.

Inclusion and Exclusion Notes

These notes provide additional information to assist the coder in determining the correct code in a specific case. Inclusion notes provide a list of synonyms or examples of similar conditions that are reported using the code. For example, the inclusion note for code category 628 (infertility, female) states:

Includes: primary and secondary sterility

If the documentation indicates that the patient has either primary or secondary sterility, a code in the 628 series is reported. Note that code category 628 is further divided into subcategories 628.0–628.9. The inclusion note is applicable to all the codes listed in the subcategories under 628.

Exclusion notes provide a list of similar or related conditions that should not be reported using the code. The note refers the coder to another section of ICD-9-CM for an appropriate code. For example, the exclusion note for code 625.6 (stress incontinence, female) states:

Excludes: mixed incontinence (788.33)
            stress incontinence, male (788.32)

If the documentation indicates that the patient has either mixed incontinence or male stress incontinence, then code 625.6 is not reported. The coder should refer to the code indicated (in this case 788.32 or 788.33) to make sure it is the appropriate code to report for this specific case.

Using More Than One Code

Sometimes two diagnostic codes are required to describe a patient's condition completely. ICD-9-CM uses three different phrases to indicate that two codes are necessary and which code should be reported first.

"Code first underlying condition" means that the code for the underlying condition is listed before this code. It is assumed that the underlying cause is known. For example, under code 628.1 (infertility, female, of pituitary–hypothalamic origin), is the statement: "Code first underlying cause, as:

   Adiposogenital dystrophy (253.8)
   Anterior pituitary disorder (253.0–253.4)"

Therefore, a code for the cause of the infertility (253.0–253.4 or 253.8) is listed first on the claim form followed by code 628.1.

"Code, if applicable, any causal condition first" means that the code for the underlying condition may or may not be known at that time. If the underlying condition is not known or is not applicable, then this code may be reported as the first or only diagnosis. If the cause is known, then the code for the cause is reported first. For example, code category 788.3 (urinary incontinence) includes the note:

"Code, if applicable, any causal condition first, such as:

   congenital ureterocele (753.23)
   genital prolapse (618.00-61.9)"

If the patient has both genital prolapse and urinary incontinence, report first a code for the prolapse along with a code from category 788.3 for the incontinence. If she has incontinence but the cause is unknown, report a code from category 788.3 only.

"Use additional code" means that the listed code is reported first, followed by an additional code. For example, code 660.0 "Obstruction caused by malposition of fetus at onset of labor," includes a note: "Use additional code from 652.0–652.9 to identify condition." Therefore, code 660.0 is listed first on the claim form followed by a code for the malposition (652.0–652.9).

Other Specified and Unspecified Diagnoses

Even with 12,000 diagnostic codes to choose from in Volume 1, physicians or coding staff sometimes will be unable to find a code that matches the specific diagnosis for a patient. Sometimes the documentation does not include enough information to select a code. Other times, the diagnosis assigned to the patient is more specific than the terminology in the codes. For these situations, ICD-9-CM includes codes using the terms "Not Otherwise Specified," "Not Elsewhere Classified," and "Unspecified."

The term "Not Otherwise Specified" (sometimes abbreviated as NOS) means that the physician's documentation does not provide enough information to choose among several ICD-9-CM coding options. These codes should be avoided when more specific information can be obtained.

For example, a physician documents "vulvovaginitis" on his patient's chart but does not indicate an underlying cause. The choices under category 616.1 (vaginitis and vulvovaginitis) are 616.10 (vaginitis and vulvovaginitis, unspecified) and 616.11 (vaginitis and vulvovaginitis in diseases classified elsewhere). An inclusion note under 616.10 lists "vulvovaginitis NOS"; therefore, the physician's coder reports 616.10. It would be preferable, however, for the coder to seek additional information from the physician in order to select a more specific code such as 112.1 (candidiasis of vulva and vagina) or 131.01 (trichomonal vulvovaginitis).

The term "Not Elsewhere Classified (sometimes abbreviated as NEC) means that the physician's documentation may be very specific, but no ICD-9-CM diagnostic code matches the documentation. For example, a physician diagnoses a uterine cyst in her patient. The alphabetic index lists "Cyst, uterus" and refers the coder to 621.8. The description for code 621.8 in the Tabular List reads: "Other specified disorders of uterus, not elsewhere classified." The physician reports code 621.8 as the most specific code available to describe the patient's condition.

Most headings in ICD-9-CM include a category for "Other specified" conditions. The "Other specified" category is similar to the "Not Elsewhere Classified" category discussed previously. The "Other specified" category is used when the physician's documentation may be very specific, but no ICD-9-CM diagnostic code matches the documentation. Sometimes these are "catch-all" codes, with a number of inclusion terms for conditions that fit in the category but do not warrant a separate code. For example, category 643 (excessive vomiting in pregnancy) includes codes 643.0–643.2 to report mild hyperemesis, hyperemesis with metabolic disturbance, and late vomiting. In addition, code 643.8 is used to report other vomiting complicating pregnancy, and has inclusion terms for vomiting due to organic disease or other cause. Use of this code is not limited to the codes listed as inclusion terms. "Other specified" or "Not Elsewhere Classified" codes often end in a digit "8."

Most headings in ICD-9-CM also include a category for "Unspecified" conditions. An unspecified code is used when there is not enough information to choose between the other codes in that category. These codes should be avoided when possible. Unspecified codes may not support the medical necessity for the services rendered, which may result in delayed payment or underpayment. Unspecified codes often end with the digit "9."

The Alphabetic Index to Diseases and Injuries lists terms and subterms that identify diseases, conditions, and symptoms.

Volume 2: Alphabetic Index to Diseases

The Alphabetic Index has three parts: 1) the Index to Diseases, 2) the Table of Drugs and Chemicals, and 3) the Alphabetic Index to External Causes of Injury and Poisoning. Obstetrician–gynecologists primarily will use the Index to Diseases.

The Alphabetic Index to Diseases lists terms and subterms that identify diseases, conditions, and symptoms. Terms in the index can be nouns, adjectives, or eponyms. This volume includes many more diagnostic terms than found in the Tabular List. Many conditions are listed in more than one place in the Alphabetic Index. For example, obstructed labor is listed under both the term "delivery" and the term "obstruction."

A neoplasm table and a hypertension table also are included in the index. The neoplasm table is addressed later in this chapter.

Main Terms

Main terms are printed in bold-face type and may denote:

- Diseases (eg, trichomoniasis, pneumonia)
- Conditions (eg, inflammation, injury)
- Nouns (eg, delivery, iron)
- Adjectives (eg, high, triple)

Anatomic terms are listed in the index, but only to refer the coder elsewhere. For example, a coder may be looking for a code for inflammation of the cervix. If he or she looks under the main term "cervix" the index simply states "see condition." The coder would then look under "cervicitis" to locate the appropriate code.

Sometimes terms listed in the Alphabetic Index will not be included in the Tabular List. For example, the index listing for "Headache, spinal, complicating labor and delivery" refers the coder to 668.8. The Tabular List describes this code as "Other complications of anesthesia or other sedation in labor and delivery," but does not specifically mention headache. However, because the index directs the user to this code, it is the correct one to report.

ICD-9-CM Coding Conventions for Volume 2

Specific coding conventions are used in Volume 2. The conventions include essential and nonessential modifiers.

Essential Modifiers

Most main terms are followed by indented subterms that describe different conditions or other factors that will determine the correct code in a specific case. These subterms are called "essential modifiers" because the condition must be documented in a patient's record in order for the code to be reported.

Sometimes there are several levels of indentation. For example, the index lists three columns of indented terms under the main term "Inflammation," including:

Inflammation
    genital organ, female 614.9
        complicating pregnancy, childbirth, or puerperium 646.6
            affecting fetus or newborn 760.8

If the patient is female but was not pregnant, then code 614.9 is reported. If the patient was female, pregnant, and the inflammation was affecting the pregnancy, then code 646.6 is reported. Code 760.8 would be used if the inflammation was affecting the fetus (thus complicating the pregnancy).

Two main entries in the index, Hypertension and Neoplasm, have subterms located in tables. The tables make it easier to find the multiple coding options for these conditions. Specific issues related to coding for neoplasms will be addressed later in the chapter.

Nonessential Modifiers

Many main terms or subterms are followed by words or phrases in parentheses that provide additional information to the coder but do not necessarily affect code selection in a specific case. These are called "nonessential modifiers" because they may or may not be documented in a patient's record. For example, the index lists:

Inflammation
    labium (majus) (minus) 616.10

The nonessential modifiers "(majus) (minus)" assure the coder that 616.10 is the correct diagnostic code for an inflammation of the labia, whether it is documented by the physician as labium minus, majus, or neither. Note that "labium" is an essential modifier under the term "Inflammation."

Basic Guidelines for ICD-9-CM Coding

Most editions of ICD-9-CM contain the "Official ICD-9-CM Guidelines" as approved by the U.S. Public Health Service, Centers for Medicare and Medicaid Services, and the parties involved in developing and maintaining ICD-9-CM. These instructions provide the underlying principles for using and reporting ICD-9-CM codes. These basic guidelines for reporting physician services are:

- Do not select a code using only the Alphabetic Index (Volume 2).
- Read all notes and instructions found in both the Alphabetic Index and the Tabular List.
- Select the most specific code for each service.
- Do not report a diagnosis as "Rule out, Probable, or Suspected."

- Indicate the primary diagnosis for each service.
- Report only relevant diagnoses.

Following is a summary of the underlying principles for these guidelines:

- Do not select a code using only the Alphabetic Index (Volume 2).

  Sometimes a code listed in the index will appear to be the correct one for the condition described. However, the Tabular List may provide additional information that indicates that another code would be a better, more specific diagnosis. For example, an entry in the Alphabetic Index for "Lesion, vagina" refers the coder to 623.8. However, code 623.8 is defined in the Tabular List as "other specified noninflammatory disorders of vagina." The coder can look at the related codes in the same category and may find a more specific code, such as vaginal hematoma (623.6) or polyp of vagina (623.7), that better describes the patient's condition.

- Read all notes and instructions found in both the Alphabetic Index and the Tabular List.

  These notes and instructions provide information to help the user choose the most appropriate code. This includes the conventions listed previously and instructions regarding selection of fourth or fifth digits. Selection of digits is described below.

- Select the most specific code for each service.

  When the exact diagnostic term is not listed, the coder should look for another code that includes the condition. For example, the term "corpus luteum insufficiency" is not in the index because the condition may have several different underlying causes. The coder should look up a term in the index that indicates the cause of the condition, such as "dysfunction, ovary" or "deficiency, hormone" to find an appropriate code.

Selecting the most specific code also means using the maximum number of digits available in a category. The fourth and fifth digits in a code generally add specific information about the condition. For example, code 633 (ectopic pregnancy) is reported with a fourth digit of "1" if the ectopic pregnancy is tubal, but a fourth digit of "2" if the ectopic pregnancy is ovarian. Code 633.2 (ovarian ectopic pregnancy) is reported with a fifth digit of "1" if the pregnancy includes both an ovarian and intrauterine pregnancy, but a fifth digit of "0" if it does not.

If the codes in the category can be expanded to five digits, five digits must be reported. Some code categories have only three digits (eg, 220, benign neoplasm of ovary) or four digits (eg, 623.0, dysplasia of vagina) and cannot be expanded.

Always report the maximum number of digits available in a code category but no more. Many editions of ICD-9-CM use special symbols to indicate which codes require fourth or fifth digits or both. Many payers, including Medicare, will not pay for services unless the diagnosis has been carried to the highest number of digits possible.

The fourth or fifth digits may be listed in the Tabular List of ICD-9-CM codes or in a separate table. In the previous example of ectopic pregnancy, the additional digits are included in the Tabular List:

633 Ectopic pregnancy

   633.0 Abdominal pregnancy

      633.00 Abdominal pregnancy without intrauterine pregnancy

      633.01 Abdominal pregnancy with intrauterine pregnancy

In other instances, fifth digit options are in a separate table at the beginning of a chapter, section, or category. For example, the Tabular List includes:

789.3 Abdominal or pelvic swelling, mass, or lump

789.4 Abdominal rigidity

These codes require a fifth digit that is selected from a table at the beginning of the category (789, "Other symptoms involving abdomen and pelvis"). The fifth digit identifies the location of the swelling, mass, or lump. For example, the fifth digit "6" indicates epigastric, while the fifth digit "1" indicates right upper quadrant. In other sections, the fifth digit provides other types of information.

Most of the codes in the obstetric chapter of ICD-9-CM include fifth digits to indicate the current status of a pregnancy. These are addressed in Chapter 10.

- Do not report a diagnosis as "Rule out, Probable, or Suspected."

A physician may document a condition as a suspected one and use terms such as "rule out," "suspected," or "probable" in the patient's record. There are no ICD-9-CM codes to report these diagnoses. Until there is a definitive diagnosis, the physician can report only a code for the sign or symptom. For example, a patient may be seen by a physician for an ill-defined symptom such as "pelvic pain." The physician may suspect a specific condition such as endometriosis or a urinary tract infection and order studies to aid in making a diagnosis. However, until he has a confirmed diagnosis of endometriosis or urinary tract infection, he should report a code for the symptom, pelvic pain (625.9). Reporting a suspected condition as confirmed can complicate the patient's insurance coverage. In these instances, the physician might report codes for the presenting signs or symptoms as a provisional diagnosis or wait for the test results before submitting the claim.

Categories 780–799 describe provisional diagnoses that can be used until all the facts are obtained. Other provisional diagnoses can be found in the specific disease chapters. For example, urinary frequency is reported using code 788.41 and lump in the breast can be reported as 611.72. Neither code assigns a definitive condition to the patient but accurately reflects the reason for the patient encounter. If appropriate, the physician in the previous example can add a V code to provide additional information to the insurance company (eg, to indicate observation for suspected neoplasm [V71.1 series], family history [V16 series], or personal history [V10 series] of a malignant neoplasm).

If test results are available, code for the definitive diagnosis confirmed by the test. If the test findings are nonspecific, then report a code for the sign or symptom or both. Generally, it is not recommended to delay submission of claims until test results are received from an outside laboratory.

- Indicate the primary diagnosis for each service.

Often a patient may have more than one diagnosis. In this case, report the primary diagnostic code first, followed by the second most important one. The primary diagnosis is the one chiefly responsible for the services provided. Up to four diagnoses can be submitted on a claim form. It is important to prioritize and link diagnostic codes accurately. Some payers read only the first diagnosis linked to an individual CPT-4 code when processing the claim. If this first diagnosis does not indicate the medical necessity for the procedure or service, the claim may be denied or delayed. For example, a woman, who has a previously diagnosed ovarian cyst, came to a physician's office with findings consistent with vaginitis. At the same encounter, the physician decided to perform an ultrasound examination to assess the size of the cyst. The primary diagnosis for the visit was a code for vaginitis (616.10). The secondary diagnosis was the code for ovarian cyst (620.2).

- Report only relevant diagnoses.

Coding guidelines state that only current conditions should be reported. This may be either the conditions that prompted the patient's visit or the one that was treated on that occasion. Report also coexisting conditions that affect the treatment of the patient. The physician should not code conditions that were previously treated but no longer exist. Instead, codes V10–V19 (personal or family history of a condition) can be reported as secondary diagnoses if the previous condition has an impact on the current care or influences treatment. For example, in the case addressed previously, the primary diagnosis for the ultrasound examination was an ovarian cyst (620.2). It had been treated during a previous encounter and was the reason the ultrasound examination was performed but not the primary reason the patient was seen that day. Once it has been determined that the cyst has been treated successfully, that diagnosis would not be reported for future encounters.

Special Coding Issues

Coding for Neoplasms

Coding for neoplasms causes special problems for coders in three areas:

1. Defining terms found in ICD-9-CM
2. Deciding when to report a neoplasm diagnosis and when to report a history of neoplasm diagnosis
3. Selecting and sequencing diagnoses

Definitions of Terms

Neoplasm codes are listed in a table in the Alphabetic Index (Volume 2). This table lists codes for different types of neoplasms according to anatomic sites. Table 3–1 is a partial entry from the neoplasm table. The terms in the heading of this table are defined as follows:

- Malignant neoplasms are cancerous and capable of dissemination and/or local infiltration. They are divided into three types:

—Cancer in situ is cancerous but primary neoplasms are the original site of the neoplasm.

—Secondary neoplasms are a second cancerous neoplasm appearing at a body site other than the original one. This description is used for all secondary cancers, even when the primary malignancy appears to have been arrested.

—Cancer in confined or "noninvasive" in nature.

- Benign neoplasms are noncancerous.

Table 3–1. Partial Entry From Neoplasm Table

	Malignant					
	Primary	Secondary	Cancer in situ	Benign	Uncertain Behavior	Unspecified
Cervix (cervical) (uteri) (uterus)	180.9	198.82	233.1	219.0	236.0	239.5
Canal	180.0	198.82	233.1	219.0	236.0	239.5
Contiguous sites	180.8	—	—	—	—	—
Endocervix (canal) (gland)	180.0	198.82	233.1	219.0	236.0	239.5

- Uncertain behavior means the tissue has neoplastic characteristics, but the type of behavior cannot yet be determined. Further testing by the physician is required. An example of this category is borderline ovarian tumor.

- Unspecified behavior means the nature of the neoplasm is undetermined pending laboratory test results.

The primary site of the tumor may not be the primary diagnosis for a specific encounter. Report as the primary diagnosis the code for the site receiving the most definitive treatment on that day. This may be either the primary or the secondary neoplasm.

Neoplasm versus "Personal history of ..."

It is sometimes unclear when a patient's diagnosis changes from a cancer diagnostic code (codes 140–239) to a code for "personal history of..." (V10.XX). There are no universally accepted rules to determine when the patient ceases to have cancer and converts to a "personal history of..." diagnosis. Often the "personal history of..." cancer code is used when the patient's treatment has been completed.

If the physician is providing treatment (such as chemotherapy or radiotherapy) that is directed toward a specific site, he or she should report a cancer code. This is true even if the cancer at that site has been removed.

If the treatment has been completed, the physician may see the patient to monitor her medication. In this case, he or she reports a code in the V10 series of codes along with a code for the medication. For example, a patient is taking tamoxifen after a mastectomy. Her physician reports V10.3 (personal history of breast cancer) plus V58.69 (current use of high-risk medication).

Selecting and Sequencing Codes

Coding options may depend on 1) whether the global surgical package period has been completed and 2) whether the patient has symptoms that indicate she may still have cancer. The global surgical package is addressed in Chapter 8. Coding options are as follows:

- If a patient is seen within the postoperative global surgical package period and she is receiving ongoing treatment, correct coding depends on the nature of the visit.

  —If the visit is for routine follow-up, it usually is considered part of the global surgical package and not reimbursed or reported separately. In most cases, surgery performed for cancer diagnoses will include routine postoperative services for 90 days after the surgery.

  —If the visit is for treatment of a complication of either the surgery or other treatment, report a diagnostic code for the complication or other problem along with a cancer code.

  —If the visit is for treatment of a problem unrelated to the surgery, report a diagnosis for the problem. If the cancer is affecting treatment of that problem, report also the cancer diagnosis.

- If a patient is seen after the global surgical period has ended, correct coding depends on whether there are any symptoms at the time of the visit or the reason for the visit.

  —If no symptoms exist and there is no clinical evidence for residual cancer, report a code from the V10 series (personal history of cancer) with V71.1 (observation for suspected malignant neoplasm).

  —If symptoms exist or if the primary reason for the visit is to reassess the status of a previously diagnosed cancer, report all relevant symptom codes or the cancer diagnosis.

- If a patient is seen for a preventive or other unrelated visit and the physician wants to document that she had (but no longer has) cancer, report the appropriate V code (personal history of cancer) as the secondary diagnosis.

Carcinoma in Situ/Dysplasia/Abnormal Pap Tests

In 2005, these codes were modified and new codes added to more clearly indicate when to report an abnormal Pap test result, histological finding of dysplasia and carcinoma. The general rule is that the diagnostic code should reflect the reason the patient is being seen for that visit (eg, for an annual visit, because of an abnormal Pap test result from the previous visit). Figure 3–1 shows the sequence for this coding.

Reporting Complications

A complication is a new medical problem that developed as a result of previous medical or surgical treatment. Most complications are classified as either mechanical or nonmechanical and are listed in the section "Complications of Surgical and Medical Care, Not Elsewhere Classified" (codes 996–999). Obstetric complications, however, are listed in the obstetric chapter (codes 670–677, Complications of the puerperium).

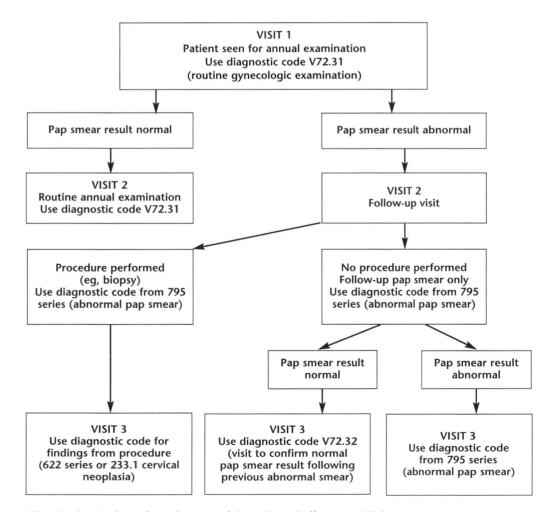

Fig. 3–1. Coding for Abnormal Pap Test Follow-up Visits

When coding for complications, report as the primary diagnosis the immediate problem being treated...

A mechanical complication is a displacement, malfunction, or infection caused by an artificial implant inside the body, an internal prosthesis, or an external prosthesis. The implant may be a urethral catheter, suture, cardiac pacemaker, or breast implant. These codes are listed in the category 996 (complications peculiar to certain specified procedures). This category includes distinct codes for complications of cardiac devices, implants, and grafts; genitourinary devices, implants, and grafts; and breast prostheses. An infection caused by an intrauterine contraceptive device (996.32) is considered a mechanical complication.

Other complications are classified as nonmechanical complications. These codes are listed in three different categories of diagnoses not elsewhere classified (NEC) in ICD-9-CM:

1. The 997 category (complications affecting specified body system, NEC). This category includes distinct codes for complications such as those affecting the nervous, digestive, or urinary systems.

2. The 998 category (other complications of procedures, NEC). This category includes distinct codes for complications such as a hematoma, accidental laceration during procedure, and postoperative shock.

3. The 999 category (complications of medical care, NEC). This category includes distinct codes for complications such as air embolism, anaphylactic shock caused by serum and Rh incompatibility reaction.

When coding for complications, report as the primary diagnosis the immediate problem being treated, and then, if necessary, a secondary diagnostic code identifying the problem as a complication. Complications are referenced in the ICD-9-CM index under main terms such as complications, inflammation, infection, and hemorrhage. For example, an encounter with a patient treated because of an acute infection caused by an intrauterine device is reported using codes for inflammatory diseases of uterus, acute (615.0) plus 996.32 (mechanical complication of IUD).

Chapter 3 Quiz: Basics of ICD-9-CM Coding

True or False:

1. Physician practices use all three volumes of ICD-9-CM to identify reasons for health care encounters.

2. V codes are used to report factors influencing the patient's health and reasons for health encounters other than signs, symptoms, or actual illness.

Choose the best answer.

3. Essential modifiers are:

    a. Necessary for proper code selection

    b. Indented under the main term in the Index

    c. Similar to inclusion/exclusion notes

    d. All of the above

4. Basic guidelines for ICD-9-CM coding include:

    a. Read all notes and instructions

    b. Report only relevant diagnoses

    c. Select the most specific code for each service

    d. A and C

    e. All of the above

5. Selecting the most specific code for an individual service means:

    a. Identifying the most accurate code for the circumstances

    b. Selecting the maximum number of digits available in the category

    c. Identifying the appropriate ICD-9-CM code for each CPT-4 code

    d. All of the above

6. The term NOS indicates:

    a. The physician's documentation is not sufficient enough to report a more specific code.

    b. More information is necessary to select the proper ICD-9-CM code

    c. The code should be used as the primary diagnosis

7. The neoplasm table:

    a. Includes only malignant conditions

    b. Can be used alone to select an ICD-9-CM code

    c. Is located in the Index and lists different types of neoplasms by anatomic site

Answers are listed on page 179.

Chapter 4

Evaluation and Management Services

Although learning how to use evaluation and management (E/M) codes is probably the most difficult part of coding, it can be the most rewarding. Reporting the appropriate level of E/M service and backing it up with the necessary documentation can increase a physician's revenue and protect him or her from charges of fraud.

This chapter describes CPT rules for selecting E/M services to report problem-oriented visits. Medicare rules are addressed in Chapter 6. Preventive care is discussed in Chapter 7. This chapter addresses:

- The organization of E/M codes
- Definitions of commonly used terms in E/M codes
- Guidelines for selecting E/M codes

Following completion of the chapter, the reader should be able to:

- Select the appropriate category of E/M services
- Distinguish between the types of E/M services
- Understand how to select the appropriate E/M service based on CPT guidelines

Organization and Structure of E/M Services

In 1992, CPT introduced new codes called "Evaluation and Management Services" codes to report patient visits. These E/M codes were developed to correlate with the federal government's 1992 Resource-Based Relative Value Scale system for physician payment. This system bases reimbursement on the costs of providing a service rather than on physician charges (see Chapter 1). Most E/M service codes are used to report services provided in the diagnosis and treatment of illness, disease, and symptoms. Other E/M services describe preventive, counseling, or other nonprocedural services.

CPT-4 codes and definitions for E/M services are found in the E/M section in the front of the CPT-4 book. The E/M services are divided into broad categories based on the location of the service (such as office, other outpatient facility, or inpatient facility) and type of service (such as consultations, preventive care, or counseling). These categories are further divided into subcategories (such as new or established patient or initial or subsequent visit) and then finally into levels of service based on the resources required to provide the service.

Some areas within a facility (such as emergency departments, observation areas, and outpatient surgical centers) also are considered outpatient areas.

To select the appropriate CPT code, physicians must:

- Identify the category/subcategory of service
- Review CPT instructions
- Select an appropriate level of service

Most problem-oriented E/M codes designate a specific location where the patient was treated as well as the type of patient. For example, the category "Office or Other Outpatient Services" has subcategories for new and established patient encounters. The category "Consultations" includes different codes according to the location (inpatient or outpatient) of the service.

Many categories of E/M services have special instructions in the introductory section for that category. These instructions provide important information and guidelines for using the codes in that category. For example, the introduction to the Initial Hospital Care codes gives instructions on how to report other E/M services and an initial hospital admission provided on the same date.

Important Definitions

It is necessary to understand some key terms in order to select the appropriate category or subcategory of E/M codes. Words whose meanings seem obvious (eg, outpatient/inpatient or new/established patient) may have specific and somewhat unexpected definitions when used in CPT.

Outpatient/Inpatient

According to CPT-4, a patient is an outpatient until she is admitted to a health care facility as an inpatient. A physician's office is an outpatient area. Some areas within a facility (such as emergency departments, observation areas, and outpatient surgical centers) also are considered outpatient areas. The same outpatient E/M codes used in a physician's office are used to report services in these locations.

New and Established Patients

Some outpatient problem-oriented codes differentiate between new and established patients. These are defined as follows:

- A new patient has not received any professional services from the physician or another practitioner of the same specialty who belongs to the same group practice within the past 3 years. New patients are typically self-referred or are sent by another physician for treatment.

- An established patient has received professional services from the physician or another practitioner of the same specialty who belongs to the same group practice within the past 3 years.

A professional service is defined as a face-to-face service provided by a physician and reported by a specific CPT code. In covering situations, the patient–covering physician relationship is reported as if the primary physician had seen the patient. For example, physician A is covering for physician B. Physician A sees physician B's established patient. Physician A reports the encounter as an established patient visit, even if physician A has never seen this patient before.

A patient's status as new or established does not depend on whether her previous medical records are available or whether she is being seen for a new problem. It is determined only by the period of time since she was last seen if ever, and her relationship to the physician and the group practice. Following are some examples of new and established patients.

A patient was seen in the emergency department by Suskind. Dr. Suskind asked the patient to come to her office for follow-up. In the office, the patient completed a patient information form because she had never been to Dr. Suskind's office. The patient was seen by Dr. Manley, Dr. Suskind's partner. The patient is Dr. Manley's established patient.

A patient has been seeing Dr. Powers for years. Dr. Powers leaves the Armstrong Medical Group and joins the Amityville Medical Group. The patient comes to the new practice to see Dr. Powers within 3 years of her last visit. The patient is Dr. Powers established patient.

A patient has been seeing Dr. Braverman for years. Dr. Braverman leaves the Armstrong Medical Group. The patient then sees Dr. Loveless, another general gynecologist at the Armstrong Medical Group. The patient is Dr. Loveless' established patient.

A patient has been seeing Dr. Weisman for years. He leaves the Armstrong Medical Group. The patient develops acute cystitis and is seen by Dr. Fonda, Dr. Weisman's partner in the new practice since Dr. Weisman's schedule is fully booked. The patient is Dr. Fonda's new patient because she has never been seen in the new practice.

Dr. Albright and Dr. McGiver are both in solo practice. Dr. Albright goes on vacation and asks Dr. McGiver to cover for her. During that time, Dr. Albright's patient, sees Dr. McGiver. This patient is Dr. McGiver's established patient.

A patient had been seeing Dr. Meeks for years. Dr. Meeks leaves Mercy Medical Group and joins the Foxworthy Ob/Gyn Associates Group. The patient comes to Dr. Meeks' new practice 18 months later. The patient is his established patient because he had seen her within a 3-year period.

A patient moved to the community from out-of-state and needed a refill of her oral contraceptive prescription. She called Dr. Manners' office for an appointment and discovered that it would be 3 weeks before she could be seen. Dr. Manners agreed to call in a 1-month supply after the patient had her blood pressure checked by the nurse. When the patient saw Dr. Manners 3 weeks later, she was a new patient. No face-to-face service had been provided by Dr. Manners and no E/M service had been reported previously.

Consultation

Physicians often use the term "consultation" to indicate conversations with patients or other physicians. CPT-4 defines a consultation differently. Consultation codes are reported when:

- A physician is asked for his or her opinion or advice. This request may come from another physician or other appropriate source, such as a nurse–midwife or physician assistant not part of the requesting physician's practice.

- Both the request and need for the consultation are documented in the patient's medical record.

- The consulting physician prepares a written report describing his or her findings and any services ordered or performed. The report is sent to the requesting health care provider.

According to CPT-4 guidelines, the consultant may initiate diagnostic and/or therapeutic services either at the same visit or a subsequent one. These services would be reported with the appropriate code for the other service along with the code for a consultation. However, if at some point the consultant assumes responsibility for management of all or a portion of the patient's care, he or she no longer reports consultation codes. Instead, the physician reports the appropriate outpatient or inpatient E/M codes.

For example, a patient had seen Dr. Goodwin, her primary care physician, for a routine visit. Her Pap test result was abnormal. Dr. Goodwin asked Dr. Wright, a gynecologist, to see her. Dr. Goodwin suggested that Dr. Wright might perform a colposcopy. Dr. Wright reviewed the patient's history and discussed the diagnostic and management possibilities with her. Based on the discussion, Dr. Wright performed a colposcopy and biopsy during the visit. Dr. Wright reported an outpatient consultation code and a CPT code for the colposcopy. The biopsy results indicated cervical intraepithelial neoplasia III. Dr. Wright sent a report describing her findings to Dr. Goodwin. The patient returned to Dr. Wright's office to discuss the findings and treatment options. At this follow-up visit, Dr. Wright reported an established outpatient E/M service because she had assumed responsibility for the care of the patient's problem.

The requesting physician does not always send a formal, written request for the consultation. In these instances, the consulting physician can document that the request was made, why it was made, and the name of the requesting physician in the note for the encounter.

The consultant's report back to the requesting physician can be a copy of the office notes, a formal letter, or a report. The medical record must clearly indicate that a written communication was sent to the requesting physician.

It is important to document a service as a consultation using words such as "consult," "opinion," "evaluation," or "recommendation," and not the term "referral." Payers often interpret "referral" to mean a transfer of care from one physician to another. Thus, in the event of a record review, a payer may deny a consultation code if the documentation does not specifically state that the encounter was a consultation.

It sometimes is difficult to distinguish between a consultation or a new patient visit. The primary distinction is the intent of the requesting physician. Is physician A asking for physician B's opinion or advice, or is physician A asking physician B to provide care for a problem? For example, a patient saw her internist Dr. Fairchild regularly for management of her hypertension and diabetes mellitus. Dr. Fairchild, however, does not perform wellwoman examinations and sent the patient to Dr. Morales, a gynecologist. Dr. Morales reported a preventive visit, not a consultation code.

In another example, a patient saw her family physician, Dr. Nobel, and reported irregular uterine bleeding. Dr. Nobel sent the patient to Dr. Carrington, a gynecologist, for consultation and evaluation. Dr. Carrington took additional history and performed a physical examination. She diagnosed chronic anovulation and treated the patient with medroxyprogesterone acetate. This was documented in her chart and in a formal consultation letter to Dr. Nobel. Dr. Carrington reported an outpatient consultation code.

Selecting Levels of E/M Services

Each category or subcategory of E/M service has three to five levels of care. The levels represent the variations in skill, effort, and medical knowledge needed to evaluate and treat the patient. The definitions for the levels of service are not consistent across the categories and subcategories. That is, the requirements for an outpatient level-3 new patient service are different than requirements for either a level-3 established patient service or a level-3 inpatient admission.

Seven components are used to select the appropriate level of E/M code. In most cases, the level of service will be based on three elements that are considered the key components. They are:

1. History

2. Examination

3. Medical Decision Making

Three additional components contribute to the level of service:

1. Counseling

2. Coordination of care

3. Nature of presenting problem

The final reference component is:

• Time

The history and physical examination components have the same levels of service:

• Problem-focused

• Expanded problem-focused

• Detailed

• Comprehensive

The medical decision making component has these levels of service:

• Straightforward

• Low

• Moderate

• High complexity

Most problem-oriented E/M services codes require a specific level of the three key components. For example, a level-4 outpatient visit (code 99204) requires a comprehensive history and examination and medical decision making of moderate complexity.

Not all E/M services categories require documentation of all three key components at the specified level. For example, new patient office visits, consultations, and observation services require documentation of all three key components. Established patient office visits and initial and subsequent hospital visits require documentation of only two of the three components.

Under some circumstances, a code may be selected based solely on the time spent with the patient instead of the key components. Reporting services using only time will be discussed later in this chapter.

Determining the Extent of the Key Components

History

The physician's clinical judgment and the nature of the patient's problem(s) determine the level of history needed in a particular case. Depending on the level of service, some or all of the following elements must be documented:

• Chief Complaint—a statement describing the reason for the encounter

• History of Present Illness—a clear, chronological narrative of the patient's present illness(es) either from the onset of the sign or symptom to the time of the encounter or from the previous encounter to the present

• Review of Systems—a series of questions concerning the signs and/or symptoms the patient is or has been experiencing

• Past, Family, and Social History includes the following information:

—Past History—a summary of the patient's experience with illnesses, injuries, operations, medications, and treatments

The level of history needed in a particular case is determined by the physician's clinical judgment and the nature of the patient's problem(s).

—Family History—a review of medical events in the patient's family, including diseases that may be hereditary or place the patient at risk

—Social History—an age-appropriate review of past and current activities, including marital status, employment, drug and alcohol use, education, sexual history, or other relevant social factors

The four levels of history are: 1) problem-focused, 2) expanded problem-focused, 3) detailed, and 4) comprehensive. Each level is subdivided into the four elements described previously (chief complaint; history of present illness; review of systems; and past, family, and social history). Not all levels of service require all four elements. The requirements for each level are:

1. Problem-focused:

   • Chief complaint

   • Brief history of present illness

2. Expanded problem-focused:

   • Chief complaint

   • Brief history of present illness

   • Problem pertinent system review

3. Detailed:

   • Chief complaint

   • Extended history of present illness

   • Problem pertinent system review extended to include a review of a limited number of additional systems

   • Pertinent past, family, and/or social history directly related to the patient's problem

4. Comprehensive:

   • Chief complaint

   • Extended history of present illness

   • Review of systems directly related to the problem(s) identified in the history of the present illness plus a review of all additional body systems

   • Complete past, family, and social history

Physical Examination

The level of physical examination needed in a particular case depends on how extensive an examination was necessary to establish a diagnosis or treat the patient. This examination must be documented using the appropriate body areas or organ systems selected from the following list:

Body Areas:

   • Head, including face

   • Neck

   • Chest, including breasts and axilla

   • Abdomen

   • Genitalia, groin, and buttocks

   • Back

   • Each extremity

Organ Systems:

- Eyes

- Ears, nose, mouth, and throat

- Cardiovascular

- Respiratory

- Gastrointestinal

- Genitourinary

- Musculoskeletal

- Skin

- Neurologic

- Psychiatric

- Hematologic/lymphatic/immunologic

The levels of physical examination are the same as those used for the history component. The requirements for each level are:

1. Problem-focused—A limited examination of the affected body area or organ system

2. Expanded problem-focused—A limited examination of the affected body area or organ system and any other symptomatic or related body area(s) or organ system(s)

3. Detailed—An extended examination of the affected body area(s) or organ system(s) and other symptomatic or related body area(s) or organ system(s)

4. Comprehensive—Either a general multisystem examination or a complete examination of a single organ system plus other symptomatic or related body area(s) or organ system(s)

Medical Decision Making

Medical decision making concerns the complexity of establishing a diagnosis or selecting a management option or both. Medical decision making is based on these elements:

- Number of possible diagnoses and/or management options

- Amount and/or complexity of data, such as medical records, diagnostic tests, and other information that is obtained, reviewed, and analyzed

- Risk to the patient of significant complications, morbidity, and/or mortality, as well as comorbidities, associated with the presenting problem(s), diagnostic procedure(s), and the possible management options.

The four levels of medical decision making are: 1) straightforward, 2) low complexity, 3) moderate complexity, and 4) high complexity. Each level is subdivided into the three elements described previously (number of diagnoses or management options, amount and/or complexity of data to be reviewed, and risk of complications and/or morbidity or mortality). Two of the three elements must be met or exceeded to qualify for a given level of decision making. The level of service cannot be based on only one of these elements. The requirements for each level are shown in Table 4–1.

Reporting E/M Services Using Time

Many, but not all, E/M codes list typical times for their services. These times are only averages; the actual time spent providing the service may be more or less depending on actual

Table 4–1. Medical Decision Making

Type of Medical Decision Making	Number of Diagnoses or Management Options	Amount or Complexity of Data to Be Reviewed	Risk of Complications or Morbidity or Mortality
Straightforward	Minimal	Minimal or none	Minimal
Low complexity	Limited	Limited	Low
Moderate complexity	Multiple	Moderate	Moderate
High complexity	Extensive	Extensive	High

clinical circumstances. In most instances, time is used only as a reference and does not influence code selection.

Sometimes, however, time is the determining factor in code selection. CPT-4 states: "When counseling and/or coordination of care dominates (more than 50%) the physician patient and/or family encounter (face-to-face time in the office/outpatient setting or floor/unit time in the hospital…), then time may be considered the key or controlling factor to qualify for a particular level of E/M service. This includes time spent with parties who have assumed responsibility for the care of the patient or decision making whether or not they are family members (eg, foster parents…). The extent of counseling and/or coordination of care must be documented in the medical record."

Obstetricians and gynecologists often spend significant amounts of time counseling patients. A physician may perform a physical examination and obtain a history, but then may spend most of the time with the patient providing counseling or coordination of care. A physician also may spend all of the visit providing counseling to the patient and/or her family and perform no physical examination at all. In both of these cases, time alone determines the level of service reported.

CPT defines counseling as a discussion with a patient and/or her family about:

- Diagnostic results, impressions, and/or recommended studies
- Prognosis
- Risks and benefits of management (treatment) options
- Instructions for management (treatment) and/or follow-up
- Importance of compliance with chosen management (treatment) options
- Risk factor reduction
- Patient and family education

Time is measured differently depending on the location of the service:

- Office and other outpatient visits—Physician time spent face-to-face with the patient and family. This includes the time in which the physician obtains a history, performs a physical examination, and counsels the patient.
- Inpatient, hospital observation, and nursing facility encounters—Physician time spent both with the patient and on the patient's floor or unit. This includes the time in which the physician establishes or reviews the patient's chart, examines the patient, writes notes, and communicates with other professionals and the patient's family.

When reporting services using time as the controlling factor, physicians should document in the patient's medical record the total time spent with the patient, time spent counseling or coordinating care, and a description of the content of the counseling or coordinating activity.

The level of service is based either on the key components (history, examination, medical decision making) or time (when counseling/coordination of care activities comprises most of the service). Following are some examples of coding using time.

A 56-year-old established patient, came to her physician's office to discuss the findings of a bone mass measurement study that was ordered at the time of her well-woman visit. The findings indicated significant osteopenia. Her history was significant in that her mother and older sister are being treated for osteoporosis. The physician met with the patient for 25 minutes to discuss the findings and treatment options. The physician counseled the patient regarding her test results and treatment options but did not perform any of the key components of an E/M service. The physician reported CPT code 99214 and documented in the patient's chart the time spent with the patient in addition to the issues that were discussed. Code 99214 lists 25 minutes as its typical time.

A 22-year-old new patient came to a physician's office reporting menorrhagia and dysmenorrhea. Her menstrual cycle had always been slightly irregular, but the bleeding had increased over the past 2–3 months. The dysmenorrhea occurred only during the first 2 days of her cycle. The patient was not using any birth control and had recently become sexually active. The physician performed an expanded problem-focused history and examination plus straightforward decision making. He then discussed the available treatment and contraceptive options and counseled her on sexually transmitted diseases. The physician spent a total of 45 minutes with the patient, including 30 minutes spent discussing these issues and addressing her questions and concerns. The physician reported CPT code 99204 based on the total time spent with the patient. He also documented the total encounter time and indicated that counseling activities were more than 50% of the total visit with the patient. If the physician had selected a code based on the key components rather than time, he would have reported a lower level of service, code 99202.

If the level of service is selected according to the key components, the physician is not required to meet the typical time listed for that code. However, if the level is based on the typical time for the code, the physician is not required to meet the requirements for the key components.

Sometimes the services provided meet both the E/M code's requirements for the key components and the typical time associated with the code. In this case, the level of care is supported using either criteria. The physician reports only the appropriate level of care. Additional codes, such as prolonged services codes, generally cannot be reported. Prolonged services codes are discussed in Chapter 5.

Sometimes it takes longer than usual to perform the key components. For example, the patient had an extensive history that was reviewed, or she was a poor historian, or she had physical restrictions that prolonged the physical examination. In these situations, it is not appropriate to report the service according to time; the level must be selected based only on the key components. Time is used only when counseling the patient comprised more than 50% of the visit, not when the visit is longer because of other factors.

Determining the Level of Care

The level of E/M service is determined by the services provided by the physician and the particular level of service required by a category or subcategory of E/M services. The following chapter provides an overview of the requirements for key E/M categories and subcategories used most often by obstetrician–gynecologists.

Chapter 4 Quiz: Evaluation and Management Services

True or False:

1. E/M codes can be selected based only on the extent of the history, examination, and medical decision making.

2. E/M codes selection depends on the category and subcategory of service as well as the level of care provided and documented.

Choose the best answer.

3. Documentation in a new patient's medical record must meet or exceed the criteria for the following elements in order to qualify for a particular E/M level of service:

   a. history and examination only

   b. history, examination, and medical decision making

   c. examination and medical decision making only

4. Documentation in an established patient's medical record must meet or exceed the criteria for the following elements in order to qualify for a particular level of service:

   a. all three key components (history, examination, and medical decision making)

   b. medical decision making only

   c. two of the three key components (history, examination, and medical decision making)

5. Elements that distinguish a consultation from other types of E/M services include:

   a. the service is requested by a physician or other appropriate source. The request is documented in the patient's medical record

   b. does not involve ongoing management of the patient's care, although the consultant may initiate diagnostic or therapeutic services

   c. the consultant's opinion or advice must be communicated to the requesting physician

   d. all of the above

6. Time may be used to determine the level of E/M service if:

   a. More than 50% of the encounter is spent providing counseling/coordination of care

   b. the time spent with the patient and the topics discussed are documented in the medical record

   c. the requirements for the history, examination, and medical decision making are also met for the level of service

   d. A and B

7. The elements for determining the appropriate level of medical decision making are:

   a. number of diagnostic tests ordered/reviewed and length of current illness

   b. number/type of current illnesses and management plan

   c. number of diagnosis/management options, complexity of data, and risk to the patient

   d. complexity of problems, length of illness, risk assessment

Answers are listed on page 179.

Chapter 5

Applying E/M Services Codes

The previous chapter addressed in general terms the three key components used in most problem-oriented evaluation and management (E/M) services codes: history, physical examination, and medical decision making. This chapter addresses the specific rules for different categories of E/M services, with examples of how to report the codes in clinical practice. The rules discussed are primarily CPT rules, but Medicare rules also are discussed when they differ from CPT's rules. This chapter addresses:

- The proper use of the types of E/M services
- The requirements for selecting codes within the E/M categories/subcategories
- General documentation requirements

Following completion of the chapter, the reader should be able to:

- Apply the categories and subcategories of E/M services to clinical practice
- Determine how to report E/M codes when more than one service is provided on the same date
- Understand the requirements for proper code selection

Proper Use of E/M Services Codes

Every category of E/M services codes has a unique use and specific guidelines. Much of this information can be found within the code descriptors and the instructions in the beginning of each section of CPT. Being familiar with these CPT guidelines and instructions enables physicians to select the proper category and level of care in a specific case. Following is a discussion of each code category and its specific guidelines.

Office or Other Outpatient Services Codes (99201–99215)

Office or other outpatient services codes are used to report services provided either in a physician's office or in an outpatient or other ambulatory facility. There are different codes for new and established patient encounters. The correct code is determined in most cases by documentation of all three key components, although time alone can be used in some cases.

New Patient Encounters

New patient encounters include five levels of service. Table 5–1 shows the different levels of the components required.

Table 5–1. Requirements for New Patient Encounter Services

E/M Components	99201	99202	99203	99204	99205
History	Problem-focused	Expanded problem-focused	Detailed	Comprehensive	Comprehensive
Physical examination	Problem-focused	Expanded problem-focused	Detailed	Comprehensive	Comprehensive
Medical decision making	Straightforward	Straightforward	Low	Moderate	High
Typical face-to-face time	10 minutes	20 minutes	30 minutes	45 minutes	60 minutes

Document either all three key components (history, examination, and medical decision making) at the required level or total time spent with patient (counseling longer than 50% of encounter). If any one of the key components is less extensive or complex than the others, then the lesser component determines the level of care.

For example, a physician treated a new patient. Based on the patient's presenting complaint, the physician obtained a comprehensive history, performed a comprehensive examination, and considered the medical decision making involved to be of moderate complexity. The encounter was reported using code 99204. The comprehensive history and physical examination met the requirements for code 99205. However, the medical decision making (moderate complexity) was less than the high-complexity medical decision making required to report code 99205. Therefore, the physician reported code 99204.

Established Patient Encounters

Established patient encounters also include five levels of service. Table 5–2 shows the different levels of the components required.

Document either two of three key components (history, examination, and medical decision making) at the required level or total time spent with patient (counseling longer than 50% of encounter). The level is determined in most cases by any two of the three key components.

If the patient in the previous example had been an established patient, then the correct code would be 99215. Because only two of the three components are required and the comprehensive history and physical examination met the requirements for code 99215, it does not matter that the medical decision making did not reach the required level (eg, the decision making was moderate, not high, complexity).

Code 99211 is unique among E/M services. This code is commonly reported when a nurse, technician, or other provider in the practice sees the patient at her physician's request. Examples of the services provided are blood pressure check, review of medication usage, or patient education. According to the CPT definition, the presence of a physician is not required when the service is provided. This is supported by another statement in the descriptor: "typically 5 minutes are spent performing or supervising these services."

This code can be reported only for established patients. No documentation of any key components is required. However, the nurse or other provider must document the encounter with the patient. At a minimum, the documentation should include sufficient information to support the reason for the encounter and service(s) provided. Medicare requires that a physician be present in the office suite when someone other than the physician provides services.

Table 5–2. Requirements for Established Patient Encounter Services

E/M components	99211*	99212	99213	99214	99215
History	Not required	Problem-focused	Expanded problem-focused	Detailed	Comprehensive
Physical examination	Not required	Problem-focused	Expanded problem-focused	Detailed	Comprehensive
Medical decision making	Not required	Straightforward	Low	Moderate	High
Typical face-to-face time	5 minutes	10 minutes	15 minutes	25 minutes	40 minutes

*Medicare requires that a physician be in the office suite during the E/M service.

Hospital Inpatient Services Codes (99221–99239)

Hospital inpatient services codes are used to report services provided when the patient has been admitted to an inpatient facility. There are different codes for initial care, subsequent care, and discharge care services. There also are codes for observation and inpatient care when admission and discharge occur on the same date. These codes will be discussed in the section on observation services.

Initial Hospital Care (99221–99223)

The admitting physician uses the initial hospital care codes to report his or her first encounter with the patient. These codes are reported once during the patient's hospital stay. Use these codes when the initial care and subsequent care or discharge services are on different dates. These codes do not differentiate between new and established patients. The correct code is determined in most cases by the documentation of all three key components, although time alone can be used in some cases.

Initial hospital care codes include three levels of service; all three components must be met. If any one of the key components is less extensive or complex than the others, then the lesser component determines the level of care.

The physician may have initiated care in another location, such as his or her office, emergency department, or observation area and then decided to admit the patient on the same day. In this case, only an initial hospital care code is reported. A separate code for the outpatient visit is not reported. These services are included in the level of service reported for the admission. That is, if the physician performs an expanded problem-focused examination in the office and then an additional examination of symptomatic or related organ systems on admission, he or she can report a detailed examination for that day.

If another physician (who did not admit the patient) sees her during the hospital stay, he or she reports inpatient consultation or subsequent hospital care codes.

Table 5–3 shows the different levels of the components required. Document all three key components (history, examination, and medical decision making) at the required level or time spent either with the patient and/or time spent on the unit/floor. Note that the history and examination must be detailed, even for the lowest-level admission code. The higher levels require a comprehensive history and examination and vary according to the complexity of the medical decision making.

For example, a physician saw a patient in her office. After an evaluation, she decided the patient should be admitted to the hospital. The physician documented a comprehensive

Initial hospital care codes are used by the admitting physician to report his or her first encounter with the patient.

Table 5–3. Requirements for Initial Inpatient Care Services

E/M Components	99221	99222	99223
History	Detailed/comprehensive	Comprehensive	Comprehensive
Physical examination	Detailed/comprehensive	Comprehensive	Comprehensive
Medical decision making	Straightforward/low	Moderate	High
Floor/unit time	30 minutes	50 minutes	70 minutes

examination and history with moderate complexity medical decision making. She sent the documentation and admission orders with the patient to the hospital. After the physician finished in the office, she went to the hospital to check on the patient. The physician reported code 99222 (initial hospital care, comprehensive history and examination, and moderate medical decision making). The level of service documented during the office visit is used to determine the level of service for the initial hospital care code.

For example, a physician was called to the emergency department to see a patient, who reported pelvic pain and elevated temperature. The physician evaluated the patient and was concerned that she had pelvic inflammatory disease. He documented a detailed history, performed a comprehensive physical examination with moderate medical decision making, and admitted her to the hospital. The encounter was reported using code 99221. The comprehensive examination and moderate medical decision making met the requirements for code 99222. However, the detailed history was less than the required history for code 99222. The physician did not report an E/M service for the evaluation in the emergency department because the work performed there was included in the hospital admission code.

Subsequent Hospital Care (99231–99233)

Subsequent hospital care codes are used by the admitting physician to report inpatient services provided after the date of admission and by any other physicians who see the patient during her hospital stay. These codes do not differentiate between new and established patients. The correct code is determined in most cases by the documentation of any two of the three key components, although time alone can be used in some cases.

The history component is described as an "interval history," meaning the physician's work for obtaining any new information since the last encounter. It is not necessary to repeat the past, family, and/or social history for each hospital day because a significant change is unlikely. These codes include reviewing the medical record, results of diagnostic tests, and changes in the patient's status since the last assessment.

More than one physician can report these subsequent hospital care codes on the same day for the same patient. This is called concurrent care and will be addressed later in the chapter.

Subsequent hospital care codes include three levels of service. If a physician sees the patient more than once during the day, all the day's services are combined into a single E/M code. Table 5–4 shows the different levels of the components required. Document two of the three key components (history, examination, and medical decision making) at the required level or time spent with the patient or on the unit/floor.

For example, the patient from the previous example received intravenous antibiotics at the time of her admission. The day after the admission, the physician reviewed the laboratory studies and performed a detailed examination and interval history and medical deci-

Table 5–4. Requirements for Subsequent Hospital Care Services

E/M Components	99231	99232	99233
History	Problem-focused	Expanded problem-focused	Detailed
Physical examination	Problem-focused	Expanded problem-focused	Detailed
Medical decision making	Straightforward/low	Moderate	High
Floor/unit time	15 minutes	25 minutes	35 minutes

sion making of moderate complexity. He reported code 99233. The code selection was based on only two of the three components, in this case the detailed history and examination. Code 99233 can be reported even though high-complexity medical decision making was not performed.

Hospital Discharge Services Codes (99238–99239)

Hospital discharge day management codes are used to report the final hospital discharge activities when provided on a day other than the day the patient was admitted. These codes do not differentiate between new and established patients. There are no requirements for documentation of the key components. The correct code is determined only by total time spent providing discharge management. The time does not have to be continuous but can occur during several episodes on the same day.

These codes include the final examination of the patient, discussion of the hospital stay, instructions for continuing care to all relevant caregivers, and preparation of discharge records, prescriptions, and referral forms.

Table 5–5 shows the different codes for discharge management. For example, the patient from the previous case remained in the hospital for a total of 6 days. She was discharged on day 6 with a prescription for antibiotics and instructions for follow-up in the office. The physician reported subsequent hospital care codes for the 4 days after the date of admission. On the day of discharge, he reported the discharge day management code 99238.

Observation Care Codes (99217–99220)

Observation care codes are used to report services provided to a patient who has been designated a status of being in observation. These patients are being observed to determine if they should be admitted to the hospital, moved to another facility, or discharged home. It is not necessary for the patient to be located in a designated observation area of the hospital. If the facility does not have a separate observation area, other areas of the hospital, such as the emergency department, can be used for observation services.

Table 5–5. Codes for Hospital Discharge Services

Codes	Time Involved in Discharge Day Management
99238	30 minutes or less
99239	Greater than 30 minutes

There are different codes for initial observation care and observation care discharge on a different date. These codes do not differentiate between new and established patients. Initial observation care codes require documentation of all three key components. If any one of the key components is less extensive or complex than the others, then the lesser component determines the level of care. The observation discharge code is determined by time only.

Note that there are separate codes to report when a patient is admitted and discharged from observation care on the same date. These codes are addressed later in this section.

Only one physician can report an observation care code each day. If other physicians also see the patient on that day, they report outpatient E/M services.

Initial observation care includes three levels of service. These codes have the same key component requirements as the initial inpatient care codes. Like the hospital admission codes, documentation of at least a detailed history and examination is required to report these codes. Table 5–6 shows the different codes for observation care. Document all three key components (history, examination, and medical decision making) at the required level.

The physician may have initiated care in another location, such as his or her office, emergency department, and then decided to admit the patient to observation care on the same day. In this case, only an observation care code is reported; a separate code for the other visit is not reported. These services are included in the level of service reported for the admission to observation care. That is, if the physician performs an expanded problem-focused examination in the office and then an additional examination of symptomatic or related organ systems on admission to observation care, he or she can report a detailed examination for that day.

If the physician initiates observation care and then admits the patient as an inpatient on the same day, then he or she reports only the initial hospital admission code. The services provided in observation care are included in the level of service reported for the inpatient admission code.

If the inpatient admission and initiation of observation care occurs on different days, then both services can be reported. The medical record must support the need for both services and the selected levels of care. If the physician does not need to perform a detailed history and examination (the minimum requirements for an initial inpatient care code), he or she should report a subsequent hospital care code.

For example, on 12/13/03, a patient, who was at 12 weeks of gestation, came to the emergency department at 5:00 PM with complaints of vomiting for the past several hours. She stated that she had been nauseated for several days and able to eat and drink only small amounts. The emergency department physician called her obstetrician to the hospital after starting intravenous fluids and ordering electrolytes.

The physician saw the patient at 6:30 PM and performed a detailed history and examination. She decided to admit the patient to observation care. The physician reviewed the

Table 5–6. Requirements for Observation Care Services

E/M Components	99218	99219	99220
History	Detailed/ comprehensive	Comprehensive	Comprehensive
Physical examination	Detailed/ comprehensive	Comprehensive	Comprehensive
Medical decision making	Straightforward/low	Moderate	High

laboratory test results and ordered repeat electrolytes to be run at 11 PM. The patient remained nauseated and although her electrolyte count improved, she was still unable to tolerate oral fluids.

At 1:00 AM on 12/14/03, the physician admitted the patient to the hospital as an inpatient, continued her intravenous fluids, and ordered another set of electrolytes for 7 AM. She also ordered a trial of fluids by mouth every 2 hours as tolerated. The physician left the hospital at 1:30 AM.

The physician reported code 99218 on 12/13/03 for the initiation of observation care services. She did not report a separate code for the services provided before the admission to observation. On 12/14/03, the physician reported an initial inpatient care code (99221–99223) or a subsequent care code (99231–99233) for the services to admit her patient to inpatient status.

Observation Care Discharge Services Code (99217)

Observation care discharge services codes are used when the initiation of observation care and the discharge from observation occur on different days. This code does not require documentation of any of the three key components or time spent with the patient.

Code 99217 includes all services provided by the physician on the day of discharge from observation status (eg, the final examination of the patient, discussion of the hospital stay, instructions for continuing care to all relevant caregivers, and preparation of discharge records).

The observation discharge code is not reported if the physician initiates observation care on one day and then admits her directly to inpatient status on a different day. The physician reports only the hospital admission code on that day because the discharge services are included in the initial inpatient care code.

Observation or Inpatient Care Services Codes (99234–99236)

Observation or inpatient care services codes are used to report the admission and discharge of a patient only when these events occur on the same day. The same set of codes is used for either observation or inpatient services. These codes bundle all the E/M services for an admission and for discharge services into a single code. The correct code is determined by documentation of all three of the key components. If any one of the key components is less extensive or complex than the others, then the lesser component determines the level of care. These codes have the same key component requirements as the initial inpatient and observation care codes.

Same day admission and discharge services include three levels of service. Table 5–7 shows the different levels of the components required. Document all three key components (history, examination, and medical decision making) at the required level.

Table 5–7. Requirements for Same Day Admission and Discharge Services

E/M Components	99234	99235	99236
History	Detailed/ Comprehensive	Comprehensive	Comprehensive
Physical examination	Detailed/ comprehensive	Comprehensive	Comprehensive
Medical decision making	Straightforward/low	Moderate	High

For example, if the physician in the previous case had admitted and discharged her patient from inpatient services on 12/14/03, she would report a code describing admission and discharge on the same day of service (99234–99236) instead of an admission code (99221–99223) and a discharge code (99238–99239).

Medicare has special requirements for reporting an admission and discharge from observation or inpatient care on the same day. The physician must:

- Satisfy the documentation requirements for both the admission and discharge

- Document the length of time the patient was on observation or inpatient status

If the patient spends less than 8 hours in observation or inpatient care, then only an admission code is reported. No discharge management is considered necessary.

CPT, however, does not specify a minimum period for these same day admission and discharge codes. Thus, the same service might be reported differently to Medicare than it is to a payer following CPT rules. Following are two examples:

1. A physician admitted his patient to observation care on Tuesday at 10:00 am and discharged her on the same date at 5:00 PM (a 7-hour stay). Under CPT rules, the physician would report the appropriate same day admission/discharge code (99234–99236). Under Medicare rules, the physician would report only the admission code (99218–99220) because the patient was in observation care for less than 8 hours on 1 day.

2. A physician admitted her patient to observation care on Thursday at 8:00 AM and discharged her on the same day at 9:00 PM (a 13-hour stay). Under either CPT or Medicare rules, the physician would report the appropriate same day admission/discharge code (99234–99236).

Consultation Codes (99241–99275)

Consultation services codes are used when the physician has been asked for his or her opinion regarding a specific problem(s). There are different codes for outpatient and initial inpatient consultations. Confirmatory and follow-up inpatient consultations were deleted from CPT in 2006. Consultation codes do not differentiate between new and established patients. The correct code is determined in most cases by documentation of all three key components, although time alone can be used in some cases. If any one of the key components is less extensive or complex than the others, then the lesser component determines the level of care.

Outpatient Consultations (99241–99245)

Outpatient consultation codes are used when the services were provided in an outpatient setting. This includes the physician's office, emergency department, observation areas, and other ambulatory facilities. These codes can be used for either the initial or subsequent outpatient consultations. That is, if the requesting physician asks the consultant for his or her opinion or advice on the patient a second time, then another outpatient consultation code can be reported. The second request can be for the same problem or for a new one. However, if the consultant either initiates the second visit or is providing ongoing management of the patient's problem, then he or she reports an established patient E/M code, not a consultation code.

Outpatient consultation codes include five levels of service. Table 5–8 shows the different levels of the components required. Document either all three key components (history, examination, and medical decision making) at the required level or total time spent with patient (counseling longer than 50% of encounter).

Table 5–8. Requirements for Outpatient Consultation Services

E/M Components	99241	99242	99243	99244	99245
History	Problem-focused	Expanded problem-focused	Detailed	Comprehensive	Comprehensive
Physical examination	Problem-focused	Expanded problem-focused	Detailed	Comprehensive	Comprehensive
Medical decision making	Straightforward	Straightforward	Low	Moderate	High
Face-to-face time	15 minutes	30 minutes	40 minutes	60 minutes	80 minutes

For example, Dr. Brown sent his patient to Dr. Pinkston for evaluation of irregular uterine bleeding. Dr. Pinkston completed a comprehensive history, performed a detailed physical examination, and started the patient on medication. The medical decision making was moderately complex. He sent a written report to Dr. Brown. Dr. Pinkston reported code 99243. The requirements for the history (comprehensive) and medical decision making (moderate) components for code 99244 were met. However, the examination component (detailed) was at the level of code 99243. Because all three components must meet or exceed the criteria, code 99243 was reported.

Inpatient Consultation Codes (99251–99263)

Inpatient consultation codes are used when the services are provided in an inpatient, nursing facility, or partial hospital setting. Unlike outpatient consultation services, there are different codes for initial and subsequent inpatient consultations.

The initial consultation codes (99251–99255) are reported the first time a physician is asked for his or her opinion during the patient's hospital stay. A physician can report only one initial inpatient consultation code per admission.

Initial inpatient consultation codes have five levels of service. The key component requirements are the same as for outpatient consultations. The correct code is determined in most cases by documentation of all three key components, although time alone can be used in some cases. If any one of the key components is less extensive or complex than the others, then the lesser component determines the level of care. Table 5–9 shows the different levels of the components required. Document either all three key components (history, examination, and medical decision making) at the required level or total time spent with

Table 5–9. Requirements for Initial Inpatient Consultation Services

E/M Components	99251	99252	99253	99254	99255
History	Problem-focused	Expanded problem-focused	Detailed	Comprehensive	Comprehensive
Physical examination	Problem-focused	Expanded problem-focused	Detailed	Comprehensive	Comprehensive
Medical decision making	Straightforward	Straightforward	Low	Moderate	High
Floor/unit time	20 minutes	40 minutes	55 minutes	80 minutes	110 minutes

Inpatient consultation codes are used to report E/M services for consultations provided to hospital inpatients, nursing facility residents, or patients in a partial hospital setting.

patient (counseling longer than 50% of encounter). If the consultant either initiates a second visit or is providing ongoing management of the patient's problem, then he or she reports a subsequent hospital care code.

In general, Medicare follows CPT guidelines and criteria concerning consultations. However, Medicare created additional, more specific guidelines to ensure that payments for consultations provided in different areas of the country are equivalent. In August 1999, Medicare clarified its policy on the use of these codes. Several specific issues were further explained and additional information provided to help physicians use consultation codes appropriately. A summary of Medicare's policies follows.

A consultation code can be reported when the requesting and consulting physicians are within the same group practice and even the same specialty. However, the patient's problem must be outside the area of expertise of the requesting physician. For example, a general gynecologist sends a patient to a gynecologic oncologist within the same practice for recommendations concerning the patient's treatment. The gynecologic oncologist reports the service using an outpatient consultation code.

A consultation code can be reported when a surgeon requests a preoperative clearance or a postoperative consultation. It does not matter if the physician has seen the patient before the consultation (eg, whether she is the physician's new or established patient). However, if the physician has reported a preoperative clearance, he or she cannot also report a postoperative consultation. If the consultant assumes management for any portion of the patient's care, a subsequent hospital care code, not a consultation code, is reported.

Medicare also established documentation requirements for reporting consultation codes when the medical record is shared and when it is not. In each of these instances, all criteria for the use of consultation codes must be met.

If the medical record is shared among several physicians (eg, in an inpatient setting or group practice), the request for the consultation may be documented as:

- Part of a plan written in the requesting physician's progress note, or
- An order in the medical record, or
- A specific written request for consultation

The consultant's report may be an entry in the common record.

If the medical record is not shared among the physicians (eg, separate group practices), the request must be documented as:

- A specific written request from the requesting physician or
- A specific reference to the request in the consultant's record

The consultant's report must be a separate document communicated to the requesting physician.

Emergency Department Services Codes (99281–99285)

Emergency department services codes are used when the services are provided in an emergency room setting. CPT defines an emergency department as: "an organized hospital-based facility for the provision of unscheduled episodic services to patients who present for immediate medical attention. The facility must be available 24 hours a day." The emergency department is considered an outpatient area. These codes can be used only in an area meeting the previous definition. These codes do not differentiate between new and established patients. The correct code is determined by the documentation of all three key components. These codes cannot be reported using time. Many payers reimburse only one physician for emergency services for a given episode of care.

In most cases, an obstetrician–gynecologist is not the first physician to see a patient in the emergency department. Therefore, an obstetrician–gynecologist would report a different E/M service (eg, an outpatient consultation, outpatient E/M service, initial inpatient, or observation care), not an emergency department code.

If, for the convenience of either the patient or the physician, a patient is seen in the emergency department rather than the physician's office, then a code from the category "Office or Other Outpatient E/M Services" is reported.

Emergency department services include five levels of services. Table 5–10 shows the different levels of the components required. Document all three key components (history, examination, and medical decision making).

Prolonged Services Codes (99354–99360)

Prolonged services codes are used when E/M services last longer than the typical physician time needed to provide the service. CPT includes codes for prolonged services that are face-to-face and for those that are not. If the additional time to provide the service is less than 30 minutes longer than the typical time, the prolonged services codes are not reported.

The correct code is not determined by documentation of key components but by time only. There are three subcategories of prolonged services in CPT:

1. Prolonged Physician Services With Direct (Face-to-Face) Patient Contact

2. Prolonged Physician Services Without Direct (Face-to-Face) Patient Contact

3. Physician Standby Services

Prolonged Physician Services With Direct (Face-to-Face) Patient Contact Codes (99354–99357)

These codes are used when the prolonged services involve direct (face-to-face) patient contact. Codes 99354 and 99355 are reported for prolonged services in an office or other outpatient settings. Codes 99356 and 99357 are reported for inpatient prolonged services. These are CPT add-on codes. Therefore, the code is reported in addition to other physician service(s) codes, including any level of E/M service. Examples of services that may require additional time with the patient are described in the prolonged services codes as:

- Prolonged care and treatment of an acute asthmatic patient in an outpatient setting

- Physiologic monitoring

- Prolonged care of an acutely ill inpatient

Codes 99354 (office or other outpatient service) and 99356 (inpatient service) are used when the prolonged services last a total time of 30–60 minutes on a given date. These codes are reported only once per day.

Sometimes the prolonged service lasts longer than 1 full hour. If the service is provided in the office or other outpatient setting, report code 99354 for the first 60 minutes plus

Prolonged services codes are used to report E/M services provided beyond the usual service.

Table 5–10. Requirements for Emergency Department Services

E/M Components	99281	99282	99283	99284	99285
History	Problem-focused	Expanded problem-focused	Expanded problem-focused	Detailed	Comprehensive
Physical Examination	Problem-focused	Expanded problem-focused	Expanded problem-focused	Detailed	Comprehensive
Medical Decision Making	Straightforward	Low	Moderate	Moderate	High

code 99355 for each additional 30 minutes. If the service is provided in an inpatient setting, report code 99356 for the first 60 minutes plus code 99357 for each additional 30 minutes. The additional service must be at least 30 minutes beyond the first hour.

Codes 99355 or 99357 also are reported for the final 15–30 minutes of prolonged services on a given date. If the final minutes are fewer than 15, these codes are not reported.

Prolonged services codes can be reported only with E/M codes that include a typical time in their code description. A typical time is listed for office and other outpatient services, hospital care, and most consultation codes. No typical time is listed for observation care, emergency department, and critical care services codes. Prolonged services codes cannot be used with E/M services that include multiple encounters (such as global obstetric codes) or that are selected solely based on time (such as inpatient discharge services).

For example, a physician's established patient, returned to discuss the findings of the endometrial biopsy performed at the time of her well-woman examination. The findings were positive for uterine cancer. The physician discussed the findings with the patient as well as the options for treatment. She was quite upset and called her daughter to come to the physician's office. The physician again reviewed the findings and treatment options with the patient and her daughter. The physician spent a total of 80 minutes face-to-face with her patient. The physician reported codes 99215 and 99354. The typical time for code 99215 is 40 minutes. The remaining 40 minutes were reported using code 99354 (prolonged services, first hour, initial 30–74 minutes).

CPT provides guidelines to help calculate prolonged services. Table 5–11 indicates coding for various periods of prolonged face-to-face services in either an outpatient or inpatient setting.

Prolonged Physician Services Without Direct (Face-to-Face) Patient Contact Codes (99358–99359)

These codes are used to report prolonged services that do not involve direct (face-to-face) care. The same codes are used for inpatient and outpatient prolonged services. These are CPT add-on codes. Therefore, the code is reported in addition to other physician service(s) codes, including any level of E/M service. Examples of the service include review of extensive records and tests and communication with other professionals and the patient/family.

Like the face-to-face prolonged services codes, time is reported based on the first hour and each additional half hour. Table 5–12 indicates coding for various periods of prolonged non–face-to-face services in any setting. Medicare will reimburse for documented face-to-face prolonged services, but will not reimburse for prolonged services without direct patient contact.

Physician Standby Services (99360)

This code is used when one physician is asked by another to provide standby services, including prolonged physician attendance but no direct (face-to-face) patient contact.

Table 5–11. Codes for Prolonged Face-to-Face Services

Minutes	Code for Outpatient Services	Code for Inpatient Services
30–74	99354	99356
75–104	99354 × 1 plus 99355 × 1	99356 × 1 plus 99357 × 1
105–134	99354 × 1 plus 99355 × 2	99356 × 1 plus 99357 × 2
135–164	99354 × 1 plus 99355 × 3	99356 × 1 plus 99357 × 3
165–194	99354 × 1 plus 99355 × 4	99356 × 1 plus 99357 × 4

Table 5–12. Codes for Prolonged Non-Face-to-Face Services in Any Setting

Minutes	Code for Inpatient or Outpatient Services
30–74	99358
75–104	99358 × 1 plus 99359 × 1
105–134	99358 × 1 plus 99359 × 2
135–164	99358 × 1 plus 99359 × 3
165–194	99358 × 1 plus 99359 × 4

Examples include standby for operative procedures (eg, cesarean or high-risk delivery). Unlike the other prolonged services codes, these codes are not add-on codes and can be reported alone.

Do not report physician standby services codes if the physician standing by is:

- Involved in performing a procedure after the standby period
- Rendering an opinion or advice to the operating surgeon
- Proctoring another physician
- Involved in other patient care activities while he or she is standing by
- Not in physical proximity to the patient

Standby services codes are not reported if the services last less than 30 minutes. If subsequent periods of standby are provided, each period must last a full 30 minutes in order to be reported. Medicare does not reimburse for standby services.

Case Management Services Codes (99361–99373)

Case management services codes are reported when a physician coordinates and controls access to health care services or initiates or supervises a patient's health care services. The physician providing case management services is responsible for direct care of the patient. These codes do not require documentation of key components. There are two types of case management services: team conference and telephone calls.

Team Conferences Codes (99361–99362)

Team conferences codes are used to report coordination of patient care using medical conferences with either an interdisciplinary team of health professionals or representatives of community agencies. The patient is not present during the conference. These codes are reported by time only. Code 99361 is reported if the conference lasted approximately 30 minutes; code 99362 is reported if the conference lasted approximately 60 minutes.

Telephone Call Codes (99371–99373)

Telephone call services codes are used to report physician calls to a patient or other health care professional for consultation, medical management, or coordinating medical care. The codes are described as simple or brief (99371), intermediate (99372), and complex or lengthy (99373) but do not include specific time periods. Examples of each type of call are included in the code descriptions.

Most payers, including Medicare, do not reimburse separately for telephone calls. Many payers consider telephone calls to be a noncovered service; in some instances, the physician may be able to bill the patient. Medicare, however, considers telephone calls as bundled in the E/M service(s) that immediately precedes or follows the call. Physicians cannot bill a Medicare patient for a telephone call.

> *Concurrent care occurs when more than one physician provides similar services to the same patient on the same day.*

Special Issues in E/M Coding

Concurrent Care

Concurrent care occurs when more than one physician provides similar services to the same patient on the same day. Payers may not reimburse more than one physician to see an inpatient for the same type of service for the same problem. However, both physicians may be paid if:

- Each physician is rendering a different type of patient care on the same day even if they are treating the same diagnosis(es). For example, one physician reports a consultation, while the other reports a hospital admission.

- Each physician is rendering the same type of patient care on the same day for the same diagnosis(es) but each physician is a distinctly different specialty. For example, one physician is a gynecologist and the other is a general surgeon.

- Each physician is rendering the same type of patient care on the same day but each is treating different problem(s) and reporting different diagnoses. For example, a gynecologist is providing subsequent hospital care for one diagnosis and a general surgeon is providing subsequent hospital care for another diagnosis.

No modifiers or additional documentation are required when reporting concurrent care. Each physician submits his or her claim identifying the reason for his or her service using the most specific ICD-9 diagnostic code(s) available.

More Than One E/M Service on the Same Day

In general, payers do not reimburse a physician for more than one E/M service provided to the same patient on the same day. As noted in the sections on hospital and observation services, all E/M services provided on the same date as a hospital admission are reported using the one code for the admission. Similarly, if the physician sees an inpatient or outpatient multiple times on the same day, all E/M services are combined and reported using a single code.

There are some exceptions. For example, a patient was seen by a physician on hospital rounds in the morning and later developed an acute problem requiring critical care services. A physician reported a subsequent hospital care code for the morning visit and critical care services for the encounter in the afternoon.

Another example is a patient, who was seen by Dr. Vermillion in the outpatient setting. Later that same day, she is seen in the emergency department. The emergency physician called Dr. Vermillion to see her. Dr. Vermillion would report an outpatient code for the office visit and another outpatient code (established patient or consultation) for his emergency department services. In both these examples, the payer may ask for supporting documentation.

Another exception occurs when a problem-oriented E/M service is provided at the same time as a preventive medicine service. This situation is addressed in Chapter 7.

E/M Services and Procedures on the Same Day

CPT rules state that a separate visit can be reported on the same day as minor surgery or procedures if the patient's condition requires a significant, separately identifiable E/M service. This service must be above and beyond the usual preoperative and postoperative care provided with that procedure. The E/M service and the procedure can have the same diagnosis. Modifier –25 (significant and separately identifiable E/M service on the day of another service) is added to the E/M service to indicate that these services were distinct from the procedure. The documentation should clearly support the need for and the content of each service.

Not all payers accept these CPT guidelines. Medicare will reimburse for both services if the documentation clearly indicates that two separate services were provided and the E/M code is reported with a modifier –25. This modifier is discussed more fully in Chapter 9.

Documentation of E/M Services

Evaluation and management services codes were revised in 1992 to standardize the selection of codes across specialties and to better delineate variations in the amount of physician work. At the same time, the American Medical Association released its "Principles of Medical Record Documentation." Representatives from the insurance industry, the payer industry, and providers jointly developed these principles to respond to issues surrounding documentation requirements. The Principles of Documentation first set out some general guidelines:

- The medical record must include documentation of the service(s) rendered and the symptoms and/or diagnosis(es) found.
- The CPT-4 and ICD-9-CM codes reported should match the service(s) and diagnosis(es) documented in the medical record.

The Principles of Documentation also provided more specific guidelines:
- The medical record should be complete and legible.
- The documentation of each patient encounter should include:
  —The chief complaint and/or reason for the encounter and relevant history, physical examination findings, and prior diagnostic results
  —Assessment, clinical impression, or diagnosis
  —Plan for care
  —Date and legible identity of the health care professional who provided the service.
- If not specifically documented, the rationale for ordering diagnostic and other ancillary services should be easily inferred.
- To the greatest extent possible, past and present diagnoses and conditions, including those in the prenatal and intrapartum period that affect the newborn, should be accessible to the treating and/or consulting physician.
- Appropriate health risk factors should be identified.
- The patient's progress, response to and changes in treatment, planned follow-up care and instructions, and diagnosis should be documented.
- The CPT-4 and ICD-9-CM codes reported on the health insurance claim form or billing statement should be supported by the documentation in the medical record.

The CPT-4 does not include these principles explicitly in its guidelines. However, most payers adhere to them when evaluating claims for services. These principles were explicitly incorporated into Medicare's documentation guidelines. These are discussed in detail in the next chapter.

Chapter 5 Quiz: Applying E/M Services Codes

True or False:

1. All inpatient and outpatient E/M codes include five levels of service.

2. All E/M codes distinguish between new and established patient encounters.

Choose the best answer.

3. If a new patient E/M visit is documented with an expanded problem-focused history, comprehensive examination and moderate medical decision making, the overall level of service would be:

   a. 99201

   b. 99202

   c. 99203

   d. 99204

   e. 99205

4. If an established patient E/M visit is documented with an expanded problem-focused history, comprehensive examination, and moderate medical decision making, the overall level of service would be:

   a. 99211

   b. 99212

   c. 99213

   d. 99214

   e. 99215

5. Services provided to patients seen in the physician's office and subsequently admitted to the hospital are reported using:

   a. Only the appropriate outpatient E/M code

   b. Both the appropriate outpatient E/M code and the initial inpatient care code

   c. Only the appropriate initial inpatient care code

6. The initial inpatient care codes:

   a. Can be reported only by one physician during the patient's hospital stay

   b. Can be reported by more than one physician if a transfer of care occurs

   c. Can be reported by each physician seeing the patient for the first time during the hospital stay

7. Initial observation care codes have:

   a. Three levels of service

   b. The same requirements as initial inpatient care codes

   c. A minimum requirement for a detailed history and exam

   d. All of the above

Answers are listed on page 179.

Chapter 6

E/M Services and Medicare Documentation Guidelines

Since 1992, Medicare has struggled with the task of making each evaluation and management (E/M) services code represent a clearly defined amount of physician work, regardless of the specialty of the physician providing the service. This chapter reviews the various documentation guidelines that grew out of this struggle and addresses:

- The purpose and background of the American Medical Association (AMA)/Centers for Medicare and Medicaid Services (CMS) documentation guidelines
- The distinctions between the 1995 and 1997 documentation guidelines
- The specific requirements of the documentation guidelines

Following completion of the chapter, the reader should be able to:

- Demonstrate knowledge of the guidelines for each key component of E/M services
- Recognize the distinctions between the 1995 and 1997 guidelines
- Apply the guidelines to clinical practice

History of the Documentation Guidelines

In 1992, the CPT codes for reporting medical visits were revised to standardize the services included in each code. The new E/M services codes included limited descriptions of the components (history, physical examination, and medical decision making) for each level of service. Medicare, in its effort to clearly define the content of medical services, wanted more. Therefore, Medicare incorporated the AMA's 1992 "Principles of Medical Record Documentation" into its guidelines. These principles were reviewed in the previous chapter.

Many providers, however, felt that the guidelines for documenting E/M services still were unclear, and CMS began the task of developing very specific documentation guidelines. Medicare's goal was that all carriers use the same guidelines. Therefore, payment made to a gynecologist in Vermont for an E/M service will represent equivalent work as a payment made to a pediatrician in Utah for the same E/M service.

The documentation guidelines were the joint work of CMS and the AMA. They were implemented in June 1995. The guidelines introduced the concept of "quantifying" certain aspects of medical documentation to determine levels of service. These guidelines, known

...physicians can use either the 1995 or 1997 guidelines, depending on which one is most appropriate to their practice.

as the "1995 Documentation Guidelines," defined a comprehensive examination as the documentation of findings for at least eight different organ systems. Because of this, the guidelines were criticized for not reflecting the more focused work performed by specialists who might perform a very detailed examination of one organ system.

On October 1, 1997, CMS released the "1997 Documentation Guidelines." These guidelines were developed as a cooperative effort between CMS, the AMA, and numerous specialty societies. The guidelines sought to reflect the clinical activities of specialists while maintaining work equivalency. The result was a set of 10 single-system examinations and a multisystem examination. The level of examination was determined by counting the number of specific examination elements documented.

These guidelines were criticized as being overly complicated. Rather than adopt the 1997 guidelines as a replacement for the 1995 guidelines, CMS instructed carriers to use both sets of guidelines when reviewing medical claims. As a result, physicians can use either the 1995 or 1997 guidelines, depending on which one is most appropriate to their practice. The CMS also agreed to look at alternative guidelines.

Future of the Documentation Guidelines

After several other attempts at developing new guidelines, the secretary of the Department of Health and Human Services halted the process. It was decided not to implement any changes to CPT definitions or documentation guidelines at this time. Physicians should continue to use either the 1995 or 1997 guidelines.

The introductions to both the 1995 and 1997 Documentation Guidelines incorporate AMA's 1992 "Principles of Documentation." These introductions state: "Medical record documentation is required to record pertinent facts, findings, and observations about an individual's health history, including past and present illnesses, examinations, tests, treatments, and outcomes. The medical record is used to chronologically document the care of the patient and thus contributes to high quality care." The introductions further note that medical record documentation facilitates:

- Evaluation and planning of the patient's immediate treatment and monitoring of health care over time
- Communication and continuity of care among physicians and other health care professionals involved in the patient's care
- Accurate and timely claims review and payment
- Appropriate utilization review and quality of care evaluations
- Collection of data that may be useful for outcomes research and education

The documentation guidelines recognize that medical record information may vary for certain groups of patients. Specifically, the records of infants, children, adolescents, and pregnant women may have additional or modified information recorded in the history and examination components. These variations, although not explicitly addressed in the guidelines, are considered appropriate.

The remainder of this chapter briefly describes each key component of an E/M service (history, examination, and medical decision making) and related documentation guidelines. The 1995 and 1997 requirements for the history and medical decision-making components are virtually the same. The requirements for the examination component, however, are different for the 1995 and 1997 guidelines. Summaries of the documentation requirements for different levels and types of services can be found at the end of the chapter.

Documenting the History Component

The previous chapter listed the four levels of history as described by CPT: 1) problem-focused, 2) expanded problem-focused, 3) detailed, and 4) comprehensive. Some or all of these elements determines the level of history: chief complaint (CC); history of present illness (HPI); review of systems (ROS); and past, family, or social history (PFSH).

The CMS' documentation guidelines for the history component provide additional, more specific requirements:

- The CC should be reflected clearly in the medical record and indicate the reason for the encounter.

- The CC, ROS, and PFSH may be listed separately or they all may be included in the description of the HPI.

- The ROS and/or PFSH may be recorded by ancillary staff or on a form completed by the patient. The physician must supplement or confirm information recorded by others.

- An ROS and/or PFSH recorded during a previous encounter does not have to be re-recorded. However, the physician must document that he or she reviewed and updated the information as follows:

  —Document any new ROS and/or PFSH information and note the date and location of the earlier information or

  —Note that there has been no change

- If the physician is unable to obtain a history from the patient or other source, the record should describe the patient's condition or other circumstances that preclude obtaining a history.

History of Present Illness

CPT and the documentation guidelines list specific elements used to determine the level of HPI:

- Location
- Quality
- Severity
- Duration
- Timing
- Context
- Modifying factors
- Associated signs and symptoms significantly related to presenting problems(s)

CPT describes levels of HPI as "brief" and "extended," but does not define these terms. The 1995 and 1997 documentation guidelines distinguish brief from extended by the number of the above elements required to evaluate the clinical problem(s):

- A brief HPI includes one to three elements
- An extended HPI includes four or more elements or associated comorbidities

For example, a brief HPI would state: The patient reports dysuria for the past 2 days. An extended HPI would state: The patient reports dysuria for the past 2 days, which is progressively getting worse. She denies fever or chills.

The 1997 Documentation Guidelines expanded the definition of an extended HPI to include the status of three chronic or inactive conditions instead of four or more elements if appropriate.

Review of Systems

CPT and the documentation guidelines list specific systems that determine the level of ROS:

- Constitutional symptoms (eg, fever or weight loss)
- Eyes
- Ears, nose, mouth, throat
- Cardiovascular
- Respiratory
- Gastrointestinal
- Genitourinary
- Musculoskeletal
- Integumentary (skin and/or breast)
- Neurologic
- Psychiatric
- Endocrine
- Hematologic/lymphatic
- Allergic/immunologic

CPT describes the review of systems as "problem pertinent," "extended," and "complete," but does not define these terms.

The 1995 and 1997 documentation guidelines distinguish between these terms by specifying the number of systems reviewed:

- Problem pertinent ROS includes one system (the system related to the problem)
- Extended ROS includes two to nine systems
- Complete ROS includes at least 10 systems

The complete ROS can include documentation of:
- 10 individual systems or
- Pertinent positive and negative findings, plus either:

   —statement indicating all other systems are negative or

   —notation supplementing or confirming the information recorded by others

Past, Family, and Social History

CPT and the documentation guidelines list specific areas that are used to determine the PFSH level:

- Past history—Patient's past experiences with illnesses, operations, injuries, medications, compliance, and treatments
- Family history—Review of medical events in the patient's family, including diseases that may be hereditary or place the patient at risk
- Social history—Age-appropriate review of past and current activities

CPT uses the terms "pertinent" and "complete" to describe the PFSH, but does not define them.

The 1995 and 1997 documentation guidelines distinguish between a pertinent and complete PFSH using above elements:
- A pertinent PFSH is a review of history area(s) directly related to the problem(s) identified in the HPI.

- A complete PFSH is a review of two or three of the PFSH areas, depending on the category of service. A PFSH for the code categories listed below require one specific item from personal, family, and social history. These services by their nature include a comprehensive assessment or reassessment of the patient:

  —Office or other outpatient services, new patient

  —Hospital observation services

  —Hospital inpatient services, initial care

  —Consultations (except inpatient follow-up)

  —Comprehensive nursing facility assessments

  —Domiciliary care and home care, new patients

  A PFSH for the code categories listed below require only one specific item from two of the three PFSH areas:

  —Office or other outpatient services, established patient

  —Emergency department services

  —Domiciliary care and home care, established patients

  Some codes are used to report return visits that require only an interval history. Because the PFSH is unlikely to have changed from the last encounter, no PFSH is required for these code categories:

  —Subsequent hospital care

  —Follow-up inpatient consultations

  —Subsequent nursing facility care

Table 6–1 describes the history components necessary to report a specific level of service.

All four components of the history (CC, HPI, ROS, and PFSH) must be documented at the designated level (number of elements) to qualify for a given level of history. For example, a patient is seen with a chief complaint of urinary urgency and frequency. The physician documents the chief complaint, four HPI elements (detailed), review of two systems (detailed), and three PFSH elements (comprehensive). This is a detailed history based on the level of the HPI and ROS.

Table 6–1. Levels of History

Levels	Chief Complaint (CC)	History of Present Illness (HPI)	Review of Systems (ROS)	Past, Family, Social History (PFSH)
Problem-focused	Required	Brief (one to three elements)	None required	None required
Expanded problem-focused	Required	Brief (one to three elements)	Problem pertinent (one system)	None required
Detailed	Required	Extended (four or more elements or three or more chronic or inactive conditions)	Extended (two to nine systems)	Pertinent (one element)
Comprehensive	Required	Extended (four or more elements)	Complete (10 systems)	Complete (two or more elements)

Documenting the Examination Component

Chapter 4 listed the four levels of physical examination as described by CPT: 1) problem-focused, 2) expanded problem-focused, 3) detailed, and 4) comprehensive. The 1995 and 1997 documentation guidelines use different criteria for the examination. The specific number of body area(s) and organ systems examined determines the level of physical examination under the 1995 guidelines. The specific number of elements examined within defined organ systems determines the level of physical examination under the 1997 guidelines.

Physicians can choose which set of guidelines to use for each individual patient. The 1997 guidelines often are more beneficial to obstetrician–gynecologists, especially when a pelvic examination is performed because each component of the pelvic examination is counted separately, whereas the 1995 guidelines count only one organ system (genitourinary).

1995 Documentation Requirements

These documentation guidelines use the following body areas and organ systems for the examination component:

Body Areas:

- Head, including face
- Neck
- Chest, including breast and axillae
- Abdomen
- Genitalia/groin/buttocks
- Back, including spine
- Each extremity

Organ Systems:

- Constitutional
- Eyes
- Ears/nose/mouth/throat
- Cardiovascular
- Respiratory
- Gastrointestinal
- Genitourinary
- Musculoskeletal
- Skin
- Neurologic
- Psychiatric
- Hematologic/lymphatic/immunologic

These are the same body areas/organ systems used in CPT, with the addition of constitutional organ system.

The extent of the examination performed depends on the physician's clinical judgment and the nature of the presenting problem(s). The examination ranges from a limited examination of a single body area to a general multisystem examination or a complete single organ system examination.

The 1995 guidelines, however, do not define a single organ system examination. They provide the following specific documentation requirements:

- Document the specific abnormal and relevant negative findings from the examination of the affected or symptomatic area/system. A notation of "abnormal" without elaboration is insufficient.

- Describe abnormal or unexpected findings from the examination of unaffected or asymptomatic areas/systems.

- It is sufficient to document a brief statement indicating "negative" or "normal" for normal findings related to unaffected area(s) or asymptomatic system(s).

- A general multisystem examination should include documented findings concerning eight or more of the 12 organ systems.

Table 6–2 shows the elements included in the levels of service according to the 1995 Documentation Guidelines using the body areas/organ systems listed previously. This information also is included in the tables at the end of the chapter.

Not all of these criteria are included in the official guidelines. During the discussion of proposed revisions to the 1995 guidelines, CMS indicated to specialty societies that a detailed examination included five to seven body areas/organ systems. By default, it was concluded that an expanded problem-focused examination would consist of two to four body areas/organ systems. This clarification was never included in the official guidelines. However, many specialty societies, some Medicare carriers, and other auditors use this definition of an expanded problem-focused examination.

1997 Documentation Requirements

The 1997 guidelines define a general multisystem examination plus 10 single-organ system examinations. The general multisystem examination includes elements from 10 different organ systems or body areas, including: eyes; ears, nose, mouth, and throat; and psychiatric.

The single-organ system examinations are designed to require equivalent physician work to reach a level of service. These single system examinations are:

- Skin

- Eyes

- Ears, nose, mouth, and throat

- Cardiovascular

- Respiratory

- Genitourinary (includes separate male and female examinations)

- Musculoskeletal

- Hematologic/lymphatic/immunologic

- Neurologic

- Psychiatric

The guidelines state that any physician, regardless of specialty, may perform either a general multisystem examination or any of the single-organ system examinations. Each

Table 6–2. Body Areas/Organ Systems Included in Levels of Physical Examination, 1995 Documentation Guidelines

Type of Examination	1995 Requirements
Problem-focused	One body area or organ system
Expanded problem-focused	Two to four organ systems including affected area
Detailed	Five to seven organ systems including affected area
Comprehensive	Eight or more organ systems

single-system examination includes a number of related systems in addition to the primary system being examined. For example, the psychiatric single system examination includes elements in the constitutional and musculoskeletal systems in addition to pyschiatric elements. The level of service is determined by the number of elements evaluated in one or more of the systems that are part of that single system examination. Because most obstetrician–gynecologists use the female genitourinary examination, this examination is used in the examples and tables in this chapter.

The guidelines use tables to show which organ systems and body areas are included in each single system examination. Bullets (●) identify the content or individual elements in a given area or system. Examples in parentheses clarify and provide guidance regarding documentation. Documentation must satisfy any numeric requirements listed (eg, "any three of the following seven vital signs"). Elements with multiple components but without a specific numeric requirement (eg, "examination of liver and spleen") require documentation of at least one of the components listed (eg, liver or spleen).

The general requirements associated with the 1995 guidelines (eg, describe abnormal or unexpected findings) also apply to the 1997 guidelines. Table 6–3 shows the requirements for each level of examination. Table 6–4 lists the elements included in the female genitourinary examination.

In most cases, the extent of the examination depends on the total number of bulleted elements documented in the medical record without regard to the number of body systems examined. The requirements for documenting a comprehensive level examination are different.

The female genitourinary single-organ system examination includes shaded and unshaded boxes for the various areas or systems. The shaded boxes include the constitutional, gastrointestinal, and genitourinary systems. A comprehensive female genitourinary system examination requires documentation of all the following elements:

- All bulleted elements in the constitutional and gastrointestinal systems

- Seven of the 11 bulleted elements in the genitourinary system

- One bulleted element each in the neck, respiratory, cardiovascular, chest, lymphatic, skin, and neurologic/psychiatric body areas/organ systems

Table 6–3. Elements Included in Levels of Examination, 1997 Female Genitourinary Examination

Type of Examination	1997 Requirements
Problem-focused	One to five elements from one or more organ systems
Expanded problem-focused	Six to 11 elements from one or more organ systems
Detailed	12 or more elements from one or more organ systems
Comprehensive	**Shaded boxes**
	All elements from constitutional and gastrointestinal systems
	Any seven elements in the genitourinary system
	Unshaded boxes
	One element each from neck, respiratory, cardiovascular, lymphatic, skin, and neurologic/psychiatric systems

Table 6–4. 1997 Female Genitourinary System Examination

System/Body Area	Elements of Examination*
Constitutional	• Recording of any three of the following vital signs: 1) sitting or standing blood pressure, 2) supine blood pressure, 3) pulse rate and regularity, 4) respiration, 5) temperature, 6) height, or 7) weight (may be measured and recorded by ancillary staff) • General appearance of patient (eg, development, nutrition, body habitus, deformities, attention to grooming)
Neck	• Examination of thyroid (eg, enlargement, tenderness, mass) • Examination of neck (eg, masses, overall appearance, symmetry, tracheal position, crepitus)
Respiratory	• Assessment of respiratory effort (eg, intercostal retractions, use of accessory muscles, diaphragmatic movement) • Auscultation of lungs (eg, breath sounds, adventitious sounds, rubs)
Cardiovascular	• Auscultation of the heart with notation of sounds, abnormal sounds, and murmurs • Examination of peripheral vascular system by observation (eg, swelling, varicosities) and palpation (eg, pulses, temperature, edema, tenderness)
Chest (Breast)	• See genitourinary (female)
Lymphatic	• Palpation of lymph nodes in neck, axillae and/or groin, and/or other location
Skin	• Inspection and/or palpation of skin and subcutaneous tissue (eg, rashes, lesions, ulcers)
Neurologic/ psychiatric	Brief assessment of mental status including: • Orientation (ie, time, place, and person) and • Mood and affect (eg, depression, anxiety, agitation)
Gastrointestinal (Abdomen)	• Examination of abdomen with notation of presence of masses and tenderness • Examination of liver and spleen • Obtain stool sample for occult blood test, when indicated • Examination for presence or absence of hernia
Genitourinary	• Inspection and palpation of breasts (eg, masses or lumps, tenderness, symmetry, nipple discharge) • Digital rectal examination including sphincter tone, presence of hemorrhoids, rectal masses Pelvic examination (with or without specimen collection for smears and cultures) of: • External genitalia (eg, general appearance, hair distribution, lesions) • Urethral meatus (eg, size, location, lesions, prolapse) • Urethra (eg, masses, tenderness, scarring) • Bladder (eg, fullness, masses, tenderness) • Vagina (eg, general appearance, estrogen effect, discharge, lesions, pelvic support, cystocele, rectocele) • Cervix (eg, general appearance, lesions, discharge) • Uterus (eg, size, contour, position, mobility, tenderness, consistency, descent or support) • Adnexa/Parametria (eg, masses, tenderness, organomegaly, nodularity) • Anus and perineum

*Shading in three of the boxes is important only when documenting a comprehensive examination.

The level of service can change depending on whether the physician uses the 1995 guidelines or the 1997 guidelines for the examination.

Comparison of 1995 and 1997 Documentation Guidelines

The level of service can change depending on whether the physician uses the 1995 guidelines or the 1997 guidelines for the examination. The differences between the two sets of guidelines are summarized in Table 6–5.

Following are two examples.

1. A patient was examined by her physician for irregular uterine bleeding. Her physical examination included the following findings:

   General: WDWNWF in NAD, A&Ox3

   Neck: Supple without thyromegaly

   Chest: Clear

   Breasts: No masses, glactorrhea, or retraction

   Abdomen: BS+. Soft and nontender without masses or organomegaly

   Neurologic: Grossly intact

   Pelvic: External genitalia normal. Cervix and vaginal normal. Copious, clear cervical mucous. Uterus AF, NSSC. Adnexa neg.

   Using the 1995 guidelines, the physician documented eight body areas/organ systems: constitutional, neck, respiratory, chest including breast and axillae, gastrointestinal, neurologic, genitalia/groin/buttocks, and genitourinary. This is a comprehensive examination.

   Using the 1997 guidelines for the female genitourinary system examination, the physician documented 12 bulleted elements: one each in constitutional, neck, respiratory, cardiovascular, neurologic/psychiatric, and gastrointestinal and six in the genitourinary system. This is a detailed examination.

2. A patient saw her physician for pelvic pain. The physician performed the following examination:

   Constitutional: BP 120/85, Pulse 85, Weight 125 lb, Height 64 in., patient well-groomed, well-developed

   Abdomen: No masses, no tenderness, and no enlargement of liver or spleen

Table 6–5. Comparison of Physical Examination Requirements for Medicare 1995 Documentation Guidelines and 1997 Documentation Guidelines

Level of Examination	Medicare 1995 Documentation Guidelines	Medicare 1997 Documentation Guidelines (Female Genitourinary System)
Problem-focused	One body area/organ system	One to five elements in any one or more body areas/organ systems
Expanded problem-focused	Two to four body areas/organ systems	Six to11 elements in any one or more body areas/organ systems
Detailed	Five to seven body areas/organ systems	12 and more elements in any one or more body areas/organ systems
Comprehensive	Eight and more body areas/organ systems	19 elements from nine specified body areas/organ systems

Pelvic: External genitalia: No lesions. Urethra and meatus: No lesions. Vagina: Normal appearance. Cervix: Normal appearance. Second-degree uterine prolapse. First-degree cystocele and rectocele. Bimanual: Uterus is small, anterior, mobile, and nontender. Adnexae: No masses or tenderness. Rectal: Confirms examination and first-degree rectocele.

Using the 1995 guidelines, the physician examined four body areas/organ systems: constitutional, abdomen, genitalia/groin/buttocks, and genitourinary. This is an expanded problem focused examination.

Using the 1997 guidelines, the physician documented 12 bulleted elements: two each under constitutional and gastrointestinal and eight in the genitourinary system. This is a detailed examination.

Documenting the Medical Decision Making Component

The previous chapter listed the four levels of medical decision making as described by CPT: 1) straightforward, 2) low complexity, 3) moderate complexity, and 4) high complexity.

Unlike the history and examination key components, the 1995 and 1997 documentation guidelines do not include any counting of elements or systems to determine the correct level of medical decision making. The guidelines use the same three medical decision-making components listed in CPT: 1) number of diagnoses or management options, 2) amount and/or complexity of data to be reviewed, and 3) risk of complications and/or morbidity or mortality. The levels of medical decision making are summarized in Table 6–6.

The number of possible diagnoses and/or management options considered is based on:

- Number and types of problems addressed
- Complexity of establishing a diagnosis
- Management decisions made by the physician

The complexity of medical decision making may be increased by documentation of:

- Identified but undiagnosed problem(s)
- Number and type of diagnostic tests ordered
- Need to seek advice from others
- Problem(s) worsening or failing to respond to treatment

The documentation guidelines for this component are:

- Document an assessment, clinical impression, or diagnosis for each encounter; decisions regarding management plans and/or further evaluation may be either explicitly stated or implied.
- Document presenting problems with established diagnoses as:

  —Improved, well controlled, resolving, or resolved or

  —Inadequately controlled, worsening, or failing to change as expected

- Document presenting problems without established diagnoses as differential or possible, probable, or rule out diagnoses.
- Document initiation of or changes in treatment. Treatment is defined as including patient and nursing instructions, therapies, medications, and a variety of other management options.
- Document referrals and requests for consultations or advice indicating the facilities or professionals involved.

Table 6-6. Levels of Medical Decision Making

Number of Diagnoses or Management Options to Be Reviewed	Amount and/or Complexity of Data or Mortality	Risk of Complications and/or Morbidity	Type of Medical Decision Making
Minimal	Minimal or none	Minimal	Straightforward
Limited	Limited	Low	Low complexity
Multiple	Moderate	Moderate	Moderate complexity
Extensive	Extensive	High	High complexity

Amount and Complexity of Data

The amount and complexity of data to be reviewed is based on:

- Types of diagnostic testing ordered or reviewed
- Need to obtain previous records
- Need to obtain history from other source(s)

The complexity of medical decision making may be increased by documentation of:

- Contradictory or unexpected findings
- An independent interpretation of image, tracing, or specimen by the physician ordering the study
- Discussion of results with the physician who actually performed or interpreted the study

The guidelines require documentation of:

- Any diagnostic service (test or procedure) ordered, planned, scheduled, or performed at the time of the E/M encounter; include the type of service (eg, laboratory or X-ray)
- Any review of laboratory, radiology, and/or other diagnostic tests. The physician may document the review either by making an entry in a progress note or by initialing and dating the test results report
- Any decision to obtain old records or additional history from the family, caretaker, or other source to supplement the history obtained from the patient
- Any relevant findings from the review of old records and/or receipt of additional history from family, caretaker, or other source. It is not sufficient to note the review of records or receipt of information without elaboration (eg, "old records reviewed" or "additional information obtained from family")
- Results of any discussions of laboratory, radiology, or other diagnostic test results with the physician who performed or interpreted the test(s)
- Any direct visualization and independent interpretation of tests previously or subsequently interpreted by another physician
- If no findings or additional history were reviewed, the physician should document that no relevant information was obtained

Risk of Significant Complications, Morbidity, or Mortality

The risk to the patient is based upon the highest level of risk associated with the:

- Presenting problem(s) and the risk related to the disease process anticipated between the present encounter and the next one

- Diagnostic procedure(s) and the risk during and immediately after the procedure
- Possible management options and the risk during and immediately after the treatment

The complexity of medical decision making may be increased by documenting:

- Comorbidities, underlying diseases, and identified risk factors
- Uncertain prognosis, systemic symptoms, exacerbations, and complications
- Decision to order prescription drugs, intravenous medications, parenteral controlled substances
- Decision to perform invasive tests, procedures, or major surgery

Table 6–7, excerpted from the 1995 and 1997 documentation guidelines, can help to determine the level of risk in a specific case. The table includes clinical examples for each level of risk rather than absolute measures of risk. The highest level of risk in any one category determines the overall risk. Select the highest level of risk in any one column.

Of the three components of medical decision making (number of diagnoses or management options, amount and/or complexity of data to be reviewed, and risk of complications and/or morbidity or mortality), two must be documented at the designated level to qualify for a given level of history. For example, a patient is seen by a physician with a report of bleeding and heavy menses. The physician documents multiple diagnoses (moderate complexity), extensive data review (high complexity), and moderate risk of complications (moderate complexity). This is medical decision making of moderate complexity.

CPT's Appendix C provides examples of various levels of E/M services, including all the key components. An example of a visit with straightforward medical decision making is: "Initial evaluation and management of recurrent urinary infection (code 99202)". An example of a visit with moderate medical decision making is: "Office consultation for a patient with complaint of chronic pelvic inflammatory disease who now has left lower quadrant pain with a palpable pelvic mass (code 99244)". An example of a visit with medical decision making of high complexity is: "Initial hospital visit for a 16-year-old primigravida at 32 weeks gestation with severe hypertension (200/110), thrombocytopenia, and headache (code 99223)".

> *CPT's Appendix C provides examples of various levels of E/M services, including all the key components.*

Reporting E/M Services Using Time

Both the 1995 and the 1997 documentation guidelines accept reporting of E/M services using time when more than 50% of the visit involved counseling or coordination of care. (See Chapter 4 for a more complete discussion on the use of time.) The documentation should include the total length of time of the encounter (face-to-face time in outpatient settings or floor/unit time in inpatient settings) and a description of the counseling and/or activities to coordinate care.

For example, a physician performed a level-2 history, examination, and medical decision making because the patient had a history of miscarriages. The physician spent 10 minutes performing the history, examination, and medical decision making plus another 15 minutes counseling the patient concerning possible causes of the miscarriages, for a total time spent with her of 25 minutes. The physician reports code 99214, which has a typical time of 25 minutes. She does not have to document the level of key components to report 99214. If the physician had selected the level of service based only on the key components, she would have reported code 99212.

Applying the Documentation Guidelines

The documentation guidelines were developed to provide physicians and claims reviewers with explicit rules for preparing or reviewing documentation for E/M services. Tables 6–8 to 6–15 show the documentation required for different levels of service.

Table 6–7. Examples of Levels of Risk in Medical Decision Making

Level of Risk	Presenting Problem(s)	Diagnostic Procedure(s) Ordered	Management Options Selected
Minimal	• One self-limited/ minor problem (eg, cold, insect bite, tinea corporis)	• Laboratory tests (urinalysis, KOH prep) or tests requiring venipuncture • Imaging studies (ultrasound, electrocardiography)	• Rest • Elastic bandages • Superficial dressings
Low	• Two and more self-limited/minor problems • One chronic, stable illness (eg, noninsulin dependent diabetes) • Acute, uncomplicated illness or injury	• Clinical laboratory tests using arterial puncture • Imaging studies with contrast, noncardiovascular (eg, barium enema) • Skin or superficial needle biopsy	• Minor surgery with no identified risk factors • Over-the-counter drugs • Intravenous fluids without additives
Moderate	• Undiagnosed new problem with uncertain prognosis (eg, breast lump) • One and more chronic illness with mild exacerbation/ progression, or side effects of treatment • Two and more stable, chronic conditions • Acute illness with systemic symptoms • Acute, complicated injury	• Physiologic tests under stress (eg, fetal contraction stress test) • Cardiovascular imaging studies with contrast and no identified risk factors • Diagnostic endoscopies with no identifiable risk factors • Deep needle or incisional biopsy • Obtain fluid from body cavity (eg, culdocentesis)	• Minor surgery with identifiable risk factors • Elective major surgery with no identifiable risk factors (open/percutaneous/ endoscopic) • Management of prescription drugs • Intravenous fluids with additives
High	• One or more chronic illnesses with severe exacerbation/ progression/side effects of treatment • Acute or chronic illnesses or injuries posing threat to life/bodily function • Abrupt change in neurologic status (eg, seizure/transient ischemic attack/ weakness/sensory loss)	• Cardiovascular imaging studies with contrast and identified risk factors • Diagnostic endoscopies with identified risk factors	• Elective or emergency major surgery with identifiable risk factors (open/percutaneous/ endoscopic) • Drug therapy requiring intensive monitoring for toxicity

New Patient in Office or Other Outpatient Settings

Table 6–8 shows requirements for new patients. Document either all three key components (history, examination, and medical decision making) at the required level or total face-to-face time with patient (counseling greater than 50% of encounter).

Established Patient in Office or Other Outpatient Settings

Table 6–9 shows requirements for established patients. Document either two of three key components (history, examination, and medical decision making) at the required level or total face-to-face time with patient (counseling greater than 50% of encounter).

Outpatient and Inpatient Consultations

Tables 6–10 and 6–11 show requirements for outpatient and inpatient consultations. Document either all three key components (history, examination, and medical decision making) at the required level or total time spent with patient (counseling greater than 50% of encounter).

Tables 6–12 to 6–14 show requirements for initial inpatient/initial observation/admission and discharge on same day. The levels of service are the same for these categories of E/M services. Document all three key components (history, examination, and medical decision making) at the required level.

Table 6–8. Documentation Requirements for New Patients—Office or Other Outpatient Settings

	Code				
	99201	**99202**	**99203**	**99204**	**99205**
History					
CC	Required	Required	Required	Required	Required
HPI	One to three elements	One to three elements	Greater than or equal to four elements or greater than or equal to three chronic or inactive conditions	Greater than or equal to four elements or greater than or equal to three chronic or inactive conditions	Greater than or equal to four elements or greater than or equal to three chronic or inactive conditions
ROS	Not required	One system	Two to nine systems	10–14 systems	10–14 systems
PFSH	Not required	Not required	1 elements	3 elements	3 elements
Physical examination					
1997	One to five elements	6–11 elements	Greater than or equal to 12 elements	Comprehensive single-system examination	Comprehensive single-system examination
1995	One system	Two to four systems	Five to seven systems	Greater than or equal to eight systems	Greater than or equal to eight systems
Medical decision making					
Diagnostic/ management options	Minimal	Minimal	Limited	Multiple	Extensive
Data reviewed	Minimal or none	Minimal or none	Limited	Moderate	Extensive
Risk	Minimal	Minimal	Low	Moderate	High
Typical face-to-face time	10 minutes	20 minutes	30 minutes	45 minutes	60 minutes

Abbreviations: CC, chief complaint; HPI, history of present illness; PFSH, past, family, and/or social history; ROS, review of systems.

Table 6–9. Documentation Requirements for Established Patients—Office or Other Outpatient Settings

| | Code | | | | |
Examination	99211*	99212	99213	99214	99215
History					
CC	Not required	Required	Required	Required	Required
HPI	Not required	One to three elements	One to three elements	Greater than or equal to four elements or greater than or equal to three chronic or inactive conditions	Greater than or equal to four elements or greater than or equal to three chronic inactive conditions
ROS	Not required	Not required	One system	Two to nine systems	10–14 systems
PFSH	Not required	Not required	Not required	One element	Two elements
Physical examination					
1997	Not required	One to five elements	6–11 elements	Greater than or equal to 12 elements	Comprehensive single-system examination
1995	Not required	One system	Two to four systems	Five to seven systems	Greater than or equal to eight elements
Medical decision making					
Diagnostic/ management options	Not required	Minimal	Limited	Multiple	Extensive
Data reviewed	Not required	Minimal or none	Limited	Moderate	Extensive
Risk	Not required	Minimal	Low	Moderate	High
Typical face-to-face time	5 minutes supervision	10 minutes	15 minutes	25 minutes	40 minutes

*Medicare requires that a physician be in the office suite during the E/M service.

Abbreviations: CC, chief complaint; HPI, history of present illness; PFSH, past, family, and/or social history; ROS, review of systems.

Subsequent Hospital Care

Table 6–15 shows requirements for subsequent hospital care. Document two of the three key components (history, examination, and medical decision making) at the required level or time spent face-to-face with patient and/or on unit/floor.

Table 6–10. Documentation Requirements for Outpatient Consultations

	Code				
Examination	**99241**	**99242**	**99243**	**99244**	**99245**
History					
CC	Required	Required	Required	Required	Required
HPI	One to three elements	One to three elements	Greater than or equal to four elements or greater than or equal to three chronic or inactive conditions	Greater than or equal to four elements or greater than or equal to three chronic or inactive conditions	Greater than or equal to four elements or greater than or equal to three chronic or inactive conditions
ROS	Not required	One system	Two to nine systems	10–14 systems	10–14 systems
PFSH	Not required	Not required	One element	Three elements	Three elements
Physical examination					
1997	One to five elements	Six to 11 elements	Greater than or equal to 12 elements	Comprehensive single-system examination	Comprehensive single-system examination
1995	One system	Two to four systems	Five to seven systems	Greater than or equal to eight systems	Greater than or equal to eight systems
Medical decision making					
Diagnostic/ management options	Minimal	Minimal	Limited	Multiple	Extensive
Data reviewed	Minimal or none	Minimal or none	Limited	Moderate	Extensive
Risk	Minimal	Minimal	Low	Moderate	High
Typical face-to-face time	15 minutes	30 minutes	40 minutes	60 minutes	80 minutes

Abbreviations: CC, chief complaint; HPI, history of present illness; PFSH, past, family, and/or social history; ROS, review of systems.

Table 6–11. Documentation Requirements for Inpatient Consultations

	Code				
Examination	**99251**	**99252**	**99253**	**99254**	**99255**
History					
CC	Required	Required	Required	Required	Required
HPI	One to three elements	One to three elements	Greater than or equal to four elements or greater than or equal to three chronic or inactive conditions	Greater than or equal to four elements or greater than or equal to three chronic or inactive conditions	Greater than or equal to four elements or greater than or equal to three chronic or inactive conditions
ROS	Not required	One system	Two to nine systems	10–14 systems	10–14 systems
PFSH	Not required	Not required	One element	Three elements	Three elements
Physical examination					
1997	One to five elements	6–11 elements	Greater than or equal to 12 elements	Comprehensive single-system examination	Comprehensive single-system examination
1995	One system	Two to four systems	Five to seven systems	Greater than or equal to eight systems	Greater than or equal to eight systems
Medical decision making					
Diagnostic/ management options	Minimal	Minimal	Limited	Multiple	Extensive
Data reviewed	Minimal or none	Minimal or none	Limited	Moderate	Extensive
Risk	Minimal	Minimal	Low	Moderate	High
Typical floor/unit time	20 minutes	40 minutes	55 minutes	80 minutes	110 minutes

Abbreviations: CC, chief complaint; HPI, history of present illness; PFSH, past, family, and/or social history; ROS, review of systems.

Table 6–12. Documentation Requirements for Inpatient Observation Care

	Code		
Examination	**99218**	**99219**	**99220**
History			
CC	Required	Required	Required
HPI	Greater than or equal to four elements or greater than or equal to three chronic or inactive conditions	Greater than or equal to four elements or greater than or equal to three chronic or inactive conditions	Greater than or equal to four elements or greater than or equal to three chronic or inactive conditions
ROS	Greater than or equal to two systems	10–14 systems	10–14 systems
PFSH	Greater than or equal to one element	Three elements	Three elements
Physical examination			
1997	Greater than or equal to 12 elements or comprehensive single-system examination	Comprehensive single-system examination	Comprehensive single-system examination
1995	Five to seven systems	Greater than or equal to eight systems	Greater than or equal to eight systems
Medical decision making			
Diagnostic/ management options	Minimal or limited	Multiple	Extensive
Data reviewed	None, minimal, or limited	Moderate	Extensive
Risk	Minimal or low	Moderate	High

Abbreviations: CC, chief complaint; HPI, history of present illness; PFSH, past, family, and/or social history; ROS, review of systems.

Table 6–13. Documentation Requirements for Initial Hospital Care

Examination	Code 99221	Code 99222	Code 99223
History			
CC	Required	Required	Required
HPI	Greater than or equal to four elements or greater than or equal to three chronic or inactive conditions	Greater than or equal to four elements or greater than or equal to three chronic or inactive conditions	Greater than or equal to four elements or greater than or equal to three chronic or inactive conditions
ROS	Greater than or equal to two systems	10–14 systems	10–14 systems
PFSH	Greater than or equal to one element	Three elements	Three elements
Physical examination			
1997	Greater than or equal to 12 elements or comprehensive single-system examination	Comprehensive single-system examination	Comprehensive single-system examination
1995	Five to seven systems	Greater than or equal to eight systems	Greater than or equal to eight systems
Medical decision making			
Diagnostic/management options	Minimal or limited	Multiple	Extensive
Data reviewed	None, minimal, or limited	Moderate	Extensive
Risk	Minimal or low	Moderate	High
Typical floor/unit time	30 minutes	50 minutes	70 minutes

Abbreviations: CC, chief complaint; HPI, history of present illness; PFSH, past, family, and/or social history; ROS, review of systems.

Table 6–14. Documentation Requirements for Observation or Inpatient Care Services (Including Admission and Discharge Services on the Same Day)

Examination	Code		
	99234	99235	99236
History			
CC	Required	Required	Required
HPI	Greater than or equal to four elements or greater than or equal to three chronic or inactive conditions	Greater than or equal to four elements or greater than or equal to three chronic or inactive conditions	Greater than or equal to four elements or greater than or equal to three chronic or inactive conditions
ROS	Greater than or equal to two systems	10–14 systems	10–14 systems
PFSH	Greater than or equal to one element	Three elements	Three elements
Physical examination			
1997	Greater than or equal to 12 elements or comprehensive single-system examination	Comprehensive single-system examination	Comprehensive single-system examination
1995	Five to seven systems	Greater than or equal to eight systems	Greater than or equal to eight systems
Medical decision making			
Diagnostic/ management options	Minimal or limited	Multiple	Extensive
Data reviewed	None, minimal, or limited	Moderate	Extensive
Risk	Minimal or low	Moderate	High

Abbreviations: CC, chief complaint; HPI, history of present illness; PFSH, past, family, and/or social history; ROS, review of systems.

Table 6–15. Documentation Requirements for Subsequent Hospital Care

	Code		
Examination	99231	99232	99233
History			
CC	Required	Required	Required
HPI	One to three elements	One to three elements	Greater than or equal to four elements or greater than or equal to three chronic or inactive conditions
ROS	Not required	One system	Two to nine systems
PFSH	Not required	Not required	Not required
Physical examination			
1997	One to five elements comprehensive	6–11 elements	Greater than or equal to 12 elements
1995	One system	Two to four systems	Greater than or equal to five systems
Medical decision making			
Diagnostic/ management options	Minimal or limited	Multiple	Extensive
Data reviewed	None, minimal, or limited	Moderate	Extensive
Risk	Minimal or low	Moderate	High
Typical floor/unit time	15 minutes	25 minutes	35 minutes

Abbreviations: CC, chief complaint; HPI, history of present illness; PFSH, past, family, and/or social history; ROS, review of systems.

Chapter 6 Quiz: E/M Services and Medicare Documentation Guidelines

True or False:

1. The 1995 and 1997 Documentation Guidelines are the joint work of the CMS, the AMA, and most specialty societies.

2. The Documentation Guidelines currently focus on the requirements for the key components.

Choose the best answer.

3. A complete review of systems can be documented by:

   a. Noting 10 individual systems

   b. Commenting on pertinent positive and negative findings plus a statement indicating all other systems are negative

   c. Supplementing or confirming information recorded by others along with pertinent positive and negative findings

   d. All of the above

4. Documentation of the comprehensive history requires:

   a. A review of 10 systems, an extended history of present illness, and a past, family, and/or social history

   b. A review of 10 systems and an extended history of present illness

   c. A chief complaint

   d. A and C

5. The examination requirements for the 1995 Documentation Guidelines require:

   a. Documentation of the organ systems and body areas included in the examination

   b. Documentation of 10 organ systems for a comprehensive examination

   c. Documentation of specified components of the examination

   d. A specified number of systems for a comprehensive examination

6. The examination component in the 1997 Documentation Guidelines:

   a. Defines 10 single organ system examinations and a general multisystem examination

   b. Identifies the specific content of the examination(s)

   c. Differentiates between the types of examination by the number of examination elements

   d. All of the above

7. The medical decision making component of the Documentation Guidelines:

   a. Requires the counting of elements and systems

   b. Uses a table of risk to determine overall medical decision making

   c. Includes different components than CPT

   d. None of the above

Answers are listed on page 179.

Chapter 7

Preventive Medicine Services

Physicians often find preventive care confusing because there are so many different rules for reporting these services. Commercial payers may or may not cover preventive services; Medicare covers a small part of preventive services but only some of the time. Also, the services included in a preventive visit are not defined as clearly as the other evaluation and management (E/M) services described in the previous chapters but also vary according to the patient's age and risk factors. This chapter addresses:

- CPT Preventive Medicine Services codes
- Reporting of preventive and problem-oriented services for the same encounter
- Medicare guidelines on preventive and screening services

Following completion of the chapter, the reader should be able to:

- Identify the components of a preventive medicine E/M service
- Accurately report screening services to Medicare
- Recognize the reimbursement issues relating to preventive medicine services

Purpose of Preventive Medicine Services

Obstetrician–gynecologists serve women as a primary medical resource for preventive services and early detection of disease. A woman's annual visit to her gynecologist is a time to provide routine assessment for asymptomatic women, evaluate risk factors, and counsel women to help maintain a healthy lifestyle and minimize health risks. Preventive Medicine Services are a category of E/M service that includes:

- Initial and Periodic Comprehensive E/M services
- Preventive Medicine Counseling for Individuals and Groups
- Administration and Interpretation of a Health Risk Assessment

Preventive Medicine E/M Services Codes

Obstetrician–gynecologists use the Preventive Medicine Services codes to report annual well-woman examinations. The codes are selected based on the patient's age and whether the patient is new to the practice or established. The same definitions of new and established patients that are used for problem-oriented E/M services are used for preventive medicine services.

Physicians in all specialties use the same preventive medicine codes. The exact content of the services varies depending on the patient's sex, age, and identified risk factors. Clearly, preventive medicine E/M services for a healthy 25-year-old woman will be very different from the preventive E/M services for a healthy 55-year-old man. Likewise, the services provided to a 25-year-old woman will be distinct from those provided to a 55-year-old woman. The preventive medicine E/M services include:

- Counseling/anticipatory guidance/risk factor reduction interventions
- Age and sex appropriate comprehensive history
- Age and sex appropriate comprehensive physical examination, including but not limited to:
  —Gynecologic examination
  —Breast examination
  —Collection of a Pap test specimen
  —Discussions about the status of previously diagnosed stable conditions
  —Ordering of appropriate laboratory/diagnostic procedures and immunizations
  —Discussions about issues related to the patient's age or lifestyle

The comprehensive history performed during a preventive medicine encounter is different from the one performed during a problem-oriented E/M service (99201–99350). The comprehensive history for preventive services:

- Is not problem oriented; therefore, it does not include a chief complaint or history of present illness
- Is appropriate for the patient's age, sex, and identified risk factors
- Includes a comprehensive review of systems, a comprehensive or interval past, family, and social history, and a comprehensive assessment/history of pertinent risk factors
- Does not have to meet the criteria for a comprehensive history as defined by Medicare's E/M documentation guidelines

The comprehensive examination performed during a preventive services encounter also is different than the one performed during a problem-oriented E/M service. The comprehensive examination for preventive services:

- Is multisystem, but the extent of the examination is based on the patient's age, sex, and identified risk factors
- Does not have to meet the criteria for a comprehensive examination as defined by Medicare's E/M documentation guidelines

Table 7–1 shows a comparison of preventive E/M services and problem-oriented E/M services.

Preventive services codes also include counseling and discussion of issues common to the age group. For example, issues related to contraception are discussed with women of childbearing age, and menopausal concerns are discussed with older women. Safety issues, the need for screening tests, breast self-examination, and discussions about the status of previously diagnosed stable conditions also are part of the preventive medicine service.

Ordering appropriate immunizations and laboratory or diagnostic procedures is included in the preventive service. However, performing immunizations and ancillary studies are not included in the preventive codes. These services are coded and billed separately. For example, a 28-year-old patient, came to her physician's office for her well-woman examination. An interval medical, family, and social history was reviewed and a complete review of systems obtained. A complete physical examination was performed, including a blood

Table 7–1. Comparison of Problem-Oriented Services and Preventive E/M Services

Differences	Problem-Oriented E/M Services	Preventive E/M Services
Patient status	Some services include different codes for new and established patients	All services include different codes for new and established patients
Location of service	Some services include different codes for inpatients and outpatients	Same codes used for any site of service
Time component	Most codes include a time component	No time component
Documentation required		
Key components	Most codes include history, physical examination, and medical decision making	All codes include history and physical examination only
History required	Chief complaint, history of present illness, review of systems, and past, family, and social history	Review of systems and past, family, and social history only
Physical examination requirements	Examination of affected body areas or organ systems plus other areas depending on level of service	Multisystem examination; extent depends on patient's age and risk factors

pressure check and thyroid, breast, abdominal, and pelvic examination. A Pap test specimen was obtained. The patient was taking oral contraceptives and had concerns about intermittent breakthrough bleeding. She was counseled regarding alternatives and a prescription for a new medication was written. She also was counseled about diet, exercise, substance abuse, and sexual activity. A hematocrit test was ordered.

The physician reported code 99395. The hematocrit test and Pap test were sent to the laboratory, which reported the tests directly to the payer. The laboratory was reimbursed for performing these tests. Although the patient had concerns about her current method of birth control, the associated counseling and change in medication was considered part of the usual preventive medicine services that are provided for women in her age group.

Preventive Medicine Services With Problem-Oriented Services

Often, a patient comes into the office for an annual examination but receives additional services during the same visit. These services may be provided because the patient has a significant new complaint (chest pain, irregular bleeding, or other medical problems) or because the physician finds a new condition, such as a breast lump, during the preventive examination. The visit becomes a combination of preventive and problem-oriented services. CPT guidelines suggest reporting:

- One code for the annual examination using a preventive medicine code

- Another code for the level of E/M service needed to assess the complaint or problem

A problem-oriented E/M service is reported only if the key components (history, examination, and medical decision making) of the service are performed. It is likely that a portion of these components will overlap the work performed as part of the comprehensive preventive service. Therefore, the E/M code reported is based only on the additional work performed to evaluate the problem. A modifier –25 (significant, separately identifiable E/M service on same day as another service) must be added to the problem-oriented service code to indicate that this was a separate service. Documentation for the problem-oriented part and the well-woman part of the encounter should be distinct.

For example, a physician saw a 59-year-old established patient for her well-woman examination. In reviewing her history, the physician discovered that the patient had an unexplained weight loss of 10 pounds in the past 3 months. She also complained that she had not been sleeping well and that it seemed her heart was beating too fast. The physician took additional history regarding her symptoms, carefully examined her thyroid and heart, and checked her reflexes and muscle tone. A thyroid panel was ordered. The physician documented the problem-oriented encounter and then proceeded with documentation of the well-woman examination. The physician reported code 99396 for the preventive medicine portion of the visit and code 99213–25 for the additional work required to address the problem. The laboratory reported the thyroid study.

Third-Party Coverage for Preventive Services

Preventive care may or may not be covered under a patient's insurance plan. If the service is not covered, the physician should bill the patient. Some payers provide coverage for preventive services, but may not cover both preventive and problem-oriented services on the same day.

Some third-party payers allow physicians to report both a problem-oriented E/M code and a preventive medicine code for the same visit and will reimburse the full allowable amount for both codes. Other payers allow physicians to report both codes but will carve out the payment for the problem-oriented E/M service from the payment for the well-woman examination. The total payment is equal to the fee that would have been paid for a comprehensive preventive examination alone.

Other payers do not allow physicians to report both a preventive and problem-oriented encounter on the same service day. These payers view this as double billing because portions of the preventive and problem-oriented services overlap. There are no written rules regarding coding under these circumstances. The ACOG Committee on Coding and Nomenclature suggests reporting either the preventive medicine or the problem-oriented code. The coding choice is based on which service, preventive or problem-oriented, was the primary focus of the visit and consumed the most time during the visit. That is:

- If more than 50% of the total time of the encounter was spent on preventive services, the physician reports a preventive E/M code.

- If more than 50% of the total time of the encounter was spent on the evaluation and/or management of a problem, the physician reports a problem-oriented E/M code. The level of service is determined using only the key components performed in the evaluation of the problem (not including the services that were preventive and unrelated to the problem).

- The physician may choose to provide either the preventive or problem-oriented service on that date and ask the patient to return for the other service. If the problem needs immediate attention, then the problem-oriented service is provided during the visit, and the patient is asked to return for the preventive service.

Medicare and Preventive Medicine Services

Medicare does not cover a comprehensive preventive medicine service (code 99387 or code 99397). However, coverage for certain screening services often provided during preventive visits was mandated by the Balanced Budget Act of 1997. Additional preventive services were mandated as part of the Medicare Modernization Act of 2003.

Screening services are defined as those provided in the absence of an illness, disease, sign, or symptom. Covered screening services of interest to obstetrician–gynecologists are outlined in Tables 7–2 to 7–10.

Table 7–2. Medicare Screening Pelvic Examination and Clinical Breast Check

HCPCS Codes	Coverage	Patient	Diagnostic Codes
G0101	Every 2 years	Not high risk	V72.31, V76.2, V76.47, or V76.49
	Annually	High risk	V15.89

Table 7–3. Medicare Collection of Screening Pap Smear Specimen

HCPCS Code	Coverage	Patient	Diagnostic Codes
Q0091	Every 2 years	Not high risk	V72.31, V76.2, V76.47, or V76.49
	Annually	High risk	V15.89

Table 7–4. Medicare Screening Hemoccult

HCPCS Codes	Coverage	Patient	Diagnostic Codes
G0107, G0328	Annually	50 years and older	V76.51 or V76.41

Table 7–5. Medicare Screening Mammography

CPT Code	Coverage	Patient	Diagnostic Codes
76092	Annually	40 years and older	V76.12 or V76.11

Table 7–6. Medicare Screening Bone Mass Measurement

CPT/HCPCS Codes	Coverage	Patient	Diagnostic Codes
76075, 76076, 76078, 76977, 78350, G0130, G0131, G0132	Once every 24 months	Must meet specific criteria	Determined by local carriers

Medicare covers a pelvic and clinical breast examination for all women at least every 2 years.

Table 7–7. Medicare Initial Preventive Physical Examination

HCPCS Codes	Coverage	Patient	Diagnostic Code
G0344, G0366, G0367, G0368	Once	Must be within first 6 months of Medicare coverage	V70.0

Table 7–8. Medicare Diabetes Screening

CPT Codes	Coverage	Patient	Diagnostic Code
82947, 82950, 82951	Twice in 12-month period	Must be at risk for diabetes or diagnosed with pre-diabetes	V77.1

Table 7–9. Medicare Cardiovascular Screening Blood Tests

CPT Codes	Coverage	Patient	Diagnostic Codes
82465, 84478, 83718, 80061	Every 5 years	All Medicare beneficiaries	V81.0, V81.1, or V81.2

Table 7–10. Medicare Tobacco Cessation Counseling

CPT Codes	Coverage	Patient	Diagnostic Code
G0375, G0376	Two cessation attempts in 12-month period	Patient has condition or is receiving treatment that is being adversely affected by tobacco use	Use code indicating patient's condition or treatment affected by tobacco use

Screening Pelvic and Clinical Breast Examination

Medicare covers a pelvic and clinical breast examination for all women at least every 2 years. If the patient meets the "high risk" criteria, Medicare covers the screening pelvic examination annually. The following circumstances determine if a woman is high risk:

- If a woman is of childbearing age, she is considered high risk if:
  —Cervical or vaginal cancer is present (or was present), or
  —Abnormalities were found in the preceding 3 years
- A woman of any age may be considered at high risk for cervical or vaginal cancer. A woman is considered at high risk for cervical cancer if any of these factors apply:
  —Onset of sexual activity at younger than 16 years

—Five or more sexual partners in a lifetime

—History of sexually transmitted diseases (including HIV)

—Fewer than three negative Pap tests within the previous 7 years

—No Pap tests within the previous 7 years

- A woman is considered at high risk for vaginal cancer if she was exposed in utero to diethylstilbestrol (eg, her mother took diethylstilbestrol during pregnancy)

Medicare requires that the following elements be documented to report a pelvic examination with a clinical breast examination:

- Inspection and palpation of breasts for masses or lumps, tenderness, symmetry, or nipple discharge

- Performance and documentation of any six of the following 10 elements:

  1. Digital rectal examination, including sphincter tone, presence of hemorrhoids, and rectal masses

  Pelvic examination (with or without specimen collection for smears and cultures), including:

  2. External genitalia (eg, general appearance, hair distribution, or lesions)

  3. Urethral meatus (eg, size, location, lesions, or prolapse)

  4. Urethra (eg, masses, tenderness, or scarring)

  5. Bladder (eg, fullness, masses, or tenderness)

  6. Vagina (eg, general appearance, estrogen effect, discharge, lesions, pelvic support, cystocele, or rectocele)

  7. Cervix (eg, general appearance, lesions, or discharge)

  8. Uterus (eg, size, contour, position, mobility, tenderness, consistency, descent, or support)

  9. Adnexa/parametria (eg, masses, tenderness, organomegaly, or nodularity)

  10. Anus and perineum

The screening pelvic and clinical breast examination is reported to Medicare using *Healthcare Common Procedure Coding System* (HCPCS) code G0101 and one of the following ICD-9-CM diagnostic codes:

- V72.31 (routine gynecologic examination)

- V76.2 (special screening for malignant neoplasms, cervix) if the patient has an intact cervix or uterus

- V76.47 (special screening for malignant neoplasms, vagina) or V76.49 (special screening for malignant neoplasms, other sites) for a patient who does not have a uterus or cervix

- V15.89 (other specified personal history presenting hazards to health) for a patient who is considered high risk according to Medicare criteria. (The fact that she has had a hysterectomy and, therefore, does not have a cervix or uterus is not sufficient to make her high risk and eligible for an annual pelvic examination.)

Collection of Screening Pap Test Specimen

In addition to the screening pelvic and clinical breast examination, Medicare reimburses for the collection of specimens for a screening Pap test (eg, performed in the absence of illness, disease, signs, or symptoms). Collection of specimens for a diagnostic Pap test is not reported or reimbursed separately but is included in the E/M service. An example of a diagnostic Pap test is a follow-up Pap test for dysplasia in a patient with a family history of cancer.

The collection of specimens for a screening Pap test is reported to Medicare using HCPCS code Q0091 and one of the following ICD-9-CM diagnostic codes:

- V72.31 (routine gynecological examination) is reported when the provider performs a full gynecological examination

- V76.2 (special screening for malignant neoplasms, cervix) for a patient who has an intact cervix or uterus

- V76.47 (special screening for malignant neoplasms, vagina) or V76.49 (special screening for malignant neoplasms, other sites) for a patient who does not have a uterus or cervix

- V15.89 (other specified personal history presenting hazards to health) for a patient who is considered high risk according to Medicare criteria. (The fact that she has had a hysterectomy and, therefore, does not have a cervix or uterus is not sufficient to make her high risk and eligible for an annual Pap test.)

Sometimes, a physician may provide only a pelvic examination and clinical breast check and collection of specimens for a screening Pap test. For example, an 80-year-old patient was monitored regularly by her internist for hypertension, coronary artery disease, and preventive care. The internist, however, does not perform well-woman examinations and sent the patient to a gynecologist for her pelvic and breast examinations and the collection of specimens for a screening Pap test. The gynecologist reported code G0101 for the pelvic and clinical breast examinations and code Q0091 for collection of specimens for the Pap test. The laboratory reported the appropriate code (88000 series) for the interpretation of the Pap test.

In other cases, a physician may provide both a preventive service code (99381–99397) and a Medicare-covered screening service code (G0101) during the same visit. Code G0101 includes only the examination elements listed previously. It does not include other elements normally included in a preventive examination, such as taking vital signs and examination of skin, heart, and lungs. It does not include a review of systems or past family and social history.

When the physician provides a comprehensive history and examination as part of a preventive medicine visit, the screening codes (Q0091 and/or G0101) are submitted to Medicare for payment and the preventive service code is submitted to the patient for payment. Because the screening services are a part of the preventive services, Medicare's payment amount is deducted from the amount billed to the patient for the remaining preventive services. Figure 7–1 illustrates the services included in preventive gynecologic visits.

The shaded slices of the pie chart (Pap test and pelvic and breast examination) represent portions of the services covered by Medicare. The fee for these services is submitted to Medicare. The fee for the remaining portions is submitted to the patient for payment. For example, a physician performed an annual well-woman examination. The patient had coverage that year for the collection of a screening Pap test and her pelvic examination and clinical breast check. She has an intact cervix and is not considered high risk for cervical or vaginal cancer. The physician's usual charge for an annual examination is $100. Table 7–11 shows the physician's billing for these services.

The total amount charged for this visit was $100, the physician's usual fee. Modifier –52 (reduced services) is used here only to illustrate that the patient is responsible for less than the full charge for the preventive medicine service. It is not necessary to use the modifier

Table 7–11. Billing for Well-Woman Examination

Bill to:	Diagnostic Code(s)	Description	Procedural Code(s)	Description	Charge
Patient	V72.31	Routine gynecological examination	99397–52	Preventive medicine visit, established patient	$22.00
Medicare	V72.31	Special screening for malignant neoplasms, cervix (not high risk)	G0101	Pelvic examination and clinical breast check	38.00*
			Q0091	Collection of pap smear specimen	40.00*
Total Billed					$100.00

*Medicare charges are average allowable amounts for 2005.

on the actual claim form. The physician charged the patient only that portion of the preventive visit that was not covered by Medicare (the unshaded portions of the pie chart in Fig. 7–1).

Sometimes a physician may provide two services covered by Medicare during the same visit. The two services might be a problem-oriented E/M service (codes 99201–99215) and a covered screening service (codes G0101 and Q0091). Both services may be billed to Medicare. For example, an 80-year-old patient was monitored regularly by her internist for hypertension, coronary artery disease, and preventive care. The internist, however, does not perform well-woman examinations and sent the patient to a gynecologist, for her Pap test and pelvic examination. During the examination, the gynecologist discovered a lump in the patient's right breast. She evaluated the lump and performed additional history and

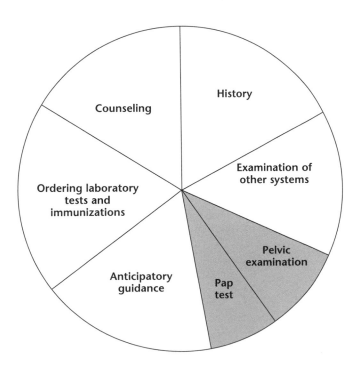

Fig. 7–1. Preventive Medicine Services

examination. Table 7–12 shows the physician's billing for these services.

In this case, Medicare reimbursed the physician the full allowable amount for each service. Modifier –25 is added to the E/M service to indicate that a significant, separately identifiable E/M service was performed on the same day as another service. Chapter 9 includes a discussion of use of this modifier.

Sometimes a physician does not know during the visit if a patient has coverage for Medicare preventive services. These may be services that are not covered every year, such as the pelvic examination and clinical breast check (G0101) and collection of a Pap test specimen (Q0091).

These HCPCS codes can be reported each year. Medicare will deny the service if it is not the patient's covered year. If the physician believes the service may be denied, he or she should ask the patient to sign an Advance Beneficiary Notice (ABN) at the time the service is provided. An ABN advises the patient that Medicare may deny payment for the service and that she will be financially responsible for any denied claims. A copy of the notice is in Appendix C. The claim is submitted with a modifier added to the HCPCS code:

- Modifier –GA is used if the patient signed an ABN and the physician is unsure whether Medicare will cover the service. For example, the physician may not know if G0101 and/or Q0091 will be covered this year. If the services are not covered, then the patient will receive an Explanation of Benefits that states she is responsible for the charges.

- Modifier –GY is used if the patient signed an ABN and the physician knows that Medicare will not cover the service. For example, Medicare never covers Comprehensive Preventive Medicine Services codes 99387 or 99397. The patient will receive an Explanation of Benefits that states the service was denied and that she may be billed. Some patients need a denial from Medicare to submit a claim to another insurer.

- Modifier –GZ is used if the patient did not sign an ABN and the physician is unsure if Medicare will cover the service or not. This is the same circumstance as listed previously for modifier –GA, but the patient did not sign a form. In this circumstance, the patient cannot be charged if Medicare denies the service.

Using the appropriate modifier ensures that the patient receives the correct information on her Explanation of Benefits. The ABN forms can be obtained from your local Medicare carrier. They are also available at www.cms.hhs.gov/medlearn/refabn.asp.

Table 7–12. Billing for Well-Woman Examination Plus Additional Services

Bill to:	Diagnostic Code(s)	Description	Procedural Code(s)	Description	Charge
Medicare	611.72	Lump in breast	99213–25	Office visit, established patient	$53.00*
Medicare	V72.31	Routine gynecological examination	G0101	Pelvic examination and clinical breast check	38.00*
			Q0091	Collection of pap smear specimen	40.00*
Total Billed					$131.00

*Medicare charges are average allowable amounts for 2005.

Medicare and Other Screening Services

Medicare also covers other screening services. They are summarized as follows.

Screening Hemoccult

Medicare covers one screening fecal occult blood test for persons aged 50 years and older once every 12 months. Samples must be obtained from two different sites and from three consecutive stools. A written order for the test must be submitted. This service is reported using HCPCS code G0107 (colorectal screening/fecal occult blood, one to three simultaneous determinations) linked to either diagnostic code V76.41 (special screening for malignant neoplasms, rectum) or code V76.51 (special screening for malignant neoplasms, colon). This code is used to report the interpretation of the cards sent home with the patient, not the test performed in the physician's office.

Screening Mammography

Medicare covers one screening mammogram for women aged 40 years or older once every 12 months. The service is reported using CPT code 76092 (screening mammography, bilateral [two-view film study of each breast]) linked to diagnostic code V76.12 (other screening mammogram). A diagnostic mammogram (when the patient has an illness, disease, or symptoms indicating the need for a mammogram) is covered whenever it is medically necessary.

Screening Bone Mass Measurement

Medicare covers one screening bone mass measurement test once every 24 months if the patient meets one of these criteria:

- Estrogen-deficient and at clinical risk for osteoporosis on the basis of medical history or other findings as determined by the physician (or other qualified nonphysician practitioner) who is caring for her
- Vertebral abnormalities (shown by X-ray) indicative of osteoporosis, osteopenia, or vertebral fracture
- Receiving (or expecting to receive) glucocorticoid therapy equivalent to 7.5 mg prednisone or greater per day for more than 3 months
- Has a diagnosis of primary hyperparathyroidism
- Being monitored to assess an osteoporosis drug therapy approved by the U.S. Food and Drug Administration

Local carriers determine the ICD-9-CM diagnostic codes that they will accept as supporting the previous criteria. In addition to meeting the coverage criteria, the test must be ordered by a physician or a qualified nonphysician practitioner who is treating the patient. Qualified nonphysician practitioners include physician assistants, nurse practitioners, clinical nurse specialists, and nurse–midwives. The test results must be needed as part of the patient's evaluation and/or formulation of a treatment plan.

The Medicare Modernization Act of 2003 provided for coverage for a number of new services beginning in 2005. These include:

- Initial preventive physical examination
- Diabetes screening
- Cardiovascular screening

Other screening services covered by Medicare include hemoccult, mammography, and bone mass measurement.

Initial Preventive Physical Examination

This examination (referred to as the IPPE or "Welcome to Medicare Exam") covers specific services for new Medicare beneficiaries. The examination is payable once and only if provided within the first six months of the beneficiary's first Part B coverage period. The usual deductible and co-insurance provisions apply.

In general terms, the IPPE includes the following:

- A physical examination (including measurement of height, weight, blood pressure, and electrocardiogram, but excluding clinical laboratory tests) with the goal of health promotion and disease detection and

- Education, counseling, and referral for screening and other covered preventive benefits separately authorized under Medicare Part B.

The service must be provided by a physician or qualified nonphysician provider. These include physician assistants, nurse practitioners, and clinical nurse specialists.

Specifically, the IPPE includes the following:

- Medical and social history: Review of patient's history with particular attention to modifiable risk factors for disease.

- Depression Risk Assessment: Review of the individual's potential (risk factors) for depression, including current or past experience with depression or other mood disorders. The patient cannot have a current diagnosis of depression. The provider may use one of the standardized screening tests designed for this purpose and recognized by national medical professional organizations.

- Functional ability and level of safety: Review based on the use of appropriate screening questions or a screening questionnaire. The provider may select from screening questions or standardized questionnaires designed for this purpose and recognized by national medical professional organizations.

- Examination: Measurements and tests including measurement of the individual's height, weight, blood pressure, a visual acuity screen, and other factors as deemed appropriate, based on her medical and social history and current clinical standards.

- Electrocardiogram: Performance and interpretation by provider.

- Education, counseling, and referral: Provided as appropriate, based on the results of the first five elements of the IPPE.

- Education, counseling and referral, including a brief written plan such as a checklist: Provided to the individual for obtaining appropriate screening and other preventive services which are separately covered under Medicare Part B benefits. Examples are vaccinations, screening mammography, screening Pap test and pelvic examination, colorectal cancer screening, diabetes self-management, bone mass measurement, glaucoma screening, medical nutrition therapy and cardiovascular screening and diabetes screening.

For the purposes of this benefit, medical history includes:

- Past medical and surgical history, including experiences with illnesses, hospital stays, operations, allergies, injuries, and treatment

- Current medications and supplements, including calcium and vitamins

- Family history, including a review of medical events in the patient's family, including diseases that may be hereditary or place the individual at risk

For the purposes of this benefit, social history includes:

- History of alcohol, tobacco, and illicit drug use
- Diet
- Physical activities

Report the examination using diagnostic code V70.0 (routine general medical examination at a health care facility). The following new HCPCPS codes are used to report these services:

- G0344—Initial preventive physical examination; face-to-face visit, services limited to new beneficiary during first 6 months of Medicare enrollment
- G0366—Electrocardiogram, routine ECG with at least 12 leads: with interpretation and report, performed as a component of the initial preventive physical examination
- G0367—Tracing only, without interpretation and report, performed as a component of the initial preventive physical examination
- G0368—Interpretation and report only, performed as a component of the initial preventive physical examination

If the physician or nonphysician provider cannot perform the ECG in the office suite, then alternative arrangements must be made with an outside entity. The primary care provider must incorporate the results of the ECG into the beneficiary's medical record to complete the IPPE.

Other covered preventive, screening, or problem-oriented services may be performed at the same encounter as the IPPE. These are reported using the appropriate codes. If reporting an E/M service, a modifier –25 must be added. The documentation for the problem-oriented portion of the encounter must support the level of service reported.

Diabetes Screening

The diabetes screening tests includes a fasting blood glucose test, post-glucose challenge tests, and either an oral glucose tolerance test with a glucose challenge of 75 grams of glucose for non-pregnant adults or a 2-hour post-glucose challenge test alone. This screening is covered twice within a 12-month period. This is not a covered benefit for individuals who previously received a diagnosis of diabetes.

Individuals are considered at risk if they have the following risk factors:

- Hypertension
- Dyslipidemia
- Obesity (body mass index of 30 or more)
- Previous identification of an elevated impaired fasting glucose
- Previous identification of impaired glucose tolerance
- At least two of the following:
  —Overweight (body mass index greater than 25, but less than 30)
  —A family history of diabetes
  —A history of gestational diabetes mellitus or delivery of a baby weighing more than 9 pounds
  —Age 65 years or older

Individuals diagnosed with prediabetes also are eligible for this benefit. Prediabetes is defined as a fasting glucose level of 100–125 mg/dL, or a 2-hour postglucose challenge of

The "Welcome to Medicare Exam" is payable once and only if provided within the first 6 months of the beneficiary's first Part B coverage period.

140–199 mg/dL. Individuals not meeting the prediabetes criteria are eligible for one screening test per year.

Medicare covers these tests when reported with diagnosis code V77.1 (screening for diabetes mellitus) and one of the following CPT codes:

82947	Glucose; quantitative, blood (except reagent strip)
82950	Glucose; post-glucose dose (includes glucose)
82951	Glucose; tolerance test, three specimens (includes glucose)

Cardiovascular screening blood tests

This benefit provides a blood test for the early detection of cardiovascular disease or abnormalities associated with an elevated risk of this disease. This benefit includes three clinical laboratory tests—total cholesterol, high density lipoprotein, and triglycerides. These tests, covered once every 5 years, can be ordered as one of each individual test or combination as a panel.

The tests must be ordered by a treating physician and used in the management of the patient. Laboratories must offer physicians the ability to order a lipid panel without the direct low density lipoprotein measurement. However, if the screening lipid panel results illustrate a triglycerides level that indicates the need for a direct low density lipoprotein measurement, the physician may order this test.

Medicare will reimburse for these tests when reported with a diagnosis code from the series V81.0–V81.2 (special screening for cardiovascular diseases) linked to either the CPT code for the lipid panel (80061) or the individual codes for the tests included in the panel (82465, 84478, or 83718).

Tobacco Use Cessation Counseling

Beginning in 2005, Medicare covers counseling for tobacco cessation for outpatients and for inpatients who have a condition or are receiving treatment that is being adversely affected by tobacco use. Inpatients are covered if counseling for tobacco use is not the primary reason for the patient's hospital stay. Medicare covers two cessation attempts per year.

The counseling during an E/M service must be either intermediate or intensive. An intermediate E/M service is described as two to three sessions of 3–10 minutes each and is reported using HCPCS code G0375. An intensive E/M service is described as four sessions of more than 10 minutes each and is reported using HCPCS code G0376. Counseling involving only one session of less than 3 minutes is included in current E/M payment and not covered separately. Each attempt may include a maximum of four intermediate or intensive counseling sessions. The total annual benefit is for eight sessions in a 12-month period. The diagnostic code should indicate the patient's condition or the treatment she is receiving that is being adversely affected by the tobacco use.

Services may be provided by a physician, physician assistant, nurse practitioner, clinical nurse specialist, qualified psychologist, or clinical social worker. Centers for Medicare and Medicaid Services does not currently have specific training requirements, but may have them in the future. The counseling must be provided face-to-face with the patient.

Other Preventive Medicine Services

Counseling and Risk Factor Reduction Intervention (99401–99412)

Codes for counseling individuals or groups are used to report services for promoting health and preventing illness or injury. These codes are not reported if the patient has current symptoms or a diagnosed illness. The services include discussion on issues such as sexual practices, family problems, or diet and exercise. These codes are not based on the key components. There are separate codes to report individual or group counseling. Both sets of codes are reported based on time only.

These codes are reported only when the counseling is provided at an encounter that is separate from either preventive medicine services or problem-oriented E/M services. Counseling that takes place during a preventive medicine or other E/M service is considered part of the E/M service.

For example, a 28-year-old patient came to see a physician for preconception counseling. She had no gynecologic or other medical problems. She had been on oral contraceptives for 5 years and had never tried to conceive. The physician spent 15–20 minutes with the patient discussing issues related to the discontinuation of birth control, medications, and diet. The patient reported code 99401 (preventive medicine counseling, approximately 15 minutes).

If a patient has symptoms or an established illness, then the appropriate problem-oriented E/M service should be reported instead of these codes. Counseling services provided to groups of patients with symptoms or illness are reported using 99078 (physician educational services rendered to patients in a group setting [prenatal, obesity, or diabetic instructions]).

Administration and Interpretation of Health Risk Assessment Instrument

CPT code 99420 is used to report the administration and interpretation of a health risk assessment instrument such as a health hazard appraisal. Obstetrician–gynecologists do not commonly perform this service.

Chapter 7 Quiz: Preventive Medicine Services

True or False:

1. The documentation requirements for a Preventive Medicine Service are the same as Medicare's Documentation Guidelines for E/M Services

2. Preventive Services can be reported in addition to other services provided on the same day.

Choose the best answer:

3. Elements of a preventive medicine service include:

   a. A chief complaint, comprehensive history and exam, ordering of laboratory and/or diagnostic procedures

   b. Comprehensive history and exam, ordering of appropriate laboratory and/or diagnostic procedures, and counseling and/or risk factor reduction

   c. An HPI, risk factor reduction, and comprehensive examination and medical decision making

4. The preventive medicine codes are selected according to:

   a. Patient gender

   b. Patient age

   c. Extent of key components

   d. Patient status (new or established)

   e. B and D only

5. Problem-oriented services can be reported with Preventive Medicine Services if:

   a. The components of an E/M service are provided and necessary for the evaluation or treatment of a distinct problem

   b. The services are clearly documented

   c. The patient has coverage for both services

   d. A and B only

6. Medicare reimburses:

   a. Comprehensive preventive services annually for high-risk women

   b. Comprehensive preventive services every 2 years for all women

   c. Certain screening services based on established criteria

   d. Only problem-oriented services

7. HCPCS code G0101:

   a. Includes a clinical breast and pelvic examination

   b. Should be used to report a comprehensive well-woman examination to Medicare

   c. Includes the examination components commonly performed at the time of a well-woman examination

   d. Includes a review of systems

8. HCPCS code Q0091:

   a. Identifies the interpretation of a Pap test

   b. Should be reported any time a Pap test is obtained

   c. Identifies the collection of a screening Pap test only

   d. Can be reported only with a preventive medicine encounter

Answers are listed on page 179.

Chapter 8

The Global Surgical Package

The idea of a global surgical package has been around for a long time. Physicians have always included some routine services performed before, during, and after a procedure in their fee for a surgery. With the advent of *Current Procedural Terminology* (CPT) and Medicare's Resource-Based Relative Value Scale, however, the need to determine exactly what was included or excluded from a surgical service became more important. Very specific definitions of the global surgical package were created for various procedures. Unfortunately, as shown in this chapter, CPT, Medicare, and other payers did not agree on one definition. It is important to understand the difference between the definitions because a physician may be able to report some additional services under CPT rules but not under Medicare rules. This chapter addresses:

- The components of a global surgical package
- The differences between the CPT and the Medicare guidelines for surgical services
- Special issues in gynecologic surgery

Following the completion of the chapter, the reader should be able to:

- Identify the primary components of a global surgical package
- Understand the concept of surgical bundling
- Recognize the differences between CPT and Medicare guidelines for reporting surgical services

Surgical Coding

Surgical coding rules apply to the codes in CPT's Surgery section. This section is divided into 18 subsections, including a section on the Female Genital System and a section on Maternity Care and Delivery. This chapter describes coding for surgical procedures according to CPT rules and Medicare rules and some commercial payers' variations on these rules.

CPT and the Global Surgical Package

Most of the services in the surgical section of CPT are based on a global package concept. A single code is reported for all necessary services normally furnished by the surgeon (or surgical group) before, during, and after the procedure. CPT's definition of the global surgical package may not be the same as the definition used by other payers. Variations in payers' global surgical package definitions are addressed at the end of this chapter.

CPT defines its global surgical package in the surgical guidelines section. The following services are always included in the code for the surgery:

- The operation per se
- Local infiltration, metacarpal/digital block, or topical anesthesia when used
- One related evaluation and management (E/M) encounter on the day immediately before or on the day of the procedure (including history and physical) if the decision for surgery has been made during a previous encounter
- Immediate postoperative care, including dictating operative notes and talking with the family and other physicians
- Writing orders
- Evaluating the patient in the postanesthesia recovery area
- Typical postoperative follow-up care

Preoperative Services

Preoperative services on the same day or day before the procedure may be reported only if they are significant and separately identifiable. These services are reported using the appropriate E/M code with a modifier –25 (this modifier will be addressed more thoroughly in Chapter 9).

For example, a physician saw an established patient for vaginal bleeding. After performing an expanded problem-focused examination and history (code 99213), he decided to perform an endometrial biopsy (code 58100). He reported code 58100 plus 99213–25.

If, however, the physician had asked the patient to return to his office next week for the biopsy, the coding would be different. If upon the patient's return the physician performed the procedure with little or no additional history or examination, then he would report only code 58100.

Postoperative Services

CPT does not assign a specific global period (number of postoperative days) to its procedures. CPT does, however, define which postoperative services are included in the follow-up care for diagnostic and therapeutic surgical procedures.

Follow-up services for diagnostic procedures include only the care related to the recovery from the procedure itself. Care of either the condition that prompted the diagnostic procedure or other conditions present are not included and may be reported separately. For example, a physician orders diagnostic ultrasonography. He or she may report both the services before the procedure that led to the decision to perform it and any E/M services provided after the procedure for the condition found.

Follow-up services for therapeutic surgical procedures include only the care that is typically a part of the surgical service. Care for other conditions and the evaluation or treatment of complications, exacerbations, or recurrence is not included and may be reported separately. Additional services are reported using the appropriate CPT code(s) that describes the care provided.

Supplies and Materials

CPT rules state that supplies normally used in conjunction with a procedure are included in the procedure code and should not be reported separately. If, however, the supplies and materials provided by a physician are over and above those usually required to perform the service, they may be reported separately. CPT does not indicate which specific procedure codes qualify for separate billing for supplies. Generally, payment for a procedure code includes payment for supplies (eg, a surgical tray) if the procedure is almost always performed in the office and always requires a sterile tray. Payment is not included if the procedure is typically performed in the hospital (where the cost of the tray is the responsibility of the facility) but in this case is being performed in an office setting (where the cost of the tray is the responsibility of the physician).

CPT includes only one code (99070) to report supplies and materials. Physicians reporting this code also should submit with the claim a list of the trays, drugs, or other supplies used.

Medicare and the Global Surgical Package

Medicare has its own definition of the global surgical package. All Medicare carriers use the same definition of preoperative, intraoperative, and postoperative services. Therefore, payments for a procedure performed in Vermont will be equivalent to payments for the same procedure performed in Utah.

Medicare divides surgical services into major and minor procedures. All major procedures have a 90-day global period. Minor procedures have either a 0-day or 10-day global period. The global period assigned to each procedure is determined by the Centers for Medicare and Medicaid Services and is published annually in the *Federal Register*. Table 8–1 shows global periods for some procedures commonly performed by ob-gyns. The American College of Obstetricians and Gynecologists (ACOG) posts the global periods and Relative Value Units (RVUs) each year on its web site (www.acog.org, Coding and Nomenclature).

Table 8–1. Medicare Global Periods

CPT Codes	General Description	Global Periods
57420–57461	Colposcopy, vagina and cervix	000
57425	Colposcopy with loop electrode conization of the cervix	090
57520–57522	Conization of cervix; cold knife, laser/loop electrode excision	090
58120	Dilation and curettage	010
58555–58563	Hysteroscopy, diagnostic and surgical (including with dilation and curettage)	000
58565	Hysteroscopy, sterilization	090
58660–58673 (Except 58661)	Laparoscopy, surgical	090
58661	Laparoscopy with removal of adnexal structures	010
58720	Salpingo-oophorectomy, complete or partial (open)	090
49320	Laparoscopy, diagnostic	010
49321–49322	Laparoscopy, with biopsy/aspiration of cyst	010
57282–57283	Colpopexy, vaginal	090
58356	Endometrial cryoablation	010
58956	Total abdominal hysterectomy, bilateral salpingo-oophorectomy, and omentectomy for malignancy	090

In many instances the global periods seem inconsistent. For example, a dilation and curettage (D&C) performed using a hysteroscope (code 58558) has a 0-day global period, but a D&C performed without a hysteroscope (code 58120) has a 10-day global period. All the surgical laparoscopy codes (58660–58673) have a 90-day global period, except code 58661 (removal of adnexal structures), which has only a 10-day period.

Knowing the global periods for procedures is important. For example, a physician may assume that code 58661 has a 90-day global period like the other laparoscopy codes and not bill for services provided 23 days after the procedure, when this is a billable service.

Medicare defines routine preoperative, intraoperative, and postoperative services differently for major and minor procedures. Physicians must understand these definitions and be aware of the global periods for the procedures that they perform to ensure proper reporting and reimbursement for their services.

Medicare's Surgical Package for Minor Procedures

Minor procedures have either a 0-day or 10-day global surgical period. These procedures include:

- Preoperative: same-day visits (unless a separately identifiable E/M service is furnished)
- Intraoperative: the procedure itself and all integral procedures, including anesthesia provided by the surgeon and, in most cases, supplies.
- Postoperative:
  —0-day global procedures: related visits on the day of the service
  —10-day global procedures: follow-up visits that are related to recovery from the surgery for 10 days after the service

Minor procedures do not include:

- Preoperative: same-day visits that are significant and separately identifiable from the procedure
- Intraoperative: unrelated procedures
- Postoperative:
  —0-day global procedures: visits after the date of the procedure
  —10-day global procedures: all related visits and any unrelated visits beyond 10 days after the service

Medicare's Surgical Package for Major Procedures

Major procedures have a 90-day global period. These procedures include:

- Preoperative: all preoperative visits by the surgeon beginning 1 day before the surgery, including the hospital admission workup
- Intraoperative: the procedure and all integral procedures, including anesthesia administered by the surgeon
- Postoperative:
  —Medical or surgical services, performed by the surgeon for complications that do not require a return trip to the operating room
  —Postoperative visits that are related to recovery for 90 days after the service

Major procedures do not include:

- Preoperative:
  —The E/M service during which the decision to perform surgery was made

—Diagnostic tests and procedures

—Treatment required to stabilize a seriously ill patient before surgery (eg, burns, trauma)

- Intraoperative: unrelated procedures
- Postoperative:

—Visits unrelated to the diagnosis linked to the surgical procedure

—Services for an added course of treatment other than normal recovery from surgery

—Treatment for postoperative complications requiring a return trip to the operating room

An example of a preoperative service that would not be included in Medicare's global surgical package: A patient comes into the emergency department with a ruptured ectopic pregnancy and is taken immediately to the operating room. The E/M service can be reported separately.

An example of an intraoperative service that would not be included in Medicare's global surgical package: A physician is performing a total abdominal hysterectomy with bilateral salpingo-oophorectomy and also performs an appendectomy because of endometriosis on the appendix. The appendectomy can be reported separately.

An example of a postoperative service that would not be included in Medicare's global surgical package: A patient is taken to the operating room for a wound dehiscence. The operating room services to manage the dehiscence can be reported separately.

Medicare's Guidelines on Supplies and Materials

According to the Resource-Based Relative Value Scale, supplies are considered part of the practice expense RVU. Medicare includes payment for supplies in the established fee for the procedure and, therefore, will not reimburse separately for surgical trays, dressings, catheters, or other similar supplies.

However, Medicare does reimburse separately for certain supplies, such as pessaries or injectable medications. The pessary supply and injectable drug products are reported to the Medicare carrier using *Healthcare Common Procedure Coding System* (HCPCS) level II codes. Reporting injectable drugs is discussed later in this chapter.

According to the Resource-Based Relative Value Scale, supplies are considered part of the practice expense RVU...However, Medicare does reimburse separately for pessaries.

Comparing the CPT and Medicare Global Surgical Packages

A comparison of the CPT and Medicare definitions of a global surgical package are shown in Tables 8–2 to 8–4. The modifiers included in the table are addressed in detail in Chapter 9. Following are two examples of how understanding the differences between CPT and Medicare definitions of the global surgical package can affect payment.

Under Medicare rules, treatment by the primary surgeon of intraoperative complications is not reported separately; however, if another physician of a different specialty provides the same treatment, it can be reported and reimbursed.

Under CPT rules, treatment of complications can be reported separately whether the treatment is provided by the primary surgeon or by another physician, regardless of the specialty. An example is a bowel inadvertently nicked during an open procedure. Under CPT rules, the gynecologist can report the repair as well as the code for the primary surgery. Under Medicare rules, the gynecologist cannot report the repair; however, if another specialist, such as a general surgeon, performs the repair, he or she may report the service.

Medicare will reimburse a primary surgeon for treatment of postoperative complications only if the treatment required a return to the operating room. Under CPT rules, treatment

Table 8–2. Comparison of CPT and Medicare Global Surgical Packages—Preoperative Services

Types of Services	CPT Surgical Package	Medicare Surgical Packages	
		Major Surgery (90 days)	Minor Surgery (0 or 10 days)
Preoperative days included in global package	Day of or day before surgery	Day of or day before surgery	Day of surgery
Related evaluation and management services*	Bill only if decision for surgery made during visit (modifier –57)	Bill only if decision for surgery made during visit (modifier –57)	Do not bill separately
Related or unrelated significant, separately identifiable evaluation and management services	Bill separately (modifier –25)	Bill separately (modifier –25)	Bill separately (modifier –25)

*Note: Significant and separately identifiable services can be reported both to CPT and Medicare (modifier –25).

Table 8–3. Comparison of CPT and Medicare Global Surgical Packages—Intraoperative Services

Types of Services	CPT Surgical Package	Medicare Surgical Packages	
		Major Surgery (90 days)	Minor Surgery (0 or 10 days)
Anesthesia performed by surgeon	Bill only for regional or general anesthesia	Do not bill separately for for any anesthesia	Do not bill separately any anesthesia
Operation itself	All integral procedures included	All integral procedures included	All integral procedures included
Complications treated by surgeon	Bill separately	Do not bill separately	Do not bill separately

of postoperative complications by a primary surgeon can be reported separately whether or not the patient was taken back to the operating room.

Surgical Bundling

The rules are fairly straightforward concerning which preoperative and postoperative services are included in Medicare's and CPT's global surgical packages. The rules for which intraoperative services are included are more complex.

Bundling is the inclusion of lesser procedures in the payment for a more comprehensive procedure performed during the same session. Only the comprehensive procedure is reported on the claim form. An example is lysis of filmy adhesions as a lesser procedure included in a myomectomy.

Unbundling is the separate reporting of two or more services that should have been bundled. Only one of the services should have been reported on the claim form. An example is billing separate codes for bilateral salpingo-oophorectomy (58720), total omentectomy (49255), and total abdominal hysterectomy (58150) for malignancy instead of code 58956, which includes all these procedures in its code description.

Table 8–4. Comparison of CPT and Medicare Global Surgical Packages—Postoperative Services

Types of Services	CPT Surgical Package	Medicare Surgical Packages		
		Major Surgery (90 days)	Minor Surgery (0 or 10 days)	
Postoperative days included in global package	Not specified	90 days postoperatively	0 day (day of procedure)	10 days postoperatively
Routine evaluation and management services	Do not bill separately	Do not bill separately	Do not bill separately	Do not bill separately
Treatment of complications	Bill separately	Bill only if patient treated in operating room (modifier –78)	Do not bill separately	Bill only if patient treated in operating room (modifier –78)
Treatment of other conditions	Bill separately (modifier –24, –58 or –79)	Bill separately (modifier –24, –58 or –79)	Bill separately (modifier –24, –58 or –79)	

Sometimes the bundles are obvious, such as when the smaller procedure is explicitly listed in the code description of a more comprehensive procedure, as in the previous example. In other instances, the bundling is not so obvious. For example, a pelvic examination under anesthesia (code 57410) is commonly performed and, therefore, included in the payment of procedures performed by obstetrician–gynecologists, even though it is not specifically listed in the description of the code.

To assist physicians in understanding some of these bundling guidelines, ACOG has developed the *Ob/Gyn Coding Manual, Components of Correct Procedural Coding 2006* (see Appendix A for ordering information). This manual, published annually, identifies the services included in each gynecologic procedure and the related services that can be reported separately.

Separate Procedure Designation

Some codes listed in CPT-4 include the phrase "separate procedure" in parentheses after the code's description. These services are similar to the bundled services discussed previously. These are smaller services commonly (but not always) considered an integral component of another more comprehensive procedure(s) performed at the same surgical session. These separate procedure codes should not be reported when they are performed as an integral component of another procedure or service.

For example, a physician performed a vaginal hysterectomy with removal of tubes and ovaries and repair of enterocele on her patient. It would not be appropriate to report codes 58263 (vaginal hysterectomy with removal of tube[s] and/or ovary[s], with repair of enterocele) and code 57268 (repair of enterocele, vaginal approach [separate procedure]). The procedure described by code 57268 is considered an integral component of CPT code 58263.

There are, however, circumstances in which separate procedural codes are reported. Sometimes a separate procedure is the only service performed during the visit. In this case, the separate procedure designation becomes irrelevant. If repair of the enterocele was the only procedure performed, then the physician would have reported code 57268.

Sometimes a separate procedure is performed with other procedure(s) but is independent, unrelated, or distinct from the other procedures. In this case, it is reported in addition to the major surgical procedure. For example, CPT code 58900 describes a biopsy of the ovary, unilateral or bilateral, and is a separate procedure code. If it were performed at the time of a sling procedure (code 57288), then both codes would be reported because an ovarian biopsy and a sling procedure are unrelated. A different ICD-9-CM code is linked to each procedure and a modifier –59 is added to procedural code 58900 (modifier –59 is addressed in more detail in Chapter 9).

Sometimes a separate procedure is performed with another procedure and may or may not be a distinct reportable service, depending on the circumstances. For example, a physician drained a right ovarian cyst (code 58800) and a left ovarian abscess (code 58820) on his patient. Code 58800 is a CPT separate procedure code. In this case, the two procedures are distinct because they were performed on different ovaries. The physician would report both codes and add a modifier –59 to 58800. If both procedures had been performed on the same ovary, then only the one code would be reported.

Medicare's Correct Coding Initiative

Medicare developed detailed definitions of the global surgical package to ensure that payments for procedures are equivalent regardless of where they are provided. Medicare has taken this a step further and created the Correct Coding Initiative (CCI) to ensure that all Medicare carriers are consistent in their bundling and unbundling of services. The CCI is updated quarterly and receives input from the medical community. A copy of the latest version of the CCI is available on ACOG's web site (www.acog.org) under the Department of Coding and Nomenclature.

The CCI lists "code pairs," procedural codes that may not be reported together if performed at the same operative session by the same surgeon. These codes are considered bundled. In most cases, when code pairs are reported together, one of the codes will be denied.

The guiding principle of the CCI is that all services integral to accomplishing a procedure are bundled into that procedure. For example, abdominal surgical procedures include the incision, local anesthesia, exploratory laparotomy, and examination under anesthesia as integral parts of the procedure. The CCI provides its criteria for deciding which services should be bundled:

- Standards of medical/surgical practice. The lesser procedure:
  - —Represents the standard of care in accomplishing the comprehensive procedure
  - —Is necessary to successfully accomplish the procedure (failure to perform the lesser service may compromise the success of the comprehensive one)
  - —Is not a separately identifiable procedure unrelated to the comprehensive one
- Medical/surgical package definitions. See the previous discussion of Medicare's global package.
- CPT descriptions indicating a comprehensive/lesser service (eg, partial vulvectomy and complete vulvectomy)
- Sequential procedures (eg, an attempted laparoscopy followed by an open procedure). This is referred to as "most extensive procedure" rule.
- CPT separate procedure codes

Both CPT and CMS use codes designated as "separate procedures" in their bundling. However, CPT and CMS define separate procedures differently. This difference can affect their bundling decisions.

CPT defines a separate procedure as one that is "commonly carried out as an integral component of a total service or procedure." A separate procedure can be reported with other procedures if it "is carried out independently or considered to be unrelated or distinct from other procedures/services provided at that time..."

The CCI defines a separate procedure as one that "should not be reported when performed along with another procedure in an anatomically related region through the same skin incision or orifice." A separate procedure can be reported with other procedures if it "is performed on the same day but at a different session, or at an anatomically unrelated site." If appropriate, report the separate procedure code using a modifier –59.

Exceptions to the Bundling Rules

There are exceptions to the code pairs listed in CCI. Medicare may reimburse for some code pairs if the physician documents that they were distinct procedures. In most cases, these circumstances relate to separate patient encounters, separate anatomic sites, or separate specimens.

A modifier must be used to indicate that the procedures in this specific instance were distinct and reportable; that is, not bundled. The only modifiers accepted by Medicare for reporting "bundled" services are: HCPCS anatomic modifiers (eg, LT and RT); CPT modifier –58 (staged procedure); or CPT modifier –59 (distinct procedure).

There are some codes that Medicare will never reimburse when reported when listed as code pairs, even if a modifier is used and documentation submitted with the claim. For example, Medicare will never reimburse code 51701 (insertion of non-indwelling bladder catheter) when reported with code 58550 (laparoscopic vaginal hysterectomy, for uterus 250 g or less).

The section above on bundles based on separate procedures discusses the use of modifier –59 when the services are distinct. Following are some other examples of when adding a modifier to a bundled code may or may not be appropriate.

Different Sides of the Body

Two codes may be bundled if they are performed on one organ, but sometimes they are not. For example, code 58805 (drainage of ovarian cyst, abdominal approach) is bundled into 58940 (oophorectomy). These are sequential procedures, and therefore bundled.

If the drainage of the cyst was performed on the right ovary and the oophorectomy was performed on the left ovary, both codes are reported. Use LT and RT modifiers on the codes.

Biopsy of Lesions

Two biopsies performed during the same session may be bundled, but sometimes they are not. If a single lesion is biopsied multiple times, report one biopsy code. However, if multiple distinct lesions are biopsied, physicians can report each biopsy separately with a modifier –59. This indicates that a different service was performed or that a different site was biopsied.

If the multiple biopsies were performed using an endoscope, report only one biopsy code. If a nondiagnostic biopsy is performed and then the lesion is removed or destroyed, the biopsy is not reported separately.

Endoscopy Performed at the Same Time as an Open Procedure

An endoscopic procedure performed prior to an open surgical procedure may be bundled into the open procedure, but sometimes it is not. If the endoscopy is a distinct diagnostic service and is the basis for the decision to perform the open procedure, both the endoscopy and the open procedure are reported. A modifier –58 is added to the endoscopy code.

Payers consider office medical supplies to be a practice expense and will not reimburse separately for them...In some instances, injectable medications, intrauterine devices, and pessaries may be reimbursed by the payer but at an amount less than the cost to the practice.

If the endoscopy is performed to establish a location of the lesion, confirm its presence, define its extent, or to establish anatomic landmarks, the endoscopic service is not reported separately. It is considered a medically necessary part of the overall service. If the endoscopy is attempted but unsuccessful and another surgical service is necessary, only the successful service is reported.

The proper use of surgical modifiers can have a significant effect on reimbursement. For example, a physician took her patient to the operating room for a diagnostic D&C and possible hysterectomy. The findings from the D&C indicated endometrial cancer. The physician performed a total abdominal hysterectomy at the same encounter. The physician reported codes 58150 and 58120–59. In most cases, a D&C is bundled into a hysterectomy. In this case, however, it is a distinct service and can be reported separately with the modifier –59. CPT modifiers and their use with surgical services are addressed in detail in Chapter 9.

Other Payers and the Global Surgical Package

Definition of Global Surgical Package

It is important to know which definition of the global surgical package payers are using: CPT's, Medicare's, or their own. Some payers purchase commercial software to determine payment for multiple surgical procedures. Physicians must monitor the Explanation of Benefits to understand how a particular payer reimburses for surgical procedures and to evaluate the contract with that payer.

Although CPT does not set a specific number of follow-up days for each procedure (a global surgical period), most insurance companies do. During this global surgical period, no additional payment will be made for typical postoperative care provided by the surgeon. Code 99024 (postoperative follow-up visit included in the global service) may be used within the physician's office to document a follow-up visit that is part of a global surgical package. This code generally is not reported to the insurer but is useful for internal tracking purposes.

Supplies and Materials

Many payers consider the cost of office medical supplies such as surgical trays or dressings as included in the payment for the procedure. In some instances, injectable medications, intrauterine devices, and pessaries may be reimbursed by the payer but at an amount less than the cost to the practice. Some payers request that HCPCS level II codes be used to identify the drug or supply used. (HCPCS codes are discussed in Chapter 1). It may be necessary to attach an invoice to the claim indicating the cost of the supply. Physicians need to be familiar with the policies of their payers.

Special Issues in Gynecologic Surgery

Endoscopic/Laparoscopic Versus Open Procedures

Endoscopic codes are located in the appropriate anatomic subsection and include terminology indicating the use of an endoscope. Codes that are not listed under a heading of endoscopy, laparoscopy, or hysteroscopy, or that do not include the use of an endoscope, are open surgical procedures. Open surgical codes should not be used to report an endoscopic approach. If there is no specific code for the endoscopic/laparoscopic procedure performed, then an unlisted endoscopic procedure code should be used (see Chapter 3 for discussion of unlisted codes).

Endoscopic Procedure and Open Procedure During the Same Surgical Session

Sometimes a diagnostic endoscopy is performed because of a symptom(s). As a result of the findings from that diagnostic procedure, an open therapeutic procedure is performed during the same surgical session. Also, sometimes it is not possible to complete a procedure through the scope and an open procedure is performed. Both CPT and Medicare have rules about reporting an endoscopic and an open procedure during the same surgical session, but the rules are not the same. Medicare's rules are discussed in the section of this chapter on the Correct Coding Initiative. The following example illustrates coding for these circumstances.

A physician planned a laparoscopic vaginal hysterectomy on her patient, who had a left ovarian mass and pain. However, exploration of the pelvic anatomy through the scope revealed an enlarged, complex cyst and numerous pelvic adhesions. She attempted to lyse some of the adhesions using the laparoscope. Because of the extent of the adhesions, the physician converted to an open procedure and performed a total abdominal hysterectomy.

Under CPT rules, the physician may report both procedures. She may either:

- Report the open procedure code alone and attach a modifier –22 (unusual service): 58150–22 or

- Report both procedures and attach a modifier –59 (distinct service) to the endoscopy code:

    —8150

    —58660–59

In this instance, the physician should use ICD-9-CM code V64.41 (laparoscopic surgical procedure converted to open procedure) on the claim to clarify the unusual situation.

Under Medicare rules, however, a "most extensive procedure" rule applies. This means that in most circumstances, the endoscopy is bundled into the open procedure and cannot be reported separately. If the patient had been a Medicare patient, the physician would have reported only code 58150 because CCI rules state that codes 58150 and 58660 are never reimbursed when performed at the same surgical session.

The only exception is when the CCI indicates that the diagnostic and the open procedure may be reported together (are not bundled). If the physician had performed endoscopy code 49320 (diagnostic laparoscopy), she could report both codes 58150 and 49320–51 because these codes are not listed as bundled in the CCI.

Lysis of Adhesions

Lysis of adhesions may be carried out by itself, as a component of another procedure, or independent and distinct from other procedures performed at the same session. The correct method for reporting lysis depends on the circumstances.

Sometimes lysis of ovarian or tubal adhesions is the only procedure performed. In this case, it is reported using code 58660 (for a laparoscopic approach) or code 58740 (for an open approach).

Sometimes simple lysis of adhesions is performed with other procedures. The lysis of adhesions requiring little additional time or effort is considered to be integral to (bundled into) the other procedures.

Open surgical codes should not be used to report an endoscopic approach. If there is no specific code for the endoscopic/laparoscopic procedure performed, then an unlisted endoscopic procedural code should be used.

Sometimes, however, the lysis of adhesions is independent of the other procedure(s) performed during the same session and requires significant physician work. This implies that the adhesions are dense, vascular, and anatomy distorting, or significantly increase the operative time and risk to the patient. In this case, the surgeon may seek additional reimbursement.

There are two methods for reporting the additional work:

1. Report the CPT-4 code specific to the lysis (eg, 44005, 44200, 58559, 58740) with either modifier –59 (distinct surgical procedure) or –51 (multiple procedure), or

2. Add a modifier –22 (unusual procedural service) to the other, larger surgical procedure performed

When using a modifier in this situation, the physician should send in a copy of the operative report and a cover letter to substantiate the claim. The claim may be denied initially and the surgeon may need to submit an appeal or provide additional information to be paid appropriately.

Physicians Performing Less Than the Full Surgical Package

Sometimes, different physicians provide different parts of a single global surgical service (preoperative, intraoperative, or postoperative services). CPT has modifiers to indicate this circumstance, but does not indicate how payment should be divided. Medicare has very specific rules. Commercial payers' rules vary.

CPT defines services included in its global surgical package but does not have specific rules about how to divide up payment for the package when several physicians provide different parts of it. In common practice, however, coding depends on whether or not there is a reciprocal billing relationship (covering arrangement):

- Reciprocal billing relationship—the physician who provides the preoperative and/or postoperative services does not submit a claim to the payer; the surgeon codes and bills for the entire global surgical package.

- No reciprocal billing relationship—each physician reports the same procedure code with the appropriate modifiers: –54 (surgical care only), –55 (postoperative management only), or –56 (preoperative management only). Many third-party payers, however, do not recognize these modifiers, and a cover letter may be necessary to obtain appropriate reimbursement for both physicians.

Medicare may reimburse for the preoperative, intraoperative, and postoperative services according to a percentage of the RVUs designated for the total global surgical package. The Medicare Physician Fee Schedule lists the percentage of the total RVUs assigned to each component of the surgical package. For example, roughly 40% of the codes in the Female Genital System section and the Maternity Care and Delivery section assign 12% for preoperative work, 74% for intraoperative work, and 14% for postoperative work. One third of the codes in these sections do not list any percentages for preoperative, intraoperative, and postoperative work. The percentages for codes commonly reported by obstetrician–gynecologists are listed on the ACOG's web site under Coding and Nomenclature, Payment Indicators.

The payment to each physician involved in the case may not exceed the amount Medicare would have paid if a single physician had provided all the care. Reimbursement is based on whether care has been formally transferred to another physician and the relationship between the physicians. When appropriate, the services are reported using modifiers –54 (surgical care only), –55 (postoperative management only), or –56 (preoperative management only).

A formal transfer of care has occurred when there is a written transfer agreement included in the medical record. In this case, each physician reports the same surgical code with an appropriate modifier. The claim form must state the date on which care was relinquished or assumed. The receiving physician bills only after he or she has provided at least one service to the patient.

Coding when no formal transfer of care has occurred depends on whether the physicians are within the same group practice. If the physicians are within the same group practice and are of the same specialty, the group bills for the entire global package.

If the physicians are within the same group practice but are of different specialties, each physician reports the same surgical code with an appropriate modifier. If the physicians are in different, unaffiliated practices and have a reciprocal billing relationship (covering relationship), the primary physician bills the entire global package. If the physicians are in different, unaffiliated practices and do not have a reciprocal billing relationship, each physician reports the same surgical code with an appropriate modifier.

The rules listed previously apply only to routine intraoperative or postoperative services. If another physician treats a problem or complication related to the surgery, he or she may bill separately for those services using E/M or procedure codes as appropriate. The surgeon bills the global package and receives the full global fee. The other physician bills and receives payment for services outside the global package. This applies if the patient is covered by Medicare or another insurer.

Chapter 8 Quiz: The Global Surgical Package

True or False:

1. The hospital admission workup provided the day prior to surgery is included in both the CPT and Medicare definitions of the global surgical package.

2. CPT defines the global period for all surgical CPT codes.

3. According to CPT, routine follow-up care can be reported separately for starred procedures.

4. Inappropriate unbundling occurs when routine services in a major procedure are reported separately.

Choose the best answer:

5. The evaluation and treatment of postoperative complications can be reported separately:

   a. Under CPT guidelines

   b. Under Medicare guidelines

   c. Under Medicare guidelines only if managed in the operating room

   d. A and B

   e. A and C

6. The visit at which the decision to perform surgery can be reported:

   a. Only if it occurs more than 1 day before surgery

   b. Only if Medicare rules are applied

   c. Regardless of when it occurs under both CPT and Medicare rules

7. Intraoperative bundling rules may be determined by:

   a. CPT guidelines and definitions

   b. Separate procedure designations

   c. Correct Coding Initiative

   d. Commercial software and internal payer rules

   e. All of the above

Code the following scenarios:

8. A physician performs an exploratory laparotomy, a total abdominal hysterectomy, a left salpingo-oophorectomy, and simple adhesiolysis on his patient. What CPT code or codes should he report?

9. A 28 year-old established patient was seen with complaints of vulvar pain and swelling. After the physician took an appropriate history and performed an examination, a Bartholin's gland abscess was diagnosed and the physician performed an incision and drainage. The following day, the patient returned because she was concerned about the amount of drainage she was having from the abscess site. How should the physician report the services provided to the patient?

Answers are listed on page 179.

Chapter 9

Modifiers

Proper use of modifiers can have a big impact on a physician's reimbursement and sometimes make the difference in whether services are reimbursed at all. Modifiers provide payers with a little extra information. Examples of such information include whether the service involved more than the usual physician work, less than the usual physician work, involved more than one physician, or is not bundled into the other services provided at the same time. This chapter addresses:

- The purpose of modifiers and their importance in the coding system
- The proper application of modifiers in the clinical setting

Following completion of the chapter, the reader should be able to:

- Identify key surgical and nonsurgical modifiers
- Understand how to apply modifiers to the practice setting
- Recognize the impact of modifiers on physician reimbursement

Understanding and Using CPT Modifiers

CPT developed modifiers as a way to indicate that a service or procedure has been altered by some specific circumstance yet not to the extent that the service or procedure itself has changed. CPT modifiers are two-digit numeric codes added to the end of a five-digit code when used for billing purposes. A complete listing of the modifiers and their definitions can be found in Appendix A of the CPT book.

Purpose

Modifiers are used to indicate that more than one physician performed the service, that the physician's work is more or less than usual, that multiple procedures were performed, or that the services were unusual in some way. They also are useful in identifying services that should be considered excluded (reimbursed separately) from the global surgical package. These examples illustrate that the proper use of modifiers can have a significant impact on payment for physician services.

Table 9–1 shows current CPT modifiers. Many of these will be addressed in this chapter along with examples illustrating their use.

Modifiers are used to indicate that more than one physician performed the service, that the service has been increased or decreased, that multiple procedures were performed, or that the services were unusual in some way.

Table 9–1. CPT Modifiers

Modifier	Definition	Modifier	Definition
–21	Prolonged Evaluation and Management Services	–57	Decision for Surgery
–22	Unusual Procedural Services	–58	Staged or Related Procedure or Service by the Same Physician During the Postoperative Period
–23	Unusual Anesthesia	–59	Distinct Procedural Service
–24	Unrelated Evaluation and Management Service by the Same Physician During a Postoperative Period	–62	Two Surgeons
–25	Significant, Separately Identifiable Evaluation and Management Service by the Same Physician on the Same Day of the Procedure or Other Service	–66	Surgical Team
–26	Professional Component	–76	Repeat Procedure by Same Physician
–32	Mandated Services	–77	Repeat Procedure by Another Physician
–47	Anesthesia by Surgeon	–78	Return to the Operating Room for a Related Procedure During the Postoperative Period
–50	Bilateral Procedure	–79	Unrelated Procedure or Service by the Same Physician During the Postoperative Period
–51	Multiple Procedures	–80	Assistant Surgeon
–52	Reduced Services	–81	Minimum Assistant Surgeon
–53	Discontinued Procedure	–82	Assistant Surgeon (when qualified resident surgeon not available)
–54	Surgical Care Only	–90	Reference (Outside) Laboratory
–55	Postoperative Management Only	–91	Repeat Clinical Diagnostic Laboratory Test
–56	Preoperative Management Only	–99	Multiple Modifiers

Application of Modifiers by Payers

Medicare recognizes most CPT-4 modifiers and uses them to determine payment for physician services. In addition, it has developed alphanumeric modifiers (Healthcare Common Procedures Coding System [HCPCS] modifiers) such as –RT (right) and –LT (left).

A list of the most commonly used HCPCS modifiers can be found on the inside cover of the CPT book. A complete list can be obtained from your Medicare carrier.

Some payers recognize only certain CPT-4 modifiers in their payment process and some do not recognize any modifiers. Others do not recognize only CPT-4 modifiers but also Medicare's HCPCS modifiers. When used by payers, modifiers often eliminate the necessity for additional documentation to describe the special circumstance(s) present in a specific case. It is not always clear whether a payer will use all, some, or none of CPT-4's modifiers. Physicians should review their Explanation of Benefits to determine if the payment received reflects the specific situation for which the modifier was used.

Global Surgical Package Modifiers

Some modifiers are used to indicate that a service is not part of a procedure's global surgical package. They are used for procedures performed within the preservice period (–25, –57), intraservice period (–50, –51, –59, –80, –82, –62), or postservice period (–24, –58, –78, –79). Other modifiers have different applications as discussed below.

Preservice Modifier –25 (Significant, Separately Identifiable Evaluation and Management Service by the Same Physician on the Same Day of the Procedure or Other Service)

Sometimes a physician performs both a procedure or service identified by a CPT code and a significant, separately identifiable evaluation and management (E/M) service. Modifier –25 may be used when two E/M codes are reported together. This circumstance is addressed in Chapter 7. Modifier –25 also is used to report an E/M service and a procedure on the same day. Following is a review of the latter circumstance.

It is assumed that the physician provides some E/M work directly related to the procedure on the day it is performed. This E/M work (eg, confirming the need for the procedure, assessing the patient's current status, obtaining consent, and other routine preoperative and postoperative care) is considered part of the procedure's global surgical package and, therefore, is not reported separately. However, when the E/M service is above and beyond what is usually provided for a given procedure, the services can be reported separately. The E/M service may be prompted by the symptom or condition for which the procedure and/or service was provided. Therefore, it is not necessary to report different diagnoses for the procedure and E/M service on the same date.

Generally both the E/M service and the procedure code are reported if:

- The decision to perform the procedure was made at the same encounter as the E/M service regardless of the diagnosis or
- The E/M service and the procedure have different diagnoses

For example, a patient presented with complaints of vulvar pain and swelling. After evaluation, the physician determined she had a Bartholin's gland abscess and recommended an incision and drainage. The patient agreed and the physician proceeded with the treatment. She reported an E/M service (codes 99201–99215) with a modifier –25 in addition to the CPT code for the procedure (56420).

Only the procedural code would be reported if:

- The decision to perform the procedure was made at a different encounter than the one during which the procedure was performed or
- The E/M service did not require a significant history, physical examination, and medical decision making

For example, a patient was seen on November 1 with a developing Bartholin's gland abscess. After evaluation, the physician prescribed oral antibiotics and hot baths four times daily. The patient was instructed to return in 3 days for a probable incision and drainage. On November 4, the patient returned after having followed the physician's instructions. The physician briefly examined the patient and decided to perform the procedure as planned. The physician reported an E/M service (codes 99201–99215) on November 1 and the CPT code for the procedure (56420) on November 4. A modifier is not necessary because the services were provided on separate days.

It is important to document clearly a distinct E/M service when reporting a procedure on the same day. It is advisable to separate the two notes physically by inserting a header (eg, "Procedure Note") or leaving space between the two entries. Remember, two separate services are being provided. The payer wants documentation of the work for each of them.

Preservice Modifier –57 (Decision for Surgery)

Both the Medicare and CPT global surgical package include services performed the day before or the day of surgery. An exception to this rule is when an E/M service that resulted in the initial decision to perform the operation occurs the day of or the day prior to the procedure. In such instances the E/M service is reported separately with a modifier –57.

For example, the emergency department physician called Dr. Williams to evaluate a patient who presented to the emergency room with complaints of vaginal bleeding and pelvic pain. Dr. Williams obtained a history, performed a physical examination and evaluated results of a stat human chorionic gonadotropin measurement and transvaginal ultrasonography. She diagnosed an ectopic pregnancy. The ectopic pregnancy was managed laparoscopically later that day. Dr. Williams reported an E/M service using the appropriate consultation code (99241–99245) and added a modifier –57. The appropriate surgical procedural code also was reported.

The modifier –57 tells the payer that the E/M service is excluded (reimbursed separately) from the global service because it was the encounter at which the initial decision to perform surgery was made.

Medicare has rules that differentiate the use of modifiers –57 and –25. According to Medicare, modifier –57 should only be used with an E/M services code when the decision to perform a major procedure (90-day global surgical period) is made. However, the modifier –25 should be used with an E/M services code to indicate when the decision is made to perform a minor procedure (0- or 10-day global surgical period). Other third party payers may use their own payment policy or Medicare's.

Intraservice Modifier –50 (Bilateral Procedure)

Many surgical procedures performed in the pelvis can be done either unilaterally or bilaterally (eg, oophorectomy, fimbrioplasty, etc.) Some of these procedures are coded the same whether done as a unilateral or bilateral procedure. They typically can be identified by the wording in the CPT description (eg, "unilateral or bilateral," "partial or total" or "and/or"). Others are considered unilateral codes for which additional payment is expected when performed bilaterally.

The codes for salpingostomy, fimbrioplasty, tubotubal anastomosis, tubouterine implantation, and pelvic lymph node dissection are all considered unilateral. When these services are performed bilaterally, a modifier –50 is added to the procedural code.

For example, a physician performed a laparoscopic fimbrioplasty on both the right and left fallopian tubes on her patient. She reported code 58672–50.

Intraservice Modifier –51 (Multiple Procedures)

When multiple procedures are performed at the same session by the same provider, the one with the greatest number of relative value units (RVUs) (highest valued service) is reported without a modifier. The additional procedure(s) are reported with a modifier –51 added.

Most insurers will reimburse their full allowable amount for the first procedure and a reduced amount (usually 50%) of their allowable for additional procedures. Physicians should report each procedure with their full fee and allow the payer to make any reductions.

Only those services that are not typically performed during the procedure should be listed separately. If a lesser procedure is almost always performed at the time of another procedure, it generally is included in the surgical code. See the discussion of bundling issues in Chapter 8.

Thus an exploratory laparotomy would not be reported separately when a hysterectomy also was performed during the surgical session. For example, a physician performed a vaginal hysterectomy with removal of tubes and ovaries (code 58262) and an anteroposterior colporrhaphy (code 57260) on her patient. She reported codes 58262 and 57260–51.

Some codes do not require a modifier –51 when reported with other procedures. They are "add-on" and "modifier –51 exempt" codes. A complete list of codes in these categories can be found in Appendices D and E of the CPT-4 book. These are addressed in Chapter 3.

Intraservice Modifier –59 (Distinct Procedural Service)

Modifier –59 is one of the most poorly understood modifiers, yet its correct use can greatly impact physician reimbursement. The modifier indicates that a specific case has unusual circumstances involving multiple procedures performed together. These unusual circumstances warrant payment for multiple procedures in this case when in most cases they would not be paid. The special circumstances should be documented by the physician.

Three specific scenarios can illustrate the proper use of this modifier:

1. Two separate encounters in the same day with overlapping services

2. Distinct procedures on the same day. These procedures may be performed on different structures or anatomic sites, involve different incisions or excisions, or involve different lesions.

3. Overriding a CPT "separate procedure" designation or Medicare's Correct Coding Initiative (see Chapter 8)

Modifier –59 often is confused with modifier -51. If the procedures performed ordinarily would be reported separately (that is, there is no expectation that the services would be bundled), then the modifier –51 is used. Modifier –59 is used to identify services that generally are considered bundled but are distinct procedures in this case.

The following examples illustrate situations in which the modifier –59 would be used.

- Example of two separate encounters on the same day—a physician performed a fetal nonstress test (code 59025) on her pregnant patient in the morning. That afternoon, the patient tripped and fell down her front steps. She returned to the physician's office on the same day, where a biophysical profile (code 76818), which includes a nonstress test, was performed. The physician reported codes 76818 and 59025–59.

- Examples of distinct procedures on the same day—These distinct procedures may include different structures or organs. For example, a physician performed an endometrial biopsy (code 58100, separate procedure) and a breast cyst aspiration (code 19000) during the same surgical session on her patient. She reported codes 58100–59 and 19000.

When a physician serves as an assistant at surgery, either a modifier –80 or –82 will apply.

These distinct procedures may include separate incisions or excision. For example, a physician performed a marsupialization of a Bartholin's gland cyst (code 56440) and excision of a lesion on the labia majora (code 56501) during the same surgical session on his patient. He reported codes 56440 and 56501–59.

These distinct procedures may include separate lesions. For example, a physician drained an ovarian abscess (code 58820) on her patient's right ovary and drained an ovarian cyst (code 58800, separate procedure) on her left ovary. She reported codes 58820 and 58800–59. For Medicare patients, use modifiers –LT and –RT to indicate right and left sides instead of modifier –59.

- Example of overriding CPT separate procedure or Medicare's Correct Coding Initiative- a physician performed two procedures on his patient: a colposcopic examination of the cervix with cervical biopsy and endocervical curettage for a low grade squamous intraepithelial lesion Pap test result (code 57454) and a vulvar biopsy for leukoplakia (56605). Code 56605 is a CPT separate procedure code. A distinct diagnostic code is linked to each procedure and a modifier –59 is added to code 56605 to explain why both ser-vices are being reported.

Intraservice Modifiers Denoting Surgical Responsibility

Modifiers –80 and –82 (Assistant at Surgery)

When a physician serves as an assistant at surgery, either modifier –80 or –82 will apply. Which modifier is used depends on the payer and whether the service is performed in a teaching setting with a residency program. Modifier –80 is used either for non-Medicare patients or for Medicare patients who are treated in a nonteaching setting. Modifier –82 is used only for Medicare patients in a teaching setting when no qualified resident is available to assist.

For example, Dr. Norman performed a total abdominal hysterectomy (code 58150) on his patient, whose primary insurer is Medicare. Dr. Richards assisted Dr. Norman. Dr. Norman reported code 58150. Dr. Richards reported code 58150–80. If the surgery had taken place in a teaching hospital and a qualified resident was not available, Dr. Richards would have reported code 58150–82.

Modifier –62 (Two Surgeons)

On occasion, two surgeons work together as primary surgeons performing distinct part(s) of a single procedure. In this case, they are considered co-surgeons. The services provided by both physicians are described by a single CPT-4 code. Each surgeon submits this same procedural code with a modifier –62. Both surgeons are required to dictate an operative report that describes their respective portions of the operation. Both are expected to pro-vide postoperative care for the patient. Co-surgeons usually are reimbursed between 125% and 140% of the insurer's allowable. This amount is usually divided equally between the surgeons (eg, 65.5–70% each).

For example, Dr. Phillips performed a total abdominal hysterectomy with bilateral salpingo-oophorectomy on a patient with an ovarian malignancy. Dr. Sidney performed a radical dissection and removal of the metastatic implants within the pelvis and an omentectomy. Dr. Phillips and Dr. Sidney both report code 58953–62 (bilateral salpingo-oophorectomy with omentectomy, total abdominal hysterectomy, and radical dissection for debulking). Both surgeons document their portion of the operation in separate operative reports.

On occasion, two surgeons will serve as co-surgeons for one procedure but primary and assistant surgeon for another procedure during the same surgical session. In this case, the surgeon reports the appropriate CPT code for the additional procedure without a modifier while the assistant attaches either a modifier –80 or –82, depending on the circumstances.

For example, Dr. Howard performed a right hemicolectomy with reanastomosis, and wedge resection of the liver on her patient. Dr. Michaels assisted. In addition, Dr. Michaels performed a supracervical hysterectomy with bilateral salpingo-oophorectomy for ovarian metastasis, assisted by Dr. Howard.

Medicare will not reimburse for a surgeon to serve as primary surgeon and assistant surgeon during the same session, but many commercial payers will. If the patient in the previous example had been a Medicare patient, Dr. Howard could report only codes 44160 and 47100–51 and Dr. Michaels could report only code 58180.

For commercial payers, Dr. Howard reported codes both as a primary and as an assistant surgeon. As a primary surgeon, she reported codes 44160 (colectomy) and 47100–51 (liver biopsy). As an assistant surgeon, he reported code 58180–80 (hysterectomy). Dr. Michaels also reported codes as a primary and as an assistant surgeon. As a primary surgeon, he reported code 58180 (hysterectomy). As an assistant surgeon, he reported codes 44160–80 (colectomy) and 47100–80 (liver biopsy).

On occasion, two surgeons perform distinct procedures during the same surgical session for which there is no single CPT code that describes all the services provided by both physicians. In this case, each physician reports the separate, distinct CPT codes that describe his or her own work. No modifiers are needed. Distinct ICD-9-CM codes might be appropriate in this situation.

For example, Dr. Scott performs a laparoscopic colpopexy and Dr. Lee performs a laparoscopic cholecystectomy on their patient. Dr. Scott reports 57425 (laparoscopy, surgical; colpopexy) linked to diagnosis 618.5 (prolapse of vaginal vault after hysterectomy). Dr. Lee reports 47562 (laparoscopy, surgical; cholecystectomy) linked to diagnosis 574.10 (calculus of gallbladder with cholecystectomy). Neither physician uses a modifier. If they assisted each other and the patient is not a Medicare beneficiary, then Dr. Lee also can report 57425–80 and Dr. Scott also can report 47562–80.

Modifier –78 (Return to the Operating Room for a Related Procedure During the Postoperative Period)

When additional related services are provided to a patient during the global period, a modifier –78 is appended to the additional services. (If the same procedure is repeated on the same day, see modifier –76 instead of modifier –78.)

Modifier –78 was created because of Medicare's global surgical package rules (see Chapter 8). Medicare will not reimburse for postoperative complications unless the treatment was provided in the operating room. Modifier –78 indicates both that the subsequent operation is for the treatment of a direct complication of the initial surgical procedure and that the service was performed in an operating room.

For example, 3 weeks after a physician performed a transvaginal sling procedure (code 57288, which has a 90-day global period), the patient developed a graft erosion into her vaginal vault. The physician took her back to the operating room for removal of the sling. He reported code 57287–78 (removal or revision of sling for stress incontinence). The modifier –78 informs the payer that this is a related procedure performed during the global period.

Postservice Modifier –58 (Staged or Related Procedure or Service by the Same Physician During the Postoperative Period)

Additional services may be provided during a procedure's postoperative global period that were planned prospectively at the time of the original procedure (staged), are more extensive than the original procedure, or provide therapy following a diagnostic surgical procedure. A modifier –58 is used in these cases. Modifier –58 is used to report postoperative procedures performed for an added course of treatment (not for a problem or complication that is the result of a related surgical procedure).

For example, a physician examined a patient for postmenopausal bleeding and reviewed her family history of ovarian cancer. A staged workup and treatment was planned. The physician performed a dilation and curettage (code 58120, which has a 10-day global period). The pathology report revealed an endometrial carcinoma. Several days later, the physician performed a total abdominal hysterectomy with bilateral salpingo-oophorectomy and bilateral pelvic lymphadenectomy (code 58210) on the patient. The physician reported code 58120 for the first procedure and code 58210–58 for the second one. If the physician had not used the modifier –58, she might not be paid for code 58210 because it was performed within the 10-day global period for code 58120.

Postservice Modifiers –24 (Unrelated Evaluation and Management Service by the Same Physician During a Postoperative Period) and –79 (Unrelated Procedure or Service by the Same Physician During the Postoperative Period).

Additional E/M services or procedures that are unrelated to the original service may be provided during a procedure's postoperative global period. Both Medicare and CPT-4 rules consider these unrelated postoperative services to be excluded from the global surgical package and, therefore, reimbursed separately. These services might be for treatment that is completely unrelated to the original surgery or for treatment of an underlying condition. In addition to using the appropriate modifier, the diagnosis must reflect the most specific reason for the additional services.

A modifier –24 is used if an E/M service is performed during a postoperative period for a reason(s) unrelated to the original procedure. For example, the physician performed a hysterectomy on her patient who had ovarian cancer. Several weeks after the surgery, the patient came into the physician's office and discussed chemotherapy and other treatment options for 25 minutes. This discussion is considered unrelated to the surgery and is separately reportable. The physician reported an established patient office visit (code 99214). The level of service is based on the time the physician spent counseling the patient. (Using time spent counseling to determine the level of E/M service is discussed in Chapter 4.)

A modifier –79 is used if an additional surgical procedure is performed during a postoperative period for a reason unrelated to the original procedure. For example, a physician saw a patient who complained of vulvar and vaginal pain. He had performed a TAH/BSO for bilateral ovarian cystadenomas 2 months earlier. The TAH/BSO has a global surgical period of 90 days. After an examination, candidiasis was diagnosed and the patient was treated with an application of medicated solution. The physician reported code 57150–79 and an outpatient E/M service (codes 99211–99215) with a –24 modifier. He also added a –25 modifier to the E/M code to indicate that the visit was significant and separately identifiable from the procedure performed the same day.

Components of the Global Surgical Package (Modifiers –54, –55, and –56)

Sometimes several physicians in different practices will provide portions of the global surgical package (preoperative, intraoperative, and postoperative services). These three modifiers are used to report this circumstance.

When one physician performs only the intraoperative portion of a procedure, the surgeon reports the procedure code with a modifier –54 (surgical care only). When another physician performs only the postoperative management, he or she reports the same procedure code with a modifier –55 (postoperative management only). When a physician performs only the preoperative care and evaluation, he or she reports the code with a modifier –56 (preoperative management only). Modifier –56 is rarely reported by physicians providing services to Medicare patients. Medicare assumes that whenever a procedure is performed, the preservice also is provided by that same physician. For example, Dr. Albert practices in a rural community. She sent her patient to a gynecologic oncologist, Dr. Lawrence, at a nearby medical center for staging laparotomy of ovarian cancer. After discharge from the hospital, Dr. Albert provided the postoperative care. Dr. Albert reported code 58960–55. Dr. Lawrence reported code 58960–54.

These modifiers are added only to surgical procedure codes. Not all payers, however, recognize these modifiers. Physicians should check with their payers for the preferred method of reporting these circumstances.

Other CPT Modifiers

Modifier –21 (Prolonged Evaluation and Management Services)

This modifier is used when the face-to-face or floor/unit service(s) provided is prolonged or otherwise greater than usually required. It can be used only with the highest level of E/M service within a given category. For example, for initial hospital care, the modifier could be added only to code 99223 (the highest level of service in this category).

Medicare and most other payers do not accept this modifier. Physicians should use the prolonged services codes instead. See Chapter 5 for a discussion of the prolonged service codes.

Modifier –22 (Unusual Services)

Sometimes the service(s) provided is substantially more complex than that which is typical for a procedure. This circumstance is identified by adding a modifier –22 to the procedural code. This modifier is added to a procedural code (not an E/M service code) when the services:

- Are more difficult than usual
- Include components not normally part of the specific code
- Require significantly more physician work than usually necessary

It is necessary to provide a copy of the operative report that clearly indicates the additional time, effort, or services provided. It also is helpful to send a cover letter or special report summarizing the additional work and the circumstances requiring the work. An example of a letter is included in Appendix D.

For example, a physician performed a total abdominal hysterectomy on a morbidly obese patient. The surgery took much longer and was substantially more difficult than a typical hysterectomy because of her obesity. The physician reported code 58150–22.

Modifier –26 (Professional Component)

Certain procedures are composed of a professional component and a technical component. For example, certain diagnostic tests, including ultrasound examinations and fetal stress tests, include these two components. When the professional component is reported separately, the service is identified by adding a modifier –26 to the usual procedural code.

The professional component is provided by the physician and includes:

- The supervision and/or performance of the test (if any)
- The interpretation
- The written report

The technical component includes costs associated with:

- The technician salary/benefits (if any)

- The equipment
- Any necessary supplies

For example, the obstetric ultrasound code 76801 is valued at 3.59 RVUs—2.22 RVUs for the technical component and 1.37 RVUs for the professional component.

If an ultrasound examination is performed at the hospital or other facility, the physician who performs and/or interprets the test bills the ultrasound code and adds a modifier –26. The facility bills for the technical component only by adding a modifier –TC to the same code reported by the physician.

If, however, an ultrasound examination is performed at the physician's office on a machine owned by the practice and by a technician employed by the practice, the physician reports the appropriate code without a modifier.

For example, a physician performed a fetal and maternal evaluation using ultrasound in her office on the patient who is at 17 weeks of gestation. She reported code 76805. At 37 weeks gestation, the patient presented to the hospital in active labor. The physician performed a limited ultrasound examination at the hospital to determine fetal position. She reported code 76815–26. The hospital will code for the technical component (76815–TC).

Modifier –32 (Mandated Services)

Sometimes an entity may require a consultation or second opinion. This entity may be a professional review organization, third-party payer, governmental, legislative, or regulatory entity. In these cases, the physician adds a modifier –32 to the code reported. For example, a physician sees a patient for a second opinion regarding a hysterectomy recommended by her primary gynecologist. The third-party payer requires a confirmatory recommendation before approving reimbursement for the surgery. The physician reports the appropriate E/M service (a confirmatory consultation service) with a modifier –32.

Modifier –52 (Reduced Services)

Sometimes, a service or procedure is partially reduced or eliminated at the physician's discretion. Under these circumstances, the physician reports the usual procedural code but adds a modifier –52. This indicates that the physician did not perform all the components described by the code and there is no other code that more accurately describes the service actually performed. Modifier –52 usually is attached to a procedural code but may be attached to diagnostic tests as well.

For example, a physician performed a presacral sympathectomy on her patient. There is no code for this procedure; however, it is part of code 58410 (uterine suspension, with or without shortening of round ligaments, with or without shortening of sacrouterine ligaments, with presacral sympathectomy). Therefore, the physician reported code 58410–52 because she performed some but not all the components of code 58410. There is no other code in CPT that describes this service more accurately.

Modifier –53 (Discontinued Procedure)

On occasion, a physician may elect to terminate a surgical or diagnostic procedure because of either extenuating circumstances or circumstances that threaten the well-being of the patient. A modifier –53 is added to the code for the procedure that was terminated. This modifier is used when a procedure is terminated and no other procedure is performed during the surgical session. It can be used for either office- or hospital-based procedures.

The modifier provides a mechanism for the surgeon to seek partial payment for the work performed. Also, if the procedure is performed successfully at a later date, the payer will be more likely to recognize that the claim for the first procedure (reported with a modifier –53) and the claim for the second procedure are not duplicates. Documentation may be required by the payer to determine the extent of the physician work performed before termination of the procedure.

It is not always appropriate to use this modifier when a service is discontinued. Modifier –53 is not used:

- To report the elective cancellation of a procedure before the patient's anesthesia induction and/or surgical preparation in the operating suite.
- When one surgical approach is unsuccessful but then another approach is used at the same surgical session (eg, attempted vaginal hysterectomy followed by an abdominal hysterectomy).

For example, a physician attempted an endometrial biopsy (code 58100) but was unsuccessful because his patient had a stenotic cervix. The patient was scheduled for a dilation and curettage the next day. The physician reported code 58100–53. The ICD-9-CM code for the cervical stenosis (622.4) should be listed on the claim form.

Modifier –76 (Repeat Procedure by Same Physician)

Sometimes a physician needs to indicate that a procedure or service was repeated subsequent to the original procedure or service. A modifier –76 is added to the code for the repeated procedure or service.

For example, Dr. Jacobs performed a destruction of vulvar condyloma (56501 which has a 10-day global period) on his patient. Six days later, however, the patient returned to the physician's office with new lesions. Dr. Jacobs destroyed the new growths. He reported code 56501–76 for the second procedure.

Modifier –77 (Repeat Procedure by Another Physician)

On occasion, a physician needs to indicate that a basic procedure or service performed by another physician was repeated. A modifier –77 is added to the code for the repeated procedure or service. For example, the patient from the example chose to see Dr. George, Dr. Jacobs' partner, for destruction of the new lesions. Dr. George would report 56501–77.

Modifiers –76 and –77 indicate to the payer that the second procedure is not a duplicate claim. In some circumstances, the payer may request documentation supporting the need for the additional procedure.

Modifier –90 (Reference [Outside] Laboratory)

Sometimes laboratory procedures are not performed by the treating or reporting physician. A modifier –90 is added to the usual procedural code. This modifier indicates that the interpretation was performed by an outside laboratory and not in the physician's office. The physician's practice collects the payment from the third-party payer and reimburses the laboratory. Medicare does not allow physician's offices to report laboratory services in this manner. Medicare requires that only the entity performing a service report it for reimbursement. For example, a physician performs a preventive medicine examination on his patient and a pap smear specimen is collected. The specimen is sent to the laboratory for interpretation using automated thin layer preparation. The physician reports code 88142–90 to the patient's third-party payer and reimburses the laboratory for the interpretation.

Modifier –91 (Repeat Clinical Diagnostic Laboratory Test)

Sometimes in the course of treating a patient, a physician may need to repeat the same laboratory test on the same day for the same patient to obtain subsequent (multiple) test results. A modifier –91 is added to the repeated laboratory test.

Sometimes laboratory procedures are not performed by the treating or reporting physician. A modifier –90 is added to the usual procedural code.

For example, a physician saw a patient for unexplained pelvic and abdominal pain, loss of appetite, and general lethargy. A white blood count was elevated to 12,000 with a left shift. The physician repeated the test later in the day to see if the count continued to increase. She reported code 85032 for the initial white blood count and code 85032–91 for the subsequent test.

It is not always appropriate to use this modifier. It may not be used when tests are repeated to confirm initial results because of problems with specimens or equipment, or for any other reason when a normal, one-time, reportable result is all that is required. Also, this modifier is not used with other code(s) that already include a series of test results (eg, glucose tolerance tests, evocative/suppression testing).

Chapter 9 Quiz: Modifiers

True or False:

1. Modifiers are two-digit codes used only by Medicare carriers.

2. Modifiers can have a significant impact on reimbursement.

Choose the best answer:

3. Guidelines for billing an E/M visit and a procedure on the same date of service include:

   a. –25 modifier must be attached to the procedure code.

   b. Both services are billable only if the diagnosis for the E/M is different from the diagnosis for the procedure.

   c. The procedure and the E/M visit may both be billed with the same diagnosis code and during the same encounter, if the patient's condition requires a significant, separately identifiable E/M service beyond the usual preoperative and postoperative care associated with the procedure.

4. Modifier –57 is used:

   a. To identify the visit at which the initial decision for surgery is made

   b. To report a routine preoperative history and physical

   c. Only within the preoperative period of the surgery

   d. Both A and C

5. Modifier –51:

   a. Indicates that multiple different procedures have been performed at the same session

   b. Should be appended to the lesser valued procedures

   c. Should not be appended to "add-on" codes

   d. All of the above

6. Modifier –62:

   a. Should be reported only by the assistant at surgery

   b. Should be reported by both physicians acting as co-surgeons

   c. Requires documentation by only one surgeon

7. Modifiers that indicate that a service is unrelated to a previous surgery are:

   a. –79

   b. –78

   c. –24

   d. A and C

Answers are listed on page 179.

Chapter 10

Obstetric Services

On the surface, obstetric coding seems to be fairly clear—a service is either in the global obstetric package or it is not. However, the reality is different payers have their own definitions of the global package and own requirements for how maternity services should be reported. This chapter addresses:

- The global obstetric package and some common payer variations
- The methods for reporting portions of the global obstetric package
- The proper reporting of ultrasound examinations and other diagnostic tests
- Diagnostic coding for obstetric services

Following completion of the chapter, the reader should be able to:

- Identify the components of the global obstetric package
- Properly report additional related and unrelated services provided during the global period
- Understand how to report services when more than one obstetric group has provided services during the obstetric period
- Understand when to report diagnostic codes from the maternity care chapter of ICD-9-CM and when to report a "V" code

The Global Obstetric Package

CPT-4 includes four global obstetric codes that include all routine obstetric care a patient receives during her pregnancy plus the care provided for 6 weeks after she gives birth. According to the CPT book, the global obstetric codes cover the services normally provided in uncomplicated maternity cases, including antepartum care, delivery, and postpartum care. The global obstetric codes are:

- 59400—Routine obstetric care including antepartum care, vaginal delivery (with or without episiotomy, and/or forceps) and postpartum care
- 59510—Routine obstetric care including antepartum care, cesarean delivery, and postpartum care
- 59610—Routine obstetric care including antepartum care, vaginal delivery (with or without episiotomy, and/or forceps) and postpartum care, after previous cesarean delivery

According to the CPT-4 book, the global obstetric codes cover the services normally provided in uncomplicated maternity cases, including antepartum care, delivery, and postpartum care.

- 59618—Routine obstetric care including antepartum care, cesarean delivery, and postpartum care, following attempted vaginal delivery after previous cesarean delivery

These global obstetric codes are reported when one physician or group practice provides all of a patient's obstetric care. The codes are reported after the patient has given birth. Exceptions to this rule are addressed later in the chapter.

Payers

The CPT rules about the content of the global package are fairly clear. Third-party payers, however, often have their own specific guidelines on what services they include in the global obstetric package. Payers may consider all services routinely provided by obstetricians to their patients as part of the global package. Some payers, for example, include one screening ultrasound examination in the payment for global services.

Services that fall outside the global package and, therefore, are reimbursed separately, must be documented as medically necessary with an ICD-9-CM code. For example, certain screening tests may not be reimbursed separately under some insurance policies, although a test linked to a problem diagnosis might be (eg, nonspecific abnormal findings of amniotic fluid, code 792.3). Physician practices should be aware of these issues when negotiating contracts for maternity services.

In addition, third-party payers have different policies concerning how they want obstetric services reported. Payers may want obstetric claims billed at specific intervals during the pregnancy (eg, each month or each trimester) rather than all at once after delivery. Other payers want one claim submitted after delivery but each service listed separately, or one claim submitted each trimester which lists each service provided during that trimester, or a separate claim submitted for each service when it occurs.

State Medicaid programs often want claims submitted using *Healthcare Common Procedure Coding System* Level II codes. These codes usually are submitted on a service-by-service basis. For example, codes H1000 through H1005 are used to report prenatal care for at-risk patients.

The remainder of this chapter discusses CPT rules on reporting obstetric services. Physicians should check with their payers concerning any unique requirements.

Antepartum Services

Each obstetric patient is different. Patients are seen for the initial antepartum visit at different stages in the pregnancy and may give birth early, at term, or post term. The CPT's definition of routine antepartum care is based on a patient who enrolls early in the first trimester and gives birth at term. She will typically have 13 antepartum visits. CPT-4 includes the following services in the antepartum care package:

- Initial and subsequent history and physical examinations
- Weight, blood pressures, fetal heart tones, routine chemical urinalysis
- Monthly visits up to 28 weeks of gestation (5–6 visits)
- Biweekly visits to 36 weeks of gestation (4 visits)
- Weekly visits until delivery (3–4 visits)

In addition, services that a physician normally provides in uncomplicated cases are included in the global package. For example, if a physician normally screens all patients for diabetes and cystic fibrosis carrier status, these services are included in the global package.

The CPT-4 definition of global care outlines a basic set of services that are included in an uncomplicated pregnancy. This means that services not mentioned in this definition can be considered excluded (reported and reimbursed separately) from the global obstetric package.

Services that may be excluded from the global obstetric package are:

- The initial evaluation and management (E/M) service during which the pregnancy is diagnosed

- Additional E/M services for conditions related or unrelated to the pregnancy

- Inpatient hospital admission and subsequent visits for care for complications of pregnancy

- Observation or other outpatient care in addition to routine antepartum care

- Maternal and/or fetal ultrasound examination and monitoring procedures

Each of these excluded services is addressed as follows.

E/M Services to Diagnose Pregnancy

Patients experiencing symptoms associated with early pregnancy may contact the physician's office for confirmation of the pregnancy. If the physician sees the patient and provides a pregnancy test, an E/M service can be reported for that visit. The physician may provide minimal counseling, draw blood for laboratory testing, and prescribe prenatal vitamins at that time. The specific E/M code depends on the content of the service as addressed in Chapter 4. The appropriate ICD-9-CM code is V72.40 (pregnancy examination or test, pregnancy unconfirmed) or, if the pregnancy is confirmed during the visit, report code V72.42 (pregnancy examination or test, positive result).

If, however, the physician initiates the antepartum record during this encounter, the E/M service is considered part of the global obstetric package. The E/M service is not reported separately.

Additional Services Unrelated to Pregnancy

Patients may be seen during the antepartum period for conditions unrelated to the pregnancy, such as an upper respiratory infection, bronchitis, and influenza. The evaluation and treatment of these conditions may be reported using E/M services codes. These codes are reported at the time the service is provided; the physician does not have to wait until after the delivery to submit the claim. Any other services (eg, laboratory tests) also can be reported at the time they are provided. These services may be provided either during a scheduled antepartum visit or an unscheduled one. After the delivery, the global service code is reported. For example, a patient develops a urinary tract infection and is seen by a physician at a time other than her scheduled prenatal visit. The physician reports an appropriate E/M service code and diagnostic code(s) describing the unrelated condition. The ICD-9-CM code V22.2 (pregnant state, incidental) is reported as a secondary diagnosis. (Note: Some payer's software automatically will bundle any services reported with diagnostic code V22.2 into the global package. In these cases, omit the V22.2 code.)

Sometimes a patient is seen for a scheduled prenatal visit but has an unrelated condition, such as an upper respiratory infection or a breast lump. Additional services can be reported if the condition requires a significant and separately identifiable E/M service in addition to the routine prenatal care. The additional services may include an E/M service and/or diagnostic tests. The diagnostic code linked to the procedural code must clearly identify the condition being evaluated or treated. The E/M code is selected based only on the additional services provided to evaluate and treat the problem, not including the routine prenatal care.

The physician should document the additional services in a separate section of the chart, although he or she also may note the unrelated condition in the perinatal record. If a payer requests a copy of the record, documentation outside the obstetric record helps support the assertion that the services were unrelated to the pregnancy.

Additional Services Related to Pregnancy

A patient may be seen more frequently than the typical 13 antepartum visits because she has complications of the pregnancy or needs medically necessary diagnostic tests. Examples of complications might be a preexisting heart condition complicating her antepartum care or gestational diabetes. Examples of tests are ultrasound examinations or laboratory studies. Additional E/M services are reported at the time of delivery. Additional tests are reported at the time they are performed. Diagnostic tests and procedures are addressed more fully in the section on special issues later in this chapter. For example, a patient was carrying twins and received additional ultrasound services from the physician. The physician reported each ultrasound examination (or other diagnostic test performed) along with an appropriate ICD-9-CM code that demonstrated its medical necessity. She reported these tests at the time the services were rendered. If she had provided any additional E/M services over the typical 13 visits, these would have been reported at the time of delivery.

An obstetric patient may be considered high risk because she had a problem in a previous pregnancy and/or she has a medical condition that may complicate her pregnancy. The obstetrician may see her for extra visits to monitor the potential problem. However, if no problems develop in this pregnancy, the obstetrician cannot report additional visits, even if she is seen for more than 13 times. Only visits related to current complications are reported separately.

A patient may be admitted for observation or inpatient care because of complications of her pregnancy. These are not typical antepartum visits. The obstetrician reports these services at the time they occur and the appropriate global obstetric package code after she gives birth. The service must be supported by an ICD-9-CM code that describes the complications. Visits that occur within 24 hours of delivery are considered part of the delivery service. For example, a physician saw a patient at 8 weeks of gestation for her first prenatal visit. She was seen again at 10 weeks of gestation because of a urinary tract infection. At 12 weeks of gestation she was seen for her routine prenatal visit and then seen on schedule until 34 weeks of gestation. At that time she developed hypertension and the physician saw her weekly until she gave birth at 40 weeks of gestation. The patient was seen a total of 16 times during the prenatal period: 13 routine antepartum visits plus two extra visits related to the pregnancy (because of the hypertension) plus one visit unrelated to the pregnancy (for the urinary tract infection). The physician reported the visit at 10 weeks of gestation for the urinary tract infection at the time it occurred along with codes for the laboratory studies she performed. After the patient gave birth, the physician reported a global obstetric code plus two additional antepartum visits (using E/M codes) for the visits for hypertension complicating pregnancy.

Delivery Services

The length of time between when a patient arrives at the hospital and when she actually gives birth will vary. If hospital or observation care occurs during the same episode of care as the delivery and within 24 hours of delivery, it is included in delivery service.

Included Services

The following services are included in the global obstetric package:

- Admission to the hospital
- Admission history and physical examination
- Management of uncomplicated labor
- Vaginal delivery (with or without episiotomy, with or without forceps or vacuum extraction) or cesarean delivery
- Delivery of the placenta

According to the American College of Obstetricians and Gynecologists, the following services also are included:

- Induction of labor (unless the obstetrician personally starts the intravenous line and sits with the patient during the infusion; in that case, report codes 90780–90781)

- Insertion of cervical dilator on same day as delivery (code 59200)

- Simple removal of cerclage (for complicated removal of cerclage, see code 59871)

Excluded Services

The global obstetric package codes include only services provided for uncomplicated deliveries. Any additional services that are provided because of complications are reported separately. These extra services may be specific procedures or E/M services. It is important to indicate the medical necessity for any additional services by reporting a specific ICD-9-CM code(s) that describes the circumstance or complication.

Following are examples of services that might be reported in addition to the global obstetric code. (Note that some of the services can be reported only if provided on a date other than the day of the delivery.)

- External cephalic version

- Insertion of cervical dilator by the physician on a day before delivery

- E/M services provided more than 24 hours before delivery such as:

  —Observation admission and discharge services

  —Inpatient admission, subsequent visits, and discharge services

  —Same day inpatient or observation admission and discharge services

  —Critical care services

For example, a physician saw a patient in her office for a fetal nonstress test (code 59025). The patient is at 40 weeks and 2 days of gestation. The nonstress test results indicated spontaneous decelerations with reactive fetal heart tones. The patient was sent to the hospital for a contraction stress test. She had contractions every 2–6 minutes lasting 40 seconds and she was admitted to observation. The physician saw her in observation and interpreted the contraction stress test. The patient was admitted to the hospital the next morning and gave birth to a healthy infant the following day.

In addition to the global obstetric care, the physician reported code 59025 for the nonstress test provided in her office, code 59020–26 the interpretation of the contraction stress test done in the hospital, and the initiation of observation service (codes 99234–99236). Modifier –26 is discussed in Chapter 9. The admission to the hospital was not reported separately because it occurred within 24 hours of delivery and, therefore, is included in the delivery care.

Postpartum Services

Typical Services

Postpartum care includes both inpatient and outpatient services. The typical inpatient stay is 2 days for a vaginal delivery and 4 days for a cesarean delivery. Outpatient services include one visit normally provided at 6 weeks for patients who gave birth vaginally or two visits for patients who gave birth by cesarean delivery.

Excluded Services

The global obstetric package does not include inpatient or outpatient E/M services or procedures performed to treat complications, illness, or disease unrelated to routine postpartum care.

The global obstetric package does not include inpatient or outpatient E/M services or procedures performed to treat complications, illness, or disease unrelated to routine postpartum care.

Services might be provided for patients with complications such as:

- Delayed postpartum hemorrhage (666.2X)
- Infection, perineal wound (obstetric) (674.3X)
- Inflammation, perineum (686.9)
- Other medical or surgical conditions that arise during the postpartum period

These additional services may be provided in either an inpatient or outpatient setting. In the inpatient setting, additional E/M services are reported only for the hospital days beyond the typical stay for the associated delivery. However, if another physician manages all the care for the postpartum condition (complication), the obstetrician would report only the global care code. For example, a patient developed a fever on the expected day of discharge after the vaginal delivery of a healthy infant. Endometritis was diagnosed and she received intravenous antibiotics. She remained in the hospital for an additional 3 days. The physician reported a subsequent hospital care code for the additional 3 days of inpatient care with a diagnostic code for endometritis. The next week, the physician saw the patient in her office for a follow-up visit and reported an outpatient E/M service. The patient was again seen at 6 weeks. This final visit was the routine postpartum visit and, therefore, was part of the global care.

In another example, a patient had an uncomplicated cesarean delivery but developed a pulmonary embolus 3 days after delivery. Her obstetrician called in a pulmonologist to manage her care. She was discharged from the hospital a week later. The obstetrician reported only the global code for the obstetric care. The pulmonologist reported the inpatient services provided for managing the pulmonary condition.

Special Circumstances

Even when one obstetrician or physician group provides all the obstetric services, it may be unclear whether the global package rules apply. Sometimes an obstetrician provides all the antepartum care and postpartum care for a patient, but the patient gives birth prematurely. The patient is seen for fewer than the usual 13 antepartum visits. In this case, it is still appropriate to report the global obstetric code.

Sometimes the patient begins her antepartum care late in her pregnancy. In these cases, she may require more intensive management condensed into fewer visits. The care provided may match or even surpass that given in a more typical case. In these situations, it usually is appropriate to report a global package code.

Nonglobal Obstetric Services

The description of global obstetric services is used when one physician or group provides all the obstetric care (antepartum, delivery, and postpartum) for a patient. Sometimes, however, several physicians in different groups may provide part of a patient's obstetric services. This may occur when the patient:

- Transfers into or out of the practice
- Is referred to another physician at some point in the antepartum period
- Gives birth while in care of another physician not associated with, or covering for, the obstetrician
- Terminates or miscarries her pregnancy

In other cases, the patient may change insurers during her pregnancy. Under these circumstances, the global package codes are not used. Instead, report to each insurer the appropriate code(s) for the services provided under that plan:

- An E/M service code for each visit if the patient was seen for less than four visits
- An antepartum care only code (59425 or 59426) if the patient was seen for four or more visits
- Delivery only codes (59409, 59514, 59612, or 59620)
- Delivery plus postpartum care codes (59410, 59515, 59614, or 59622)
- Postpartum care only code (59430)

These codes are not used when physicians routinely cover for each other. Coverage situations are addressed in the section on special issues in this chapter.

Antepartum Care Only

Antepartum care may be reported by using E/M codes or the "antepartum care only" codes. If a patient is seen only once, twice, or three times for antepartum care, the appropriate E/M service for each of the visits is reported. The level of service is determined by using the CPT-4 definitions and guidelines for E/M services. The Centers for Medicare and Medicaid Services documentation guidelines for E/M services (addressed in Chapter 6) do not apply to routine obstetric care and are not used in these cases. Any laboratory and diagnostic testing or other separately coded services also should be reported.

If a patient is seen for a total of four or more antepartum visits, the visits are coded as follows:

- 59425 (antepartum care only; four to six total visits)
- 59426 (antepartum care only; seven or more total visits)

These codes were designed to represent a range of visits and are reported only once regardless of the actual number of visits. Some payers, however, require that the appropriate code be reported for each instance of care. For example, Dr. Lyon saw a patient for six antepartum visits. The patient then moved to another state. Dr. Cambridge saw the patient for eight additional antepartum visits before she gave birth. Dr. Lyon reported code 59425. Dr. Cambridge reported code 59426 plus the appropriate code for delivery with postpartum care. The "delivery with postpartum care codes" are addressed as follows.

Delivery Care Only

Sometimes a physician who has provided little or none of the antepartum care performs the delivery. In some instances, one provider manages the patient's prenatal care but asks an obstetrician to perform the delivery because of complications. In other situations, the patient may have received part of her prenatal care in another practice. CPT-4 has codes to describe each of these situations. The delivery-only and delivery plus postpartum care codes are:

- 59409 vaginal delivery only (with or without episiotomy and/or forceps);
  - —59410   including postpartum care
- 59514 cesarean delivery only;
  - —59515   including postpartum care
- 59612 vaginal delivery only, after previous cesarean delivery (with or without episiotomy and/or forceps);
  - —59614   including postpartum care

For example, a patient was cared for in the antepartum period by her family physician Dr. Berlin. She was admitted to labor and delivery at 40 weeks of gestation, but after a period of labor, the caput and vertex were firmly wedged in the pelvis. Dr. Orleans performed a cesarean delivery.

Dr. Orleans reported code 59515 (cesarean delivery with postpartum care). Dr. Berlin reported code 59426 (antepartum care only seven or more visits).

The delivery-only codes also are reported in cases of multiple gestations. Tables 10–1 to 10–3 illustrate coding for twin deliveries performed vaginally, by cesarean, or one each. In all these cases, only one global delivery code is billed because the mother had only one antepartum period and one postpartum period.

For twins delivered vaginally (Table 10–1), a global code and a delivery only code are reported. For twins delivered by cesarean (Table 10–2), only a global code is reported because there was only one incision. Modifier –22 (unusual services) is added to indicate the additional physician work of delivering the additional baby.

When one twin is delivered vaginally and the other by cesarean (Table 10–3), a global cesarean code is reported with a vaginal delivery only code. The global delivery code for the cesarean/repeat cesarean delivery is reported first on the claim form because these codes usually are reimbursed at a higher rate. However, physicians should check with the insurer.

Postpartum Care Only

Sometimes a physician provides only the postpartum care. In other cases, the physician provides antepartum and postpartum care but does not perform the delivery. The postpartum care services are reported using code 59430. The relative value units for code 59430 include one routine office or outpatient postpartum visit (usually, but not necessarily, performed at 6 weeks postpartum). If an obstetrician (or group) routinely performs two postpartum outpatient visits in uncomplicated cases, the extra visit is not billed separately. Any postdelivery inpatient visits are included in the delivery services codes and not reported with this code.

For example, Dr. Avignon saw a patient for 12 antepartum visits. The patient left the city to attend her sister's 40th birthday party in another state. While there, she went into labor and was admitted to the hospital. Dr. London performed a vaginal delivery of a healthy infant. The patient returned home and saw Dr. Avignon for her postpartum care.

Dr. Avignon reported code 59426 (antepartum care seven or more visits) and code 59430 (postpartum care only). Dr. London reported code 59409 (vaginal delivery only without postpartum care). The inpatient services provided by Dr. London were included in the delivery.

The codes in the Maternity Care and Delivery section of CPT are summarized in Table 10–4. If the patient was seen for one, two, or three antepartum visits only, report an E/M

Table 10–1. Coding for Vaginal Twin Deliveries

Type	Twin	Code	Extent of Service
Vaginal delivery	Baby A	59400	Global service—vaginal
	Baby B	59409–59	Delivery only—vaginal
VBAC	Baby A	59610	Global service—VBAC
	Baby B	59612–59	Delivery only—VBAC

Abbreviation: VBAC, vaginal birth after previous cesarian delivery.

Table 10–2. Coding for Cesarean Twin Deliveries

Type	Twin	Code	Extent of Service
Cesarean delivery	Baby A and baby B	59510–22	Global service— Cesarean delivery
Repeat cesarean delivery	Baby A and baby B	59618–22	Global service—Cesarean delivery after attempted vaginal delivery after previous cesarean delivery

code at the appropriate level of service for each visit. The global obstetric package codes (59400, 59510, 59610, and 59618) cannot be reported if a physician in a different practice (and not covering for the primary physician) provided any of the antepartum care.

Special Issues in Obstetric Care and Delivery

Maternity care raises some unique coding issues. The special issues addressed as follows are reporting diagnostic tests and procedures, concurrent care, covering situations, termination of pregnancy and stillbirths, and treatment of ectopic pregnancies.

Diagnostic Tests and Procedures

Diagnostic tests and procedures may be performed during pregnancy, labor, and delivery. It is important to distinguish between screening and diagnostic tests. This is best done by identifying the most specific ICD-9-CM code that explains the reason for the service.

Screening tests are those done in the absence of signs, symptoms, or other conditions. These routine screening tests may be included in the payment for the global package or may be reimbursed separately, depending on the payer's policies.

Diagnostic tests are performed when the patient exhibits signs, symptoms, or other conditions and the physician wants to diagnose or rule out specific conditions. These tests should be reimbursed by the payers when they are supported by a medical indication. For example, a patient is considered to be small for gestational age and an ultrasound examination is performed. These tests should be reported at the time they occur and should be linked to an ICD-9-CM code that demonstrates their medical necessity.

Certain diagnostic tests such as stress tests and ultrasound examinations include both a professional and a technical component. Modifiers are added to the CPT code to identify these components. These modifiers are addressed in Chapter 9.

Table 10–3. Coding for Vaginal and Cesarean Twin Deliveries

Type	Twin	Code	Extent of Service
Vaginal delivery plus cesarean delivery	Baby B	59510	Global service—cesarean delivery
	Baby A	59409–51	Delivery only—vaginal
VBAC plus repeat cesarean delivery	Baby B	59618	Global service—repeat cesarean delivery
	Baby A	59612–51	Delivery only—VBAC

Abbreviation: VBAC, vaginal birth after previous cesarean delivery.

Table 10–4. Summary of Maternity Care and Delivery Codes

CPT Code	Obstetric Services		
	Routine Antepartum Services	Routine Delivery Services	Routine Postpartum Services (Through 6 Weeks After Delivery)
E/M codes	One to three visits		
59425	Four to six visits		
59426	Seven or more visits		
59430			Office visit(s)
59400	Approximately 13 visits	Vaginal	Hospital and office visits
59409		Vaginal	
59410		Vaginal	Hospital and office visits
59510	Approximately 13 visits	Cesarean	Hospital and office visits
59514		Cesarean	
59515		Cesarean	Hospital and office visits
59610	Approximately 13 visits	VBAC	Hospital and office visits
59612		VBAC	
59614		VBAC	Hospital and office visits
59618	Approximately 13 visits	Repeat cesarean	Hospital and office visits
59620		Repeat cesarean	
59622		Repeat cesarean	Hospital and office visits

Abbreviation: VBAC, vaginal birth after cesarean delivery.

It is important to clearly document the interpretation of any tests when reporting the service to a third-party payer. Templates may be helpful in documenting the required test components and the interpretation of the findings. Interpretations recorded only by technicians or other personnel are not adequate for billing purposes. Likewise, computer generated reports without the physician's comments and interpretation do not represent adequate documentation.

Diagnostic tests commonly performed during pregnancy and labor are found in CPT in the section on Antepartum Services (59000–59076). Codes for ultrasound services are found in the Radiology section of CPT (76801–76828). Ultrasound examinations are specifically addressed in Chapter 11.

Concurrent Care for Obstetric Services

Sometimes an obstetrician provides all the routine obstetric care, but the patient also receives care from another physician, such as a maternal–fetal medicine specialist. In this case, the obstetrician reports the appropriate global obstetric package code, and the specialist reports E/M services or procedural codes. The specialist's services fall outside the global package. Payments to the obstetrician are not reduced because of the additional payments to the specialist.

For example, a patient saw Dr. Calais, an obstetrician, and also Dr. Sydney, a maternal–fetal medicine specialist, during her pregnancy. Dr. Calais provided the routine antepartum, delivery, and postpartum care. However, Dr. Sydney also monitored the patient who was considered a high-risk patient because of an early fetal death in her previous pregnancy. Some problems developed in the current pregnancy and Dr. Sydney saw the patient in his office for three visits. Dr. Calais reported the global obstetric package code. Dr. Sydney reported E/M services for his care.

Coverage

Because of the long global period and the unpredictability of labor and delivery, the physician providing the antepartum care may not be available at the time of delivery. Because of this, many practices develop covering agreements with other practices.

Over time, physicians have developed arrangements to facilitate the reporting of global obstetric codes. Some possible arrangements are described as follows.

Sometimes obstetricians from different groups routinely cover for each other. The services provided by both physicians are routine services that, if provided by only one physician, would have been reported using only a global obstetric package code. In this case, payers generally accept that the primary obstetrician will bill the global package and the covering physician will not bill separately. However, practices should check both their state laws and specific payer rules. In some cases, physicians may be required to report their services separately.

Sometimes, a covering physician provides a service that is not included in the global obstetric package. In this case, the covering physician can report the service separately under his or her own provider number. The other physician reports the global obstetric package code. For example, Dr. Kensington is out of town and being covered by Dr. Cartagena. Dr. Kensington's patient presents to labor and delivery complaining of pelvic and back pain on Saturday. Dr. Cartagena examines the patient and performs a nonstress test, which is reactive. He admits the patient to the hospital for threatened preterm labor. Dr. Cartagena again sees the patient on Sunday. Dr. Kensington resumes management of the patient's care on Monday. Because the inpatient care and nonstress test are not routine obstetric care, Dr. Cartagena reports these services separately.

> *Sometimes, a covering physician provides a service that is not included in the global obstetric package. In this case, the covering physician can report the service separately under his or her own provider number.*

Termination of Pregnancy

Correct diagnostic and procedural coding in cases of interruption of pregnancy and stillbirth depends on the following:

- Why the procedure was performed (eg, missed or incomplete abortion, pregnancy complicated by some condition of the mother or the fetus)

- When during the pregnancy the procedure was performed (eg, gestational age)

- How the procedure was performed (eg, surgical or medical abortion)

- Which specific procedure was performed (eg, dilation and curettage, dilation and evacuation, injections, or surgical treatment of incomplete or septic abortion)

The American College of Obstetricians and Gynecologists' Committee on Coding and Nomenclature states that an abortion performed after 20 weeks 0 days of gestation is reported using a delivery code. However, some state legislatures have legally defined the difference between a miscarriage and a stillbirth using the number of weeks or a specific gram weight. This legal definition may determine which CPT-4 codes are selected: abortion (codes 59812–59857) or delivery (codes 59400–59622).

The type of termination determines the selection of the proper ICD-9-CM code as well as the CPT-4 code. The primary types of abortions are:

- Missed abortion—An empty gestational sac, blighted ovum, or a fetus or fetal pole without a heartbeat before completion of 20 weeks 0 days of gestation. ICD-9-CM defines missed abortion differently; ICD-9-CM defines a missed abortion as any fetal death before completion of 22 weeks of gestation

- Incomplete abortion—The expulsion of some products of conception with the remainder evacuated surgically
- Complete abortion—The complete expulsion or retraction of a fetus or embryo
- Induced abortion—Abortion brought on purposely by drugs or mechanical means. This includes therapeutic and elective abortions. The codes for an induced abortion include the admission and visits in the hospital and the delivery of the fetus and secundines. Tables 10–5 to 10–8 summarize the proper ICD-9-CM and CPT-4 codes to report under different circumstances.

Table 10–5. Coding Missed Abortion/Fetal Demise (In Utero)

Diagnostic Codes	Description	Procedural Codes	Description
632	Missed abortion or early fetal death, before 22 weeks 0 days or	59820	Surgical abortion, before 14 weeks 0 days
		59821	Surgical abortion, 14 weeks 0 days up to 20 weeks 0 days
656.41	Intrauterine fetal demise, after 22 weeks 0 days	59850, 59851, or 59852	Non-surgical abortion, by injections, before 20 weeks 0 days
	Also report a code from 639 series for a complication if appropriate	Delivery code	Non-surgical abortion, by injections, after 20 weeks 0 days
		59855–59857	Non-surgical abortion, by suppositories, before 20 weeks 0 days
		Delivery code	Non-surgical abortion, by suppositories, after 20 weeks 0 days
		E/M services code	Spontaneous/other medical abortion, before 20 weeks 0 days
		Delivery code	Spontaneous/other medical abortion, after 20 weeks 0 days
		E/M services code plus 59414	Spontaneous abortion plus delivery of placenta, before 20 weeks 0 days
		Delivery code	Spontaneous abortion plus delivery of placenta, after 20 weeks 0 days

Table 10–6. Coding Spontaneous (Complete) Abortion

Diagnostic Code	Description	Procedural Codes	Description
634.X2	Spontaneous abortion any trimester	E/M code	—Before 20 weeks 0 days
	Use fourth digit to indicate complication	Delivery code	—After 20 weeks 0 days

Table 10–7. Coding Spontaneous (Incomplete) Abortion

Diagnostic Code	Description	Procedural Codes	Description
634. X1	Spontaneous abortion any trimester	59812	—Before 20 weeks 0 days
	Use fourth digit to indicate complication	Delivery code	—20 weeks 0 days or more

Treatment of Ectopic Pregnancy

The CPT codes 59120–59151 are reported for the surgical treatment of an ectopic pregnancy. Report separately the E/M service during which the decision to perform surgery was made. Add a modifier –57 (decision for surgery) to the E/M code if it occurred either 1 day before or the day of the surgery. Any diagnostic tests performed, such as ultrasound examinations or laboratory studies, also can be reported.

There are no specific CPT codes to report the medical treatment of an ectopic pregnancy. Correct coding depends on the actual services provided. Generally, this includes an E/M service to diagnose the pregnancy, an ultrasound examination, laboratory studies, and a series of injections. Report both an injection code and a code for any medication provided by the physician. Report the E/M services on the same day as an injection only if the E/M services are significant and separately identifiable. A physician providing these services reports the appropriate level of E/M service. Nonphysician personnel providing E/M services report code 99211.

Diagnostic Coding for Obstetric Care

Chapter 3 provided an overview of diagnostic coding. However, diagnostic coding for obstetric services has a number of unique features. Diagnostic codes are found in ICD-9-CM Chapter 11, Complications of Pregnancy, Childbirth, and the Puerperium (codes 630–677). These codes document the medical necessity for a procedure or E/M service being reported outside the global obstetric package.

Almost all codes in Chapter 11 require fifth digits. There are two sets of fifth digits with different definitions for two subcategories: pregnancy with abortive outcomes and other maternity care codes. Diagnostic codes for pregnancy with abortive outcomes (634–639) are reported with a fifth digit that indicates whether the products of conception had been completely or only partially expelled at the time of the encounter. These fifth digits are:

0   Unspecified (Note: Coders should not use this digit because it should be known whether or not the abortion was complete or incomplete.)

1   Incomplete

2   Complete

Diagnostic codes for complications related to pregnancy (640–677) are reported with a fifth digit that indicates the current episode of care. These fifth digits are:

0   Unspecified as to episode of care (Note: Coders should not use this digit because it should be known whether or not the patient has been delivered.)

1   Delivered during this episode of care; with or without mention of an antepartum condition or complication

2   Delivered during this episode of care; with mention of postpartum complication

3   Antepartum condition or complication; patient is still pregnant at the end of the encounter. This fifth-digit also is used if the fetus was aborted or miscarried.

4   Postpartum condition or complication; patient was delivered during a previous encounter and is now being seen for a condition or complication resulting from the pregnancy.

Table 10–8. Coding Induced Abortion

Diagnostic Code	Description	Procedural Codes	Description
635.XX	Legally induced abortion any trimester	59840	By D&C, any trimester
		59841	By D&E, 14 weeks 0 days up to 20 weeks 0 days
	Use fourth digit to indicate complication	59841–22	By D&E, 20 weeks 0 days or more
		59850, 59852, or 59851	By injections, before 20 weeks 0 days
	Use fifth digit to indicate complete or incomplete abortion	59855–59857	By suppositories, before 20 weeks 0 days
		Delivery code	By suppositories, after 20 weeks 0 days
	Also report a code for a complication if appropriate, eg, 642.XX, 648.XX, 651.XX, 655.XX, 656.XX, 659.XX	E/M code	Spontaneous or other medical abortion, before 20 weeks 0 days
		Delivery code	Spontaneous or other medical abortion, after 20 weeks 0 days
		E/M code plus 59414	Spontaneous abortion plus delivery of placenta, before 20 weeks 0 days
		Delivery code	Spontaneous abortion plus delivery of placenta, after 20 weeks 0 days

Abbreviations: D&C, dilation and curettage; D&E, dilation and evacuation; E/M, evaluation and management.

The following code categories require these fifth digits 0–4:

- 640-648   Complications Mainly Related to Pregnancy
- 651-659   Normal Delivery, and Other Indications for Care in Pregnancy, Labor, and Delivery
- 660-669   Complications Occurring Mainly in the Course of Labor and Delivery
- 670-676   Complications of the Puerperium

Not all fifth digits (0–4) can be reported for all the codes previously listed. Bracketed numbers are listed under obstetric codes to indicate which fifth digits can be reported with that specific code. For example:

655.8   Other known or suspected fetal abnormality, not elsewhere classified
             [0,1,3]
665.1   Rupture of uterus during labor
             [0,1]

Code 655.8 can be reported only as 655.80, 655.81, or 655.83.

Code 665.1 can be reported only as 665.10 or 665.11.

In addition to the codes in Chapter 11, there are "V" codes used for obstetric cases. These "V" codes describe routine care, the reason for a screening test, or possible risk factors.

- V22 Normal pregnancy
- V23 Supervision of high-risk pregnancy
- V24 Postpartum care and examination
- V27 Outcome of delivery
- V28 Antenatal screening
- V84 Genetic carrier status

Usually the "V" codes for routine care (codes V22 and V24) are not reported because these services are part of the global obstetric package. ICD-9-CM recommends that code V22.2 (pregnant state, incidental) be reported when a pregnant patient is seen for a problem unrelated to the pregnancy, such as flu symptoms. However, some payer's software will automatically bundle any services reported with this diagnostic code into the global package. In these cases, V22.2 can be omitted. The V24 codes (postpartum care and examination) would only be reported to the insurer if the physician did not perform the delivery but provided the postpartum care.

The V23 codes (supervision of high risk pregnancy) indicate that the patient had a problem in a previous pregnancy. Codes in this category may not be accepted by a payer as a medically necessary reason to perform a screening test or provide additional E/M services. In most cases, payers will reimburse for additional services only if there is a problem in the current pregnancy.

Some payers require that claims submitted after delivery include a V27 code (outcome of delivery) to indicate whether the pregnancy resulted in a single or multiple birth, liveborn, or stillborn infant(s).

The V28 codes (antenatal screening) are the most useful "V" codes. These codes describe screening tests (including ultrasound examinations and amniocentesis) for specific conditions (eg, V28.4 [screening for fetal growth retardation using ultrasonics] or V28.6 [screening for Streptococcus B]). If there was a condition or symptom that led the physician to believe that there may be a problem in the pregnancy, he or she reports a code for the problem or symptom plus the "V" code for the screening test. Payers will most likely not reimburse for screening tests viewed as routine.

The V84 codes are used to indicate genetic carrier status for diseases such as hemophilia or cystic fibrosis. These code also are reported to demonstrate the medical necessity for tests.

Chapter 10 Quiz: Obstetric Services

True or False:

1. Diagnostic tests can be reported outside the global package when performed for medically necessary reasons.

2. Services related to routine obstetric care are included in the global package.

Choose the best answer:

3. CPT defines the uncomplicated obstetric "global" package to include the following:

   a. Initial E/M visit during which pregnancy is diagnosed, antepartum care, delivery and postpartum care

   b. Antepartum care, delivery, and postpartum care

   c. Initial E/M visit during which pregnancy is diagnosed, one maternal echography, antepartum, delivery, and postpartum care

4. Some of the services that are excluded from the global package and may be billed separately are:

   a. Office visits in excess of 13 because of antepartum complications

   b. Hospital visits that lead to delivery within 24 hours of admission

   c. Fetal nonstress test and fetal biophysical profile

   d. A and C

5. E/M visits may be billed separately from the global package when

   a. The visit is the initial examination and pregnancy is diagnosed

   b. The total number of visits exceeds 13 because of conditions related to complications of the pregnancy

   c. The visit is for an unrelated diagnosis

   d. All of the above

6. The global obstetric codes may be reported when:

   a. One physician or group provides all the global obstetric care

   b. The primary obstetrician has an arrangement for coverage with another physician or group

   c. The patient delivers early or enters into obstetric care late in the pregnancy

   d. All of the above

7. Codes identifying non-global obstetric services are used when:

   a. The patient transfers into or out of the practice

   b. The patient is delivered by a physician not associated or covering for the obstetrician

   c. The patient changes insurers

   d. All of the above

Answers are listed on page 179.

Chapter 11

Ultrasound Coding

The physician must consider a number of factors in order to select the correct ultrasound code: why the procedure was performed (as a screening or diagnostic procedure), how it was performed (transvaginally or transabdominally), where it was performed (in a physician's office or in a facility setting), the nature of the patient (pregnant or not pregnant), and exactly what was examined (maternal and/or fetal evaluation, detailed fetal evaluation, or a limited or follow-up examination). This chapter addresses:

- Ultrasound coding for gynecology
- Ultrasound coding for obstetric services
- The professional and technical components of ultrasound codes

Following completion of the chapter, the reader should be able to:
- Appropriately select the proper ultrasound code
- Understand how to accurately use modifiers with ultrasound services
- Understand how to report ultrasound examinations and other services on the same day

Understanding Ultrasound Coding

Codes used to report gynecologic and obstetric ultrasound examinations are located in the Radiology section of CPT-4. They are listed under the section "Pelvis" and are further divided into "Obstetrical" and "Non-obstetrical" ultrasonography. There also is a section that lists "Ultrasonic Guidance Procedures," which includes codes also reported by obstetricians and gynecologists.

Gynecologic Ultrasound Examinations

Selecting the proper code largely depends on how the ultrasound examination was performed. The description of code 76830 simply reads: "Ultrasound, transvaginal." The description for code 76856 provides a bit more information: "Ultrasound, pelvic (nonobstetric), B-scan and/or real time with image documentation; complete." Code 76856 is reported for transabdominal ultrasound examinations. Both the transvaginal and transabdominal codes have the same number of relative value units. This would imply that the two codes include equivalent work but simply use different approaches, although CPT does not specifically outline which services are included in these codes. Code 76857 describes a transabdominal ultrasound, limited or follow-up (eg, for follicles), and includes slightly fewer relative value units than the other two codes.

The only other gynecologic ultrasound code is for a saline infusion sonohysterography, including color flow Doppler ultrasonography when performed (code 76831). This examination uses a transvaginal approach. Code 76830 (transvaginal ultrasound) is included in code 76831 and not reported additionally. The induction of saline or contrast material for the sonohysterogram is reported using code 58340. If a physician performs both the induction of saline or contrast material and the radiologic supervision and interpretation of the sonohysterogram, he or she reports both codes 58340 and 76831.

Obstetric Ultrasound Examinations

Unlike gynecologic ultrasound services, the obstetric ultrasound codes are very specific about the services included. Table 11–1 summarizes the codes for obstetric ultrasound procedures using a transabdominal approach.

Ultrasound Examinations for Maternal/Fetal Evaluation (76801–76810).

These ultrasound codes describe maternal and fetal evaluations based on the trimester in which the evaluation is performed and the number of gestations evaluated. The CPT rules do not restrict the number of times these codes can be reported during a pregnancy, assuming there is a medically necessary reason to do so.

Codes 76801 and 76802 describe services provided in the first trimester.

76801   Ultrasound, pregnant uterus, real time with image documentation, fetal and maternal evaluation, first trimester (less than 14 weeks 0 days), transabdominal approach; single or first gestation

+76802   Each additional gestation (list separately in addition to code for primary procedure)

Table 11–1. Obstetric Ultrasound Codes

| Code | Extent of Evaluation | | | | Trimester* | | | Gestation | |
	Maternal and Fetal Evaluation	Detailed Fetal Anatomic Examination	Limited	Follow-up	1st	2nd	3rd	Single or first fetus	Each additional fetus
76801	X				X			X	
+76802	X				X				X
76805	X					X	X	X	
+76810	X					X	X		X
76811	X	X				X	X	X	
+76812	X	X				X	X		X
76815			X		X	X	X	Report once for any number of fetuses	
76816				X	X	X	X	Report separately for each fetus with modifier –59	

*The trimesters are defined as follows:

1st trimester—First day of last menstrual period (day 0) up to and including 13 weeks 6 days of gestation

2nd trimester—14 weeks 0 days up to and including 27 weeks 6 days of gestation

3rd trimester—28 weeks of gestation and more

Code 76802 is an add-on code and can be reported only in addition to primary procedure code 76801. This add-on code is reported for the evaluation of each gestation (beyond the first) documented in the report. No modifier –51 is needed. For example, a patient was pregnant with triplets. A physician performed a fetal and maternal evaluation at 12 weeks of gestation. She reported code 76801 once and 76802 twice for the second and third fetus. In other words, three ultrasound examinations were reported. The physician documented the findings for each separate evaluation.

Codes 76801–76802 specifically include:

- Supervision of ultrasonographer performing the examination

- Determination of the number of gestational sacs and fetuses

- Gestational sac/fetal measurements appropriate for gestation

- Survey of visible fetal and placental anatomic structure

- Qualitative assessment of amniotic fluid volume/gestational sac shape

- Examination of maternal uterus and adnexa

- Preparation of the report for the medical record

Codes 76805–76810 are reported during the second and third trimesters. Code 76810 is reported in the same way as the add-on code for the first trimester (76802).

76805   Ultrasound, pregnant uterus, real time with image documentation, fetal and maternal evaluation, after first trimester (greater than or equal to 14 weeks 0 days), transabdominal approach; single or first gestation

+76810   Each additional gestation (list separately in addition to code for primary procedure)

Codes 76805 and 76810 include:

- Supervision of ultrasonographer performing the examination

- Determination of the number of fetuses and amniotic/chorionic sacs

- Measurements appropriate for gestational age

- Survey of intracranial/spinal/abdominal anatomy

- Evaluation of the four-chambered heart

- Assessment of the umbilical cord insertion site

- Survey of placenta location and amniotic fluid assessment

- When visible, examination of maternal adnexa

- Preparation of the report for the medical record

Detailed Fetal Ultrasound Examination (76811–76812)

These codes include a description for a detailed fetal ultrasound examination, which corresponds to a Level II ultrasound examination. It includes all the components of a maternal/fetal ultrasound examination as described by code 76805 plus an extensive analysis of fetal anatomy. Code 76812 is an add-on code reported in the same way as add-on codes 76802 and 76810. CPT rules do not restrict the number of times these codes can be reported during a pregnancy, assuming there is a medically necessary reason to do so.

76811   Ultrasound, pregnant uterus, real time with image documentation; fetal and maternal evaluation plus detailed fetal anatomic examination, transabdominal approach; single or first gestation

+76812   Each additional gestation (list separately in addition to code for primary procedure)

Codes for maternal–fetal and detailed fetal evaluations include add-on codes to be used in cases of multiple gestation.

The codes include:

- Supervision of ultrasonographer performing the examination
- All components of 76805 and 76810, plus
- Detailed anatomic evaluation of:
  —The fetal brain/ventricles and face
  —Heart/outflow tracts and chest anatomy
  —Abdominal organ specific anatomy
  —Number/length/architecture of limbs
- Detailed evaluation of:
  —Umbilical cord
  —Placenta
  —Other fetal anatomy as clinically indicated
- Preparation of the report for the medical record

Limited Ultrasound Examination (76815)

A limited ultrasound examination is reported when a focused, brief assessment is made of one or two elements. There is no add-on code for limited ultrasound examinations performed in cases of multiple gestations. Code 76815 is reported once per examination regardless of the number of fetuses or elements included in the examination.

76815   Ultrasound, pregnant uterus, real time with image documentation, limited (eg, fetal heart beat, placental location, fetal position and/or qualitative amniotic fluid volume), one or more fetuses

This code includes

- Supervision of ultrasonographer performing the examination
- Interpretation of the examination limited to a "quick-look" assessment of one or more of the following key elements:
  —Fetal position
  —Fetal heartbeat
  —Placental location
  —Qualitative amniotic fluid volume
- Preparation of the report for the medical record

Follow-up Ultrasound Examination (76816)

A follow-up ultrasound examination is reported when an ultrasound procedure is performed to reexamine a previously discovered condition. There is no add-on code for follow-up ultrasound examinations performed in cases of multiple gestations. However, code 76816 is reported once for each fetus being re-evaluated. A modifier –59 (distinct procedural service) is added to the code(s) for each fetus beyond the first.

76816   Ultrasound, pregnant uterus, real time with image documentation, follow-up (eg, re-evaluation of fetal size by measuring standard growth parameters and amniotic fluid volume, re-evaluation of organ system(s) suspected or confirmed to be abnormal on a previous scan), transabdominal approach, per fetus

A follow-up examination includes:

- Supervision of ultrasonographer performing the examination
- Either of the following:
  —Reassessment of fetal size and interval growth or

—Re-evaluation of one or more fetal anatomic abnormalities previously demonstrated on ultrasound

- Preparation of the report for the medical record

Fetal Doppler Velocimetry

Two new codes were added to CPT-4 in 2005 to report Doppler velocimetry procedures on the umbilical or middle cerebral artery of the fetus. There is no add-on code for velocimetric examinations performed in cases of multiple gestations. However, if the arteries of each fetus are examined, the appropriate code is reported once for each fetus. A modifier –59 (distinct procedural service) is added to the code(s) for each fetus beyond the first.

76820   Doppler velocimetry, fetal; umbilical artery

This examination includes:

- Supervision of ultrasonographer performing the examination

- Placement of duplex Doppler sampling gate over a portion of the umbilical artery

- Recording of two to four waveforms during period when fetus is inactive and fetal breathing is absent

- Measurement of peak systolic and end diastolic frequency shift

- Obtaining average of results of 2–4 waveforms

- Comparison of specific normal values to gestational age

- Preparation of the report for medical record

76821   Doppler velocimetry, fetal; middle cerebral artery

This examination includes:

- Placement of a pulsed Doppler gate over the middle cerebral artery

- Obtaining of two to four measurements

- Recording of highest velocity

- Comparison of peak systolic velocity to gestational age-specific norms

- Preparation of the report for medical record

Transvaginal Obstetric Ultrasound Examinations (76817)

This code is reported when a transvaginal ultrasound is performed on a pregnant patient. It can be reported during any trimester and may be reported in addition to a transabdominal obstetric ultrasound if medically necessary.

Some payers initially may pay for either the transvaginal or transabdominal approach but not both. It may be helpful to attach the modifier –59 (distinct procedural service) to the transvaginal code. Some payers may require a modifier –51 (multiple procedures) on the transvaginal code instead of a modifier –59.

The American College of Obstetricians and Gynecologists' coding committee has stated that the obstetric transvaginal ultrasound code includes an evaluation of the fetus and placenta as well as an evaluation of the maternal uterus and adnexa. If the patient is not pregnant, report code 76830.

Reporting Multiple Ultrasound Procedures

Each of these ultrasound codes represents a unique service. As such, it may be appropriate to report more than one ultrasound service when each provides clinically necessary information. CPT states that multiple services are reported using a modifier –51 (multiple procedures). Most payers, however, do not require the modifier for these ultrasound services

If a transvaginal ultrasound examination is performed in addition to a complete pelvic ultrasound examination, then report both codes.

and reimburse each code at the full allowable amount. Thus, if a transvaginal ultrasound examination is performed in addition to a complete pelvic ultrasound examination, then report both code 76830 (transvaginal) and code 76856 (transabdominal).

In some cases, it also is appropriate to report an ultrasound code in addition to other diagnostic services such as a fetal nonstress test or an evaluation and management (E/M) service. For example, a patient came to the office at 35 weeks of gestation with her cervix dilated to 3 cm. She was sent to labor and delivery for a nonstress test (NST). While at the hospital she began having contractions and went into active labor. The physician interpreted the NST and performed a limited ultrasound examination to determine fetal position. The physician reported both services. It is important that each service and the need for each service are clearly documented in the medical record.

Biophysical Profile (76818–76819)

A complete biophysical profile (code 76818) is a measurement of physiologic activity in the fetus. This examination consists of:

- Fetal nonstress test
- Fetal breathing movements (one or more episodes of rhythmic fetal breathing movements of 30 seconds or more within 30 minutes)
- Fetal movement (three or more discrete body or limb movements within 30 minutes)
- Fetal tone (one or more episodes of extension of a fetal extremity with return to flexion)
- Quantification of amniotic fluid volume

Code 76819 is reported for a biophysical profile (BPP) without an NST, sometimes referred to as a limited BPP. When the obstetrician performs the NST and the radiologist performs the other elements of the profile, the obstetrician codes for the NST (code 59025) and the radiologist reports code 76819. If the obstetrician performs both elements of the study, then code 76818 is reported.

Sometimes, other services are performed on the same day as a BPP. If a second NST is performed on the same day as a complete BPP (code 76818), the second NST may be reported. The documentation must clearly indicate the medical necessity for the second study. A modifier –59 is added to the NST code to clarify that this is a distinct NST in addition to the one that was a part of the BPP. The physician reports codes 76818 (BPP) and 59025–59 (NST).

Sometimes, a BPP and an ultrasound examination are performed on the same day. These are considered distinct services and both may be reported. An ultrasound examination is an anatomic examination and a BPP is a physiologic examination measuring the well-being of the fetus. The documentation must clearly indicate the medical necessity for each test. Table 11–2 shows coding for different combinations of BPP and other services.

Ultrasound Imaging and Interpretation or Guidance

Certain ultrasound services in CPT are reported using two codes: 1) a procedural code and 2) a radiologic code. The radiologic service includes imaging interpretation, supervision and/or guidance. This simplifies the reporting when one physician performs the procedure and another provides the interpretation or guidance. If one physician performs both, then he or she reports both codes. For example, code 58340 is reported for the catheterization and introduction of saline or contrast for saline infusion sonohysterography and code 76831 is reported for the radiologic supervision and interpretation of the procedure.

Table 11–2. Reporting Biophysical Profiles With Other Procedures

Procedures Performed	Timing	Code(s) Reported	Comments
Complete BPP 76818 plus nonstress test 59025	Same session, same day	76818 only	59025 is a component of 76818
Limited BPP 76819 plus nonstress test 59025	Same or different session, same day	76818 only	59025 is a component of 76818
Complete BPP 76818 plus second nonstress test 59025	Different session, same day	76818 plus 59025–59	Document medical necessity
Complete BPP 76818 plus any obstetric ultrasound code	Same or different session, same day	76818 plus code for ultrasonography	Different examinations

Abbreviation: BBP, biophysical profile

Radiologic services, including ultrasound examinations, include both a professional and a technical component.

Table 11–3 lists services commonly performed by obstetrician–gynecologists that are reported using two codes. A modifier –26 (professional component) is added to the radiologic service when it is provided in a facility other than the physician's office.

Other ultrasound codes include both the imaging and/or guidance (technical) part and the interpretation with written report (professional) part in a single code. When one physician performs the technical component and another provides the professional component, the two parts are differentiated by using modifiers. Modifier –26 identifies the physician's activities, including the supervision or actual performance of the test, the interpretation, and the written report. Modifier –TC identifies the costs associated with the technician salary and benefits (if any), the equipment, and any necessary supplies.

If the ultrasound examination is performed in a hospital or other facility, the physician reports only the professional component (modifier –26) since the facility owns the ultrasound equipment. This is true even if the physician also performed the technical part of the procedure.

If the ultrasound examination is performed in a hospital or other facility and both the radiologist and the physician document an interpretation, either the obstetrician–gynecologist or the radiologist will be paid, but not both. Payers will reimburse only one physician for the professional component of the service. Physicians need to determine in advance who will report the interpretation to avoid misunderstandings and delays in reimbursement.

If the ultrasound examination is performed in the physician's office, the physician reports the CPT code without a modifier. The physician's reimbursement would reflect the entire service because the code includes both the professional and technical components.

For example, a patient, who was at 19 weeks of gestation, had an ultrasound examination for a maternal–fetal evaluation in a physician's office because she was large for gestational age. The technician performed the test and the physician documented the interpretation. The physician reported code 76805 without a modifier because she was responsible for the supervision of the technician and the cost of the equipment. At 36 weeks of gestation, the patient presented to labor and delivery in active labor. The physician performed a limited ultrasound examination to determine fetal position. The physician reported code 76815–26. Even though she actually performed the test, the physician had to use a modifier –26 because the service was performed on equipment located in and owned by the hospital.

Table 11-3. Codes for Imaging and Interpretation or Guidance

Description	Procedural Code	Radiologic Component Code (Interpretation or Guidance)
Intrauterine fetal transfusion	36460	76941
Saline infusion sonohysterography	58340	76831
Hysterosalpingography	58340	74740
Transcervical catheterization of fallopian tube	58345	74742
Follicle puncture for oocyte retrieval	58970	76948
Diagnostic amniocentesis	59000	76946
Intrauterine cordocentesis	59012	76941
Chorionic villus sampling	59015	76945

Reporting an E/M Service With an Ultrasound Procedure

Sometimes, an E/M service and an ultrasound procedure are both performed during the same visit. The E/M service may be reported in addition to the ultrasound if it is distinct and separate from the performance or interpretation of the ultrasonography. The E/M service must be documented separately from the radiologic findings and interpretation.

For example, a patient, who had active Crohn's disease, went to a perinatologist for a complete ultrasound examination and consultation. After the performance of the ultrasound examination, the physician informed the patient of the findings. He also spent an additional 30 minutes discussing the risks to the pregnancy associated with Crohn's disease and the patient's current medications. The physician reported both the ultrasound procedure and an outpatient consultation code for the discussion after the ultrasound examination. A modifier –25 is added to the consultation code. The physician documented both services and provided copies to the patient's obstetrician.

Diagnostic Coding and Ultrasound Procedures

ICD-9-CM diagnostic codes often are not specific enough to convey to the insurer the medical need for performing a particular ultrasound procedure. The American College of Obstetricians and Gynecologists' Committee on Coding and Nomenclature has worked with the National Center for Health Statistics, which maintains ICD-9-CM, to determine the correct codes to report for specific conditions. When the only diagnosis code available is not very specific, it may be helpful to send a cover letter with the claim that further explains the clinical need for the ultrasound.

Various insurers have different rules for reimbursing ultrasound procedures. Some will cover only a certain number of these procedures, regardless of the diagnosis. Other payers consider all routine or screening ultrasound examinations as part of their obstetric global package, but may or may not reimburse for ultrasound examinations when there is a diagnosis indicating a complication. Tables 11–4 to 11–6 list specific conditions and the appropriate diagnostic code.

Table 11–4. Diagnoses for Ultrasound Examinations Performed for Known or Possible Fetal Problems

Condition	Diagnosis	
Alphafetoprotein, abnormal serum value	V28.3	Screening for malformation using ultrasonography
	796.4	Other abnormal clinical findings
	V28.1	Screening for raised alpha fetoprotein levels in amniotic fluid
Biophysical evaluation of fetus	V71.89	Observation for other suspected condition not found
	656.3X	Fetal distress
	656.9X	Unspecified fetal and placental problem
	656.8X	Other specified fetal and placental problems
Decreased fetal movement	V28.8	Other specified antenatal screening
	655.7X	Decreased fetal movement
	656.8X	Other known or suspected fetal abnormality
Decreased triple marker	V72.85	Other specified examination
History of congenital anomaly (in previous pregnancy)	655.8X	Other known or suspected fetal abnormality
	V28.3	Screening for malformation using ultrasonics
	V23.4	Pregnancy with poor obstetric history
	655.2X	Hereditary disease in family possibly affecting fetus
Determination of fetal presentation	V28.8	Other specified antenatal screening
	652.XX	Malposition or malpresentation of fetus
Estimation of fetal weight or presentation in premature rupture of membranes or premature labor	644.2X	Early onset of delivery
	644.0X	Threatened premature labor
Evaluation of fetal condition for late registrants for prenatal care	V23.7	Insufficient prenatal care
Fetal death, suspected	632	Missed abortion
	656.4X	Intrauterine death
	Code also symptoms	
Follow-up to known fetal anomaly (in current pregnancy)	655.XX	Code for specific fetal anomaly
Intrauterine device, suspected fetal problem caused by presence	V25.42	Surveillance of intrauterine contraceptive device
	655.8X	Suspected fetal abnormalities from intrauterine device
Intrauterine growth retardation	V28.4	Screening for fetal growth retardation using ultrasonography
Macrosomia	V28.8	Other specified antenatal screening
		Code also symptoms (eg, maternal diabetes, obesity, postdates)
Multiple gestation, serial evaluation of fetal growth	V28.4	Screening for fetal growth retardation using ultrasonography
	651.XX	Multiple gestation

(continued)

Table 11–4. Diagnoses for Ultrasound Examinations Performed for Known or Possible Fetal Problems *(continued)*

Condition	Diagnosis	
Multiple gestation, suspected	V28.8	Other specified antenatal screening
	651.XX	Multiple gestation
Uterine size/clinical dates discrepancy	646.8X	Uterine size/date discrepancy
	656.6X	Excessive fetal growth
	656.5X	Poor fetal growth
	793.6	Abnormal findings by ultrasound of abdominal area

Table 11–5. Diagnoses for Ultrasound Examinations Performed for Known or Possible Maternal Problems

Condition	Diagnosis	
Adjunct to placement of cerclage	654.5X	Cervical incompetence
Ectopic pregnancy, suspected	633.X	Ectopic pregnancy
	Code symptoms	
Hydatidiform mole, suspected	V72.89	Observation for suspected condition not found
	V23.1	Pregnancy with history of trophoblastic disease
	630	Hydatidiform mole
	Code also symptoms	
Pelvic mass	654.1X	Tumors of body of uterus
	654.9X	Other/unspecified abnormality of organs/soft tissues of pelvis
	789.3X	Pelvic mass (specify site)
	793.6	Abnormal findings by ultrasound of abdominal area
Uterine abnormality, suspected	654.0X	Congenital abnormalities of uterus
	654.1X	Tumors of body of uterus
	654.3X	Retroverted and incarcerated gravid uterus
	654.4X	Other abnormalities in shape/position of gravid neighboring structures
	793.6	Abnormal findings by ultrasound of abdominal area
Vaginal bleeding of undetermined etiology	641.9X	Unspecified antepartum hemorrhage
	640.9X	Unspecified hemorrhage in early pregnancy

Table 11–6. Diagnoses for Ultrasound Examinations Performed for Other Problems

Condition	Diagnosis	
Abruptio placentae, suspected	V71.89	Observation for suspected condition not found
	641.2X	Premature separation of placenta
	793.9	Abnormal placental findings by ultrasound
Adjunct to external version	652.1X	Breech or other malpresentation successfully converted to cephalic presentation
	660.0X	Obstruction caused by malposition of fetus at onset of labor
	652.2X	Breech presentation
Adjunct to amniocentesis	Code reason for amniocentesis	
	If a complete ultrasound also performed, report as appropriate:	
	V28.2	Other screening based on amniocentesis
	V28.0	Screening for chromosomal anomalies by amniocentesis
Adjunct to other specific procedures	Code for reason for specific procedure	
Confirm dates/unknown gestational age or last menstrual period	V28.8	Other specified antenatal screening
Follow-up evaluation for known placenta previa	641.0X	Placenta previa without hemorrhage
	641.1X	Hemorrhage from placenta previa
Observation of intrapartum events	V71.89	Observation for suspected condition not found
	Code for intrapartum events	
Polyhydramnios or oligohydramnios, suspected	V71.89	Observation for other specified condition not found
	657.0X	Polyhydramnios
	658.0X	Oligohydramnios
Postterm/prolonged pregnancy	645.1X	Pregnancy 40 weeks to 42 weeks of gestation
	645.2X	Pregnancy advanced beyond 42 weeks of gestation

Chapter 11 Quiz: Ultrasound Coding

True or False:

1. The professional component of an ultrasound is identified by attaching the –26 modifier to the appropriate ultrasound code.

2. Ultrasound codes in CPT represent both the professional and technical components.

Choose the best answer:

3. An ultrasound is performed during the first trimester on a patient expecting twins. The service is reported using codes:

   a. 76801 and 76802

   b. Only 76801

   c. Only 76802

4. A limited ultrasound can be reported:

   a. During any trimester

   b. Only once per test regardless of the number of gestations

   c. To observe fetal heart beat, placental location, fetal position, and/or qualitative amniotic fluid volume

   d. All of the above

5. A follow-up ultrasound can be reported:

   a. During any trimester

   b. Only once per test regardless of the number of gestations

   c. To re-evaluate fetal size by measuring standard growth parameters and amniotic fluid volume or re-evaluate organ system(s) suspected or confirmed to be abnormal on a previous scan

   d. A and C

6. A biophysical profile (76818):

   a. Includes a nonstress test

   b. Can be reported more than once during a pregnancy if medically necessary

   c. Can be reported in addition to ultrasonography performed on the same day

   d. All of the above

7. CPT specifically identifies the components included in:

   a. Transabdominal ultrasound examinations

   b. Transvaginal ultrasound examinations

   c. Detailed fetal ultrasound examinations

   d. A and C

Answers are listed on page 179.

Chapter 12

Dealing With Third-Party Payers

Learning to code correctly as described in the previous chapters is only half the battle physicians face. The other half is learning to use this knowledge to get paid appropriately and promptly—and what to do when a payment is denied or delayed. This chapter addresses:

- Different payment mechanisms for health care services
- Methods for contracting with health care plans
- Establishing office procedures for the submission and monitoring of claims
- Dealing with payment problems

Following completion of the chapter, the reader should be able to:

- Define the differences among self-payment, government programs, indemnity plans, and health maintenance organizations (HMOs)
- Review a contract with a payer prior to review by the physician's legal counsel
- Understand some basic office procedures that assist in ensuring prompt payment of claims and monitoring of insurers policies
- Know the steps for appealing a denied claim

Introduction to America's Health Care Payment System

Sixty years ago, third parties were rarely involved in health care treatment or payment—these were issues to be resolved by the physician and the patient. By the 1950s, however, patients, physicians, and hospitals realized that the cost of medical treatment prevented many Americans from getting appropriate medical care. Health insurance for employees and their families came to be an expected job benefit and the government was expected to provide coverage for those who could not otherwise afford it. Still, 17% of all Americans are uninsured today, so they either do not seek medical care, pay for their own care, or receive free care.

A physician must know whether he or she needs to obtain full or partial payment from the patient at the time of the service (eg, does she have insurance, and if so, is this service covered), whether the payer limits the amount that can be billed for a service, and any authorizations that must be obtained before the service is provided. Thus, it is necessary to understand the payment mechanisms and contracting requirements of the payers in order to be reimbursed promptly.

A physician must know whether he or she needs to obtain full or partial payment from the patient at the time of service...

Payment Mechanisms

Physicians may be paid through a variety of mechanisms, including fee-for-service (which includes traditional indemnity plans and self-payment directly from patients), HMOs (which includes payment through capitation, discounted fee-for-service, or salaries), and entitlement programs (Medicare, the federal program for older Americans; Medicaid, the joint federal-state program for low-income people; and the TRICARE system for members of the military and their dependents).

Fee-for-Service

Under an indemnity or fee-for-service plan, the patient receives a service and may or may not pay the physician immediately. The patient may pay the physician and submit a claim to her insurer. The physician may file a claim with the patient's health insurance company and receive from the patient either a copayment or nothing at all at the time of the service.

Indemnity insurance is purchased with premiums paid to the insurance company by the individual or group. Under indemnity insurance, the patient usually pays a deductible each year, which is the annual amount that a plan member must pay out-of-pocket for health care before any insurance coverage applies. In addition, the patient usually is obligated to pay a copayment, which is a percentage of the cost of each office visit.

Services usually are reimbursed by the health plan according to the insurance company's fee schedule. If a physician contracts with an indemnity insurance plan, this fee schedule will define the amount that may be charged for a service. If there is no contract between the health plan and the physician, the insurer cannot limit what the physician can bill. In this case, the patient is responsible for any charges that are higher than the insurer's allowable rate, as well as any copayment on the allowable amount, once the deductible is met.

Some patients are responsible for all fees incurred for a physician service. This may be because the service was either not covered under their insurance plan or because they do not have any medical insurance. For example, many patients who carry medical insurance must pay out of pocket the entire fee for an annual well-woman examination because the service is not covered by their health plan. Indemnity plans were the norm until the 1990s, when managed care organizations became increasingly popular among insurance purchasers.

Health Maintenance Organizations

Health maintenance organizations (HMOs) finance and oversee the delivery of health care services to an enrolled membership seeing a restricted group of physicians. In recent years, HMOs have become more flexible in allowing patients to see physicians outside the HMO network of physicians, albeit at greater out-of-pocket cost.

Under most HMO plans, a patient chooses a primary care physician (PCP), who may act as the contact point, or "gatekeeper," for the patient's access to medical care from specialists. A specialist may be reimbursed for the care provided for a patient only if her PCP has made the necessary referral and the specialist is part of the HMOs physician network. Fortunately, most HMOs either recognize obstetrician–gynecologists as PCPs or allow direct access to obstetrician–gynecologists without a gatekeeper referral.

More and more HMOs also now allow patients to self-refer to a specialist within the physician network without referral from a PCP. Even with a referral, surgical, and diagnostic procedures may require preauthorization by the HMO. It is essential for physicians to understand the requirements of their contract with the HMO.

Physicians with contracts with HMOs are reimbursed in various ways. Physicians may receive:

- A salary as an employee of the HMO (referred to as a staff model HMO)
- Payment as a contractor of the HMO

A contracting physician may be:

- Part of an association of independent practicing physicians that each contract separately with an HMO (referred to as independent physician association, or IPA, or network model)
- Part of a large multispecialty group that contracts with one or more HMOs

The contracting physicians are reimbursed for their services either by capitation or discounted fee-for-service. Under a capitation arrangement, physicians are paid a negotiated monthly per-capita rate. Under a discounted fee-for-service arrangement, physicians are paid a fee for service, but the fee is discounted. The patient usually is required to pay a set copayment for each office visit.

In any of these payment methods, physicians may be eligible for bonuses if certain goals are met. Bonuses may be in the form of "withholds," in which a portion of the physician's pay is withheld unless the financial goals for caring for a group of patients are met. For example, if hospital days per patient are kept below a certain level, physicians may receive a year-end bonus. Withholds are declining in frequency and physicians should probably avoid them if at all possible.

Government Health Programs

Government health programs include Medicaid, Medicare, and the military health care system. Under these plans, physicians usually are paid directly by the government for the services provided to covered beneficiaries. Physicians often must accept the program's discounted rates as full payment for these services.

Medicare

Medicare was established in 1965 as a social insurance program to provide older adults with health care coverage at an affordable cost. In 1972, Medicare eligibility was extended to two other groups: people with disabilities and people with end-stage renal disease. In recent years, the government has contracted with HMOs to offer a managed care alternative to Medicare and Medicaid beneficiaries—with mixed results.

The Medicare program has two parts. Under Part A, beneficiaries receive coverage for hospital care, some long-term care, and limited home health care. Part A is free to beneficiaries. Part B provides coverage for physician services and laboratory and diagnostic tests. Beneficiaries must pay a premium to enroll in Part B. Under most Part B programs, patients also pay a deductible, after which Medicare pays 80% of allowable charges. However, Medicare has added managed care options, under which patients have lower deductibles or none at all.

Because Medicare covers less than one half of the health services used by the elderly, many elderly beneficiaries choose to supplement their coverage by purchasing supplemental coverage called Medigap policies from private insurers. Local carriers can provide specific information about reporting services to Medicare.

Billing for services to Medicare patients can be a challenge. Physicians must understand Medicare rules plus any rules for any supplemental insurance the patient has purchased.

Medicaid

Medicaid is a jointly funded cooperative venture between the federal and state governments to help states provide adequate medical care to eligible low-income persons. The federal government allocates a certain percentage of Medicaid funding to each state and the state pays the remainder of the costs. The amount paid by the federal government depends on each state's per-capita income; poorer states receive more money. Each state in turn administers its own Medicaid program through its health and human services agency. States have broad authority to define eligibility for benefits and the specific benefits that are covered. It is important for physicians who provide care for Medicaid patients to obtain information about the rules from their state program.

TRICARE

TRICARE is administered by the Department of Defense and covers active duty members of the uniformed services, their families and survivors, and retired members and their families. The program provides authorized inpatient and outpatient care from civilian and military sources on a cost-sharing basis. TRICARE includes three programs:

1. TRICARE Prime, a managed care program

2. TRICARE Standard, a fee-for-service program

3. TRICARE Extra, a fee-for-service program that offers discounts to patients who use network physicians. Funding comes through Congress as part of its annual budget allocation to the Department of Defense.

Contracting With Health Plans

Physicians cannot assume that an indemnity plan offers more freedom of choice to patients than an HMO because the line between these types of insurers is increasingly blurred. Some HMOs now allow patients more leeway to select physicians through point-of-service plans and have eliminated gatekeeper requirements. Many indemnity plans now require preauthorization for many services and require physicians to accept a discounted fee schedule. Hence, the expression "managed care plan" or "managed care organization" is now more accurate and more commonly used to describe health plans. What matters is not the label applied to the health plan, but the elements of the contract.

A decade or so ago in the early days of managed care, many physicians assumed the best policy simply was to sign up with as many payers as possible and not to worry over the details of the contracts. But as widespread payment problems arose, physicians found it necessary to look hard at any contract before signing and to monitor the payments afterwards to make sure that the provisions are enforced fully.

Physicians who work with other doctors should be aware of possible antitrust violations. Consult an attorney who is knowledgeable about antitrust issues. The physician or practice administrator should perform a thorough analysis of the contract before sending it to a lawyer and incurring legal expenses.

In relation to billing, claim processing and payment, the contract should:

- Include a fee schedule for at least 30–50 of the practice's most commonly provided services and procedures. Insurers often will not provide a list of all fees. At least one state, Georgia, now requires insurers to include a fee schedule with the contract. Make sure that the fees are adequate to meet your expenses. You do not want your costs of providing care to be greater than your reimbursement.

- Bar unilateral changes to the contract by the payer, including fee schedule changes.
- Set a limit on how often the contract can be changed—preferably once but no more than twice a year. The physician must have the right to review proposed changes, with the option of canceling the contract if the changes are not acceptable.
- Define key terms such as "clean claim," "medically necessary," and "covered services." The definition of clean claim should list required data fields.
- Specify times and systems for claims submission and payments, with specific interest or penalties when payments are late.
- Clearly specify grounds and notice requirements for termination.
- Bar retrospective denial of claims for care that was preauthorized.
- State time limits for audits and reconciliation.

When reviewing a contract, the physician should:

- Check for any mention of rules on CPT code bundling in the contract, though payers are usually silent on this point.
- Avoid contracts that allow submission of bundling disputes only one at a time. This is extremely unproductive because the insurer will continue to bundle in the same way while disputes are being reviewed. If the plan reverses itself on a large batch of identically bundled claims, that decision should stand as precedent for future reimbursements.

Physicians should always keep highly detailed, readable medical documentation of each office visit or operation.

Physicians should know the insurers' mechanisms for appeal of both medical and payment decisions and use them. Resolution of disputes begins with internal reviews by the health plan. The contract should allow for an appeal to binding arbitration outside the plan if results of the internal appeal are unsatisfactory. Remember that once it is signed, the contract is legally binding to both the health plan and the medical practice.

Office Procedures for Submitting and Monitoring Claims

Physicians should make certain that coding and billing are done correctly. Physicians should make sure that their staffs are submitting claims promptly and that rejections are not caused by sloppy or incomplete claims.

Offices should have the current editions of the *ICD-9-CM Manual*, the American Medical Association's *CPT Manual*, and the American College of Obstetricians and Gynecologists' (ACOG) *Ob/Gyn Coding Manual: Components of Correct Procedural Coding*. Physicians and billing staff should attend training courses such as the workshops offered by ACOG.

The billing staff should create tables showing the different policies of their patients' insurance plans for specific services and follow these policies when billing. For example, some insurers have certain requirements for, or will not pay for, in-office services such as ultrasound examinations and laboratory work.

Also, physicians and staff should monitor payments to be sure that they receive the amounts due, that payment is made within a reasonable amount of time (which should be specified in the contract and/or by state law), and that payment is for all the services provided.

Physicians should always keep highly detailed, readable medical documentation of each office visit or operation. Do not assume the payer has information about prior visits. All of the procedures listed on a claim must correlate logically with the diagnoses. Physicians should keep track of repeated cases of identical bundling and appeal all cases at once.

*Physicians'
reimbursement
will be what they
negotiate, not
what they
deserve.*

Dealing With Payment Problems

There are several steps that a practice can take to address inappropriate coding and payment policies by insurers, beginning with the appeal process as stated in the contract. Submit pages from ACOG's *Ob/Gyn Coding Manual* to demonstrate that the claim was coded correctly. This manual is particularly valuable when there is a dispute regarding bundling of services. Services listed as included in or excluded from a procedure reflect the opinion of the members of ACOG's Committee on Coding and Nomenclature. This is the committee that develops obstetric and gynecologic codes and relative value units in conjunction with the American Medical Association, so they are the best authority on what is included with a service. The opinion of the ACOG coding committee is not always in agreement with Medicare's Correct Coding Initiative bundles. Therefore, physicians should refer to the Correct Coding Initiative for Medicare claims.

If the physician believes payment has been denied inappropriately, he or she should follow the insurer's normal appeals process. If the normal appeal process is not successful, physicians should try one or more of these options:

- Talk to the plan's medical director, either in person or via telephone, to make his or her case. When doing this, the physician should let the medical director know about the complaint beforehand and be courteous and respectful. Physicians should use concrete evidence to show why a procedure should be covered, including claims from other insurers, ACOG's *Ob/Gyn Coding Manual*, and scientific articles. A physician should conclude such meetings by asking when he or she will find out whether the procedure is approved and what to do if it is not.

- Submit information on bundling to the state medical association, a professional society, or the state insurance commissioner. As in negotiating with health plans, there is power in numbers and the more evidence that the state medical association receives, the more likely it will be able to help.

- Appeal to a state insurance department. Many states are now cracking down on slow payments and inappropriate denials. Physicians should contact their state insurance department to find out exactly what they need to do to assist them.

- Contact ACOG if there are problematic patterns that can be addressed. Although ACOG cannot require insurers to change their policies or negotiate fees due to antitrust laws, ACOG can help with correct coding and identifying unfair policies. If requesting assistance, physicians should provide adequate information, including Explanations of Benefits, claim forms, operative notes, and previous correspondence, but with patient names and other identifying information deleted. Always be aware of the need to maintain patient privacy and adhere to state and federal privacy requirements. Physicians also should identify a medical director or equivalent point of contact at the health plan when requesting assistance.

Conclusion

Dealing with third-party payers, whether insurers or government, can be a frustrating experience. To minimize problems, physicians and medical practices must keep good records, including patient charts, coding, and financial data. Physicians also should be aware that some problems are caused by their billing practices and should be prepared to address problems within their own organization. Physicians should know the health plans' policies and adhere to them, and get to know health plans' billing representatives and medical directors. If health plans' recognize that you are serious about doing your job well, they will be more helpful when you need their assistance.

Resources

The ACOG web site, www.acog.org, includes both coding and practice management information, and links to other information and sites. Look under the Practice Management heading on the home page.

Chapter 12 Quiz: Dealing With Third-Party Payers

True or False:

1. Medicare and Medicaid are government-sponsored health plans.

2. The Medicare program is for elderly patients, people with disabilities, and people with end-stage renal disease.

Choose the best answer:

3. The term managed care applies to:

   a. Health maintenance organizations

   b. Indemnity plans that require preauthorization or pay at discounted rates

   c. The elements of a contract rather than a particular plan

   d. All of the above

4. Contracts with third-party payers:

   a. Should be signed regardless of content to ensure an adequate patient volume

   b. Should be reviewed carefully by the practice and an attorney with experience in health care contracting

   c. Do not have an impact on the practice's ability to appeal a reimbursement decision

5. Inappropriate coding and payment policies by insurers can be addressed by:

   a. Following the normal appeals process established by the payer

   b. Contacting the plan's medical director

   c. Contacting the state insurance commissioner

   d. All of the above

Answers are listed on page 179.

Appendix A

ACOG Coding Resources

Publications

The American College of Obstetricians and Gynecologists (ACOG) has a number of coding publications available to Fellows. The following publications may be ordered through the ACOG Publications and Educational Materials catalog, on ACOG's web site, or from the distribution center (1-800-762-2264).

Frequently Asked Questions in Ob/Gyn Coding is a compilation of questions submitted over the years to ACOG staff by Fellows. The ACOG staff found that the same or similar questions were asked repeatedly. As a result, the Committee on Coding and Nomenclature formalized the answers to these questions in this book. This book is published in odd years.

Ob/Gyn Coding Manual: Components of Correct Procedural Coding 2006 describes the services included or excluded from the CPT codes most often reported by ob-gyns: Female Genital System section; Maternity Care and Delivery section; selected codes from the Integumentary, Radiology, Hemic and Lymphatic, Digestive, Reproductive Medicine, and Urinary System sections. Other chapters of the coding manual include the Medicare Relative Value Units for 2004, a discussion of Medicare's Correct Coding Initiative, and a discussion of CPT modifiers. The book should assist physicians who are having disputes with insurance companies about correct coding, particularly bundling issues. The 2006 version will be available in late January 2006.

The booklet *ICD-9-CM Abridged: Diagnostic Coding in Obstetrics and Gynecology* lists diagnostic codes used by ob-gyns in the same format used by the complete ICD-9-CM book. The booklet also describes new diagnostic codes added to ICD-9-CM in October 2005. This pocket-sized booklet includes lists of codes commonly reported by ob-gyns. The 2006 version became available in fall 2005.

The ACOG Outpatient Encounter Forms are available in four formats: gynecologic services only and obstetric–gynecologic services forms, each available with or without laboratory codes:

- The gynecologic services forms list procedural codes on the front of the form and gynecologic and primary care diagnoses on the back.

- The obstetric–gynecologic services forms list procedures on the front and gynecologic and obstetric diagnoses on the back.

The forms can be ordered as single laser-printer-compatible forms or two- or three-part continuous-feed, carbonless forms, and may be personalized to include office information such as address and tax identification number.

Other Resources

ACOG Internet Access

The ACOG web site, www.acog.org, includes both coding and practice management information, and links to other information and sites. Look under the "Technical Assistance" heading on the home page or under "Member Services" on the member side of the web site.

The Department of Coding and Nomenclature has two Internet sites to assist Fellows with coding and reimbursement issues. These sites are accessed through www.acog.org. The online discussion for coding has answered more than 500 coding and reimbursement questions since its beginning in July 1997. This site has a search function to allow physicians to search for a specific topic, or physicians can simply post a question.

The Coding and Nomenclature Department web page includes a list of coding resources and timely announcements concerning coding and reimbursement issues. Also posted on this site are the most recent Medicare Resource-Based Relative Value Scale values and Correct Coding Initiative, evaluation and management services documentation templates, and an intake history form developed by the ACOG Committee on Coding and Nomenclature.

Accessing these sites is easy. First register on the web site by filling out the online registration form. Next, sign in by clicking on the member access button. Then, click on either the online discussion button to access the coding conference or the Departments button to access the Department web page. If you are already registered, simply sign in using your name and password.

ACOG Staff Coding Assistance

Physicians can fax or e-mail specific coding questions to the staff of the Department of Coding and Nomenclature. There is no charge for this service. Questions are answered in the order received, usually within 4–6 weeks. Send questions to ttropin@acog.org, coding@acog.org, or fax to 202-484-7480. If sending information such as operative reports or Explanation of Benefits from insurers, be sure to block out any information that identifies the patient.

ACOG's Listserv

The American College of Obstetricians and Gynecologists' Department of Health Economics offers a free monthly e-mail news service, "The Practice Management and Coding Update." The update includes effective coding tips, practice management advice, information about regulatory issues that affect your practice, and the latest news on what ACOG is doing to help address your reimbursement concerns and improve your practice environment. To subscribe to the listserv, send an e-mail message to: majordomo@linux.acog.com. In the body of your message, type: subscribe coding.

Appendix B

Assignment of Relative Value Units

After a new code is accepted or a code is revised, the American College of Obstetricians and Gynecologists (ACOG) surveys its membership to obtain data on the physician work and the practice expenses associated with the code. The survey asks participants to evaluate how difficult the procedure is in comparison to procedures, with already-established relative value units (RVUs). The ACOG Subcommittee for the Relative Value Scale Update Committee recommends RVUs for the new or revised procedure.

The American Medical Association/Specialty Relative Value Scale Update Committee (RUC) considers the proposal from ACOG's Subcommittee. The RUC may adopt or modify ACOG's proposal.

The Center for Medicare and Medicaid Services (CMS) reviews the RVU recommendation from the RUC. The CMS makes the final determination of the RVUs assigned.

The physician fee schedule is the composed of three factors:

1. Nationally Uniform RVUs. This includes separate RVUs for physician work, practice expenses, and malpractice expenses. The physician work and the practice expense components for a code are set by the RUC. (See Chapter 1 for a discussion of the RUC.) The professional liability RVUs are set by CMS using professional liability premium data, Medicare payment data, and specialty specific data. The work and malpractice RVU components are constant for a specific code. However, practice expense RVUs vary depending on where the service is provided (eg, in a facility setting or an outpatient setting).

2. Geographic Adjustment Factor. The nationally uniform RVUs for a procedure are multiplied first by a geographic adjustment factor to increase or decrease the RVUs according to where the physician practices. That is, the total RVUs for the same procedure will be somewhat higher for physicians practicing in New York City than in North Dakota.

3. Nationally Uniform Conversion Factor. The adjusted RVUs are multiplied by a set dollar amount established by CMS (the conversion factor).

The payment for a specific service is determined by the formula shown below. Total RVUs are first adjusted for the provider's geographic location and then multiplied by the 2005 conversion factor ($37.90). The result is Medicare 's reimbursement for a physician who accepts assignment.

Formula to determine payment to Medicare:

Work RVU × work GAF + Practice expense RVU × practice expense GAF + Malpractice expense RVU × malpractice GAF = Adjusted Total RVU

Adjusted total RVU × conversion factor = Reimbursement

RVU = rrelative value units
GAF = geographic adjustment factor

Work and malpractice RVUs are constant for a specific code. However, practice expense RVUs may vary depending on the site where service is provided. If service is performed in hospital ambulatory surgical center or skilled nursing facility, use facility RVUs. If service is performed in any other setting (eg, physician office), use non-facility RVUs. Nonfacility practice expense RVUs are higher, reflecting the greater costs to physicians when service is performed in the office.

Example 1: Endometrial biopsy

The total allowable for an endometrial biopsy (58100) performed in a physician's office in Wyoming is calculated as follows:

Performed in Physician's Office

	RVUs		GAF		RVUs
Work	1.53	×	1.000	=	1.53000
Practice Expense	1.32	×	0.874	=	1.15368
Malpractice	0.18	×	0.935	=	0.16830
Total RVUs	3.03			=	2.85198
Total RVUs × Conversion Factor ($37.90)				=	$108.09

The total allowable for an endometrial biopsy (58100) performed in a facility in Wyoming is calculated as follows:

Performed in Another Setting

	RVUs		GAF		RVUs
Work	1.53	×	1.000	=	1.53000
Practice Expense	0.72	×	0.874	=	0.62928
Malpractice	0.18	×	0.935	=	0.16830
Total RVUs	2.43			=	2.32758
Total RVUs × Conversion Factor ($37.90)				=	$88.22

Therefore, a physician in Wyoming, performing the procedure in his or her office, would be reimbursed $108.09. If performed in a hospital, he or she would be reimbursed $88.22.

This same procedure performed in Los Angeles, however, leads to a different reimbursement because of different geographic adjustments for Los Angeles as compared to Wyoming:

Performed in Physician's Office

	RVUs		GAF		RVUs
Work	1.53	×	1.049	=	1.60497
Practice Expense	1.32	×	1.147	=	1.51404
Malpractice	0.18	×	0.954	=	0.17172
Total RVUs	3.03			=	3.29073
Total RVUs × Conversion Factor ($37.90)				=	$124.72

Performed in Another Setting

	RVUs		GAF		RVUs
Work	1.53	×	1.049	=	1.60497
Practice Expense	0.72	×	1.147	=	0.82584
Malpractice	0.18	×	0.954	=	0.17172
Total RVUs	2.43			=	2.60253
Total RVUs × Conversion Factor ($37.90)				=	$98.64

Therefore, a physician in Los Angeles, performing the procedure in his or her office, would be reimbursed $124.72. If performed in a hospital, he or she would be reimbursed $98.64.

Example 2: Total abdominal hysterectomy with Marshall-Marchetti-Kranz procedure

Note that there is only one practice expense figure for this procedure. This is because this procedure would never be performed in an office setting.

The total allowable for a total abdominal hysterectomy with Marshall-Marchetti-Kranz procedure (58152) performed in Wyoming would be:

Performed in Any Setting

	RVUs		GAF		RVUs
Work	20.57	×	1.000	=	20.5700
Practice Expense	9.85	×	0.874	=	8.60890
Malpractice	2.41	×	0.935	=	2.25335
Total RVUs	32.83			=	31.43225
Total RVUs × Conversion Factor ($37.90)				=	$1,191.28

Therefore, a physician in Wyoming would be reimbursed $1,191.28, regardless of where the procedure was performed. This same procedure performed in Los Angeles, however, leads to a different reimbursement because of different geographic adjustments.

Performed in Any Setting

	RVUs		GAF		RVUs
Work	20.57	×	1.056	=	21.72192
Practice Expense	9.85	×	1.139	=	11.21915
Malpractice	2.41	×	0.955	=	2.30155
Total RVUs	32.83			=	35.24262
Total RVUs × Conversion Factor ($37.90)				=	$1,335.70

Therefore, a physician in Los Angeles, performing the procedure would be reimbursed $1,335.70, regardless of where the procedure was performed. The list of RVUs for procedure codes commonly reported by obstetrician–gynecologists is available on ACOG's website (www.acog.org) at the Department of Coding and Nomenclature.

Appendix C

Advance Beneficiary Notices

Two Medicare approved beneficiary notices are on the following pages:

- The first notice is used by physicians, practitioners, suppliers and providers when the provider does not know for certain whether the service will be covered by Medicare. A modifier –GA is attached to the procedure code reported for this service.

- The second notice is used when the provider knows that the service is excluded by statute from payment by Medicare (eg, preventive services). A modifier –GY is attached to the procedure code reported for this service.

For more information and copies of the Advance Beneficiary Notices forms, visit www.cms.hhs.gov/medlearn/refabn.asp.

Patient's Name: _____   Medicare # (HICN): _____

ADVANCE BENEFICIARY NOTICE (ABN)

NOTE: You need to make a choice about receiving these health care items or services.

We expect that Medicare will not pay for the item(s) or service(s) that are described below. Medicare does not pay for all of your health care costs. Medicare only pays for covered items and services when Medicare rules are met. The fact that Medicare may not pay for a particular item or service does not mean that you should not receive it. There may be a good reason your doctor recommended it. Right now, in your case, **Medicare probably will not pay for –**

Items or Services:

Because:

The purpose of this form is to help you make an informed choice about whether or not you want to receive these items or services, knowing that you might have to pay for them yourself. Before you make a decision about your options, you should **read this entire notice carefully.**
- Ask us to explain, if you don't understand why Medicare probably won't pay.
- Ask us how much these items or services will cost you (**Estimated Cost: $_____**), in case you have to pay for them yourself or through other insurance.

PLEASE CHOOSE **ONE** OPTION. CHECK **ONE** BOX. **SIGN & DATE** YOUR CHOICE.

☐ **Option 1. YES.**   **I want to receive these items or services.**
I understand that Medicare will not decide whether to pay unless I receive these items or services. Please submit my claim to Medicare. I understand that you may bill me for items or services and that I may have to pay the bill while Medicare is making its decision. If Medicare does pay, you will refund to me any payments I made to you that are due to me. If Medicare denies payment, I agree to be personally and fully responsible for payment. That is, I will pay personally, either out of pocket or through any other insurance that I have. I understand I can appeal Medicare's decision.

☐ **Option 2. NO.**   **I have decided not to receive these items or services.**
I will not receive these items or services. I understand that you will not be able to submit a claim to Medicare and that I will not be able to appeal your opinion that Medicare won't pay.

_____   _____
    Date   **Signature of patient or person acting on patient's behalf**

NOTE: Your health information will be kept confidential. Any information that we collect about you on this form will be kept confidential in our offices. If a claim is submitted to Medicare, your health information on this form may be shared with Medicare. Your health information which Medicare sees will be kept confidential by Medicare.

OMB Approval No. 0938-0566   Form No. CMS-R-131-G   (June 2002)

NOTICE OF EXCLUSIONS FROM MEDICARE BENEFITS (NEMB)
There are items and services for which Medicare <u>will not pay</u>.

- Medicare does **not** pay for all of your health care costs. Medicare only pays for covered benefits. **Some items and services are not Medicare benefits and Medicare will not pay for them.**
- When you receive an item or service that is **not** a Medicare benefit, **you are responsible to pay for it,** personally or through any other insurance that you may have.

> The purpose of this notice is to help you make an informed choice about whether or not you want to receive these items or services, knowing that you will have to pay for them yourself. **Before you make a decision, you should read this entire notice carefully.**
> Ask us to explain, if you don't understand why Medicare won't pay.
> Ask us how much these items or services will cost you (**Estimated Cost: $_____**).

Medicare will not pay for:
_____
_____ ;

❏ **1.** Because it does not meet the definition of any Medicare benefit.

❏ **2.** Because of the following exclusion * from Medicare benefits:

❏Personal comfort items.
❏Most shots (vaccinations).
❏Hearing aids and hearing examinations.
❏Most outpatient prescription drugs.
❏Orthopedic shoes and foot supports (orthotics).
❏Health care received outside of the USA.
❏Services required as a result of war.
❏Routine physicals and most tests for screening.
❏Routine eye care, eyeglasses and examinations.
❏Cosmetic surgery.
❏Dental care and dentures (in most cases).
❏Routine foot care and flat foot care.
❏Services by immediate relatives.
❏Services under a physician's private contract.
❏Services paid for by a governmental entity that is not Medicare.
❏Services for which the patient has no legal obligation to pay.
❏Home health services furnished under a plan of care, if the agency does not submit the claim.
❏Items and services excluded under the Assisted Suicide Funding Restriction Act of 1997.
❏Items or services furnished in a competitive acquisition area by any entity that does not have a contract with the Department of Health and Human Services (except in a case of urgent need).
❏Physicians' services performed by a physician assistant, midwife, psychologist, or nurse anesthetist, when furnished to an inpatient, unless they are furnished under arrangements by the hospital.
❏Items and services furnished to an individual who is a resident of a skilled nursing facility (a SNF) or of a part of a facility that includes a SNF, unless they are furnished under arrangements by the SNF.
❏Services of an assistant at surgery without prior approval from the peer review organization.
❏Outpatient occupational and physical therapy services furnished incident to a physician's services.

* This is only a general summary of exclusions from Medicare benefits. It is not a legal document.
  The official Medicare program provisions are contained in relevant laws, regulations, and rulings.

Appendix D

Sample Special Report/Cover Letter

To Whom It May Concern:

On March 3, 200X, I performed an operative laparoscopy and hysteroscopy with division of intrauterine septum on Ms. Virginia Dare. She was experiencing increasing dyspareunia and dysmenorrhea. She wants to have children in the future. She refused treatment with oral contraceptive pills. She had a history of second trimester miscarriage with a documented intrauterine septum. Dr. John White was the assistant surgeon. A detailed operative report is attached.

These laparoscopic and hysteroscopic surgeries required nearly 4 hours. The surgery included: laparoscopic resection of dense adnexa-to-colon adhesions with suturing of the bowel serosa; ureteral dissection; and resection of deeply penetrating cul-de-sac lesions. There was significant risk of injury to the sigmoid colon, rectum, and left ureter.

Because of the additional skill, time and potential risk to the patient involved in performing these surgeries, I have coded the attached claim using a –22 modifier and am requesting additional X% reimbursement. Please consider this when determining the level of benefits to be provided for this patient. Please contact me if you need more information or additional details concerning this case.

Sincerely,

Index

Note: Page numbers followed by the letters *f* and *t* indicate figures and tables, respectively.

A

ABN. *See* Advance Beneficiary Notice
Abortion, 137
Adhesions, lysis of, 109
Advance Beneficiary Notice (ABN), 92
American Medical Association (AMA)
   CPT developed by, 3, 4
   CPT revised by, 4–5
   documentation principles of, 57, 59, 60
Antepartum services
   in global packages, 128–129
   in nonglobal care, 133
Arrows, in CPT, 16
Assistant physicians, modifiers for, 118

B

Bilateral procedures, modifiers for, 116
Biophysical profiles, 148
Bone mass screening, in Medicare, 87*t*, 93–94
Breast examination, clinical, in Medicare, 87*t*, 88–89
Bullets
   in CPT, 15
   in documentation guidelines, 66
Bundling of procedures
   in CPT, 6
   in Medicare, 104–105
   payment problems with, 160

C

Case management services, 55
CCI. *See* Correct Coding Initiative
Centers for Medicare and Medicaid Services (CMS)
   documentation guidelines by, 60
   HCPCS developed by, 3
   ICD revisions by, 6–7

Cesarean delivery, of twins, 135, 135*t*
Claims. *See also* Reimbursement
   ICD codes in, 7–8, 8*f*
   monitoring of, 159–160
   submission of, 159–160
CMS. *See* Centers for Medicare and Medicaid Services
Complete abortion, 139*t*, 140
Complications
   ICD codes for, 29
   mechanical, 29–30, 29*f*
   nonmechanical, 29–30, 29*f*
Concurrent care
   in E/M services, 56
   in obstetric services, 136–137
Conferences, team, 55
Consultations
   CPT definition of, 35–36
   documentation of, 73*t*, 74*t*, 76
   E/M services codes for, 50–52, 51*t*
   modifiers for, 121
Contracting, with health plans, 158–159
Correct coding, criteria for, 2
Correct Coding Initiative (CCI), 106–107
Counseling, in preventive medicine, 95
Cover letter, sample, 173
Covering physicians, 137
CPT-4. *See Current Procedural Terminology,* Fourth Edition
Current Procedural Terminology, Fourth Edition (CPT-4)
   appendices of, 14
   basics of, 11–16
   bundling in, 6
   category I codes in, 11
   category II codes in, 12
   category III codes in, 13
   changes in, process for, 5–6
   development of, 3
   for E/M services, 33–41
   global surgical packages in, 99–111

Current Procedural Terminology, Fourth Edition *(continued)*
   guidelines for, 15–16
   in HCPCS, 4
   index of, 13
   modifiers in, 16, 113–124
   for obstetric services, 127–141
   organization of, 11–14
   for preventive medicine, 83
   purpose of, 2, 3–4, 11
   and reimbursement, 6–7
   semicolons used in, 15
   symbols used in, 15
   for ultrasound, 143–153
   for unlisted procedures, 16

D

Decision making in E/M services
   amount and complexity of data in, 70
   documentation of, 60–73
   level of, 39, 40*t*
   risk in, 70–71, 72*t*
Delivery services
   in global packages, 129–131
   in nonglobal care, 132–133
   termination of pregnancy as, 137–138
Diagnostic tests and procedures
   ICD coding for, 19–30
   interpretation of, 135
   in obstetric services, 135, 136*t*
   versus screening services, 135
Discontinued procedures, modifiers for, 122
Documentation, of E/M services
   1992 AMA principles of, 57, 59, 60
   1995 guidelines for, 59–60, 64–65
   1997 guidelines for, 60, 65–67, 66*t*
   of consultations, 73*t*, 74*t*
   for established patients, 73, 74*t*
   history of, 59–60
   for inpatients, 76*t*
   in Medicare, 59–80

L

Laboratories, outside, modifiers for, 123

Laboratory tests, repeat clinical diagnostic, modifiers for, 123

Laparoscopic procedures, 109–110

Letter, sample cover, 173

Listserv, ACOG, 164

Lysis of adhesions, 109

M

Mammography, in Medicare, 93

Management services, case, 55

Mandated services, modifiers for, 121

Medicaid, 158
  CPT codes in, 4
  eligibility for, 158

Medicare, 157
  consultations in, 52
  documentation guidelines of, 59–80
  eligibility for, 157
  global surgical packages in, 99–111, 101t
  modifiers in, 106–107
  preventive medicine in, 87–92, 87t, 88t, 91t, 92t
  same-day admission and discharge services in, 49
  structure of, 157
  telephone calls in, 55

Missed abortion, 138, 138t

Modifiers, 113–124
  for assistant physicians, 118
  for bilateral procedures, 121–122
  in CPT, 16, 113–124
  for discontinued procedures, 121–122
  in global surgical packages, 106–107
  in HCPCS, 4
  in ICD-9-CM, 23–24
  for intraoperative services, 117–119
  for laboratories, 123
  for laboratory tests, 123
  for mandated services, 122
  in Medicare, 106–107
  for postoperative services, 119–120
  for preoperative services, 116
  for professional components, 121
  for prolonged services, 121
  for reduced services, 122
  for repeat procedures, 123
  for termination of procedures, 121–122

Multiple gestations, delivery with, 134t, 135t

Multiple physicians
  in global obstetric packages, 137
  in global surgical packages, 103–104, 112–113, 114–115

N

National Center for Health Statistics (NCHS), in ICD revisions, 6

NEC. *See* Not elsewhere classified

Neoplasms, ICD codes for, 27, 27t

New patients
  CPT definition of, 34
  documentation for, 73, 73t
  E/M services codes for, 43, 44t

NOS. *See* Not otherwise specified

Not elsewhere classified (NEC) diagnosis, 22

Not otherwise specified (NOS) diagnosis, 22

O

Observation care, E/M services codes for, 48t, 49

Obstetric services, 127–141
  antepartum, 128–129
  biophysical profiles in, 148
  concurrent care in, 136–137
  covering physicians in, 137
  delivery, 129–131
  diagnostic tests and procedures in, 135–136
  for ectopic pregnancy, 129–130
  global, 127–141
  multiple physicians in, 137
  nonglobal, 132–133
  postpartum, 131–132
  termination of pregnancy in, 137–138
  ultrasound in, 143–153

Open procedures, 109

Outpatients
  consultations on, 50–51, 51t
  CPT definition of, 34
  documentation for, 74t
  E/M services codes for, 43, 50–51, 51t

P

Pairs, code, in Medicare's Correct Coding Initiative, 106

Past, family, and/or social history (PFSH), documentation guidelines on, 62–63

Patients, CPT classification of, 33–34

Payers. *See* Third-party payers

PCPs. *See* Primary care physicians

Pelvic examination, in Medicare, 87t, 88–89

PFSH. *See* Past, family, and/or social history

Plus sign, in CPT, 15

Postoperative services
  in CPT, 100
  in Medicare, 100
  modifiers for, 120

Postpartum services
  in global packages, 131–132
  in nonglobal care, 134–135

Pregnancy. *See also* Obstetric services
  diagnosis of, 129
  ectopic, 139
  termination of, 129, 138t, 139t, 140t

Preoperative services
  in CPT, 101–103
  in Medicare, 100
  modifiers for, 116

Preventive medicine services, 83–91
  components of, 84
  counseling in, 94
  CPT codes for, 83–84
  in Medicare, 87–92, 87t, 88t
  versus problem-oriented services, 84, 85t
  problem-oriented services combined with, 85–86
  risk factor reduction intervention in, 94
  third-party coverage for, 86

Primary care physicians (PCPs), 156–157

Prolonged services, 53
  with direct contact, 53, 54t
  modifiers for, 121
  without direct contact, 54, 55t

Publications, 163–164

R

RBRVS. *See* Resource-Based Relative Value Scale

Reduced services, modifiers for, 121

Reimbursement. *See also* Third-party payers
  claims for, 7–8, 8f
  in CPT, 5–6, 7–8
  in ICD, 7–8
  problems with, 160
  role of coding in, 1–2

Relative value units (RVUs), 5, 6

Repeat procedures, modifiers for, 123

Resources, 163–164

Review of systems (ROS), documentation guidelines on, 62

Risk, in decision making, 70–71, 72t

Risk assessment instruments, administration or interpretation of, 96–97

Risk factor reduction intervention, in preventive medicine, 96–97

ROS. *See* Review of systems

RVUs. *See* Relative value units

Answers to Chapter Quizzes

Chapter 1:
Coding: An Overview

1. T
2. T
3. d
4. e
5. d
6. d
7. c
8. e

Chapter 2:
Basics of CPT Coding

1. T
2. F
3. b
4. c
5. b
6. d

Chapter 3:
Basics of ICD-9-CM Coding

1. F
2. T
3. d
4. e
5. d
6. a
7. c

Chapter 4:
E/M Services

1. F
2. T
3. b
4. c
5. d
6. d
7. c

Chapter 5:
Applying E/M Services Codes

1. F
2. F
3. b
4. d
5. c
6. a
7. d

Chapter 6:
E/M Services and Medicare Documentation Guidelines

1. T
2. T
3. d
4. d
5. d
6. d
7. d

Chapter 7:
Preventive Medicine Services

1. F
2. T
3. b
4. e
5. d
6. c
7. a
8. c

Chapter 8:
The Global Surgical Package

1. T
2. F
3. T
4. T
5. e
6. c
7. e
8. Code 58150 Question revised
9. *Day 1*: Established E/M service (99212-99215) –25 modifier 56420 (I&D of Bartholin's gland abscess)
Day 2: Established E/M service (99212-99215) if diagnosis indicating services were not routine.
If this had been a Medicare patient, then services on Day 2 would not have been reported. Code 56420 has a 10-day global period.

Chapter 9:
Modifiers

1. F
2. T
3. c
4. d
5. d
6. b
7. d

Chapter 10:
Obstetric Services

1. T
2. T
3. b
4. d
5. d
6. d
7. d

Chapter 11:
Ultrasound Coding

1. T
2. T
3. a
4. d
5. d
6. d
7. d

Chapter 12:
Dealing With Third-Party Payers

1. T
2. T
3. d
4. b
5. d